WOULD IT SURPRISE
YOU TO KNOW...?

RONNIE
ARCHER-MORGAN

WITH JANET GLEESON

WOULD IT SURPRISE
YOU TO KNOW...?

CENTURY

1 3 5 7 9 10 8 6 4 2

CENTURY
20 Vauxhall Bridge Road
London SW1V 2SA

Century is part of the Penguin Random House group of companies
whose addresses can be found at global.penguinrandomhouse.com.

Penguin
Random House
UK

First published by Century in 2022

www.penguin.co.uk

A CIP catalogue record for this book is available from the British
Library.

ISBN 9781529135879

Set in 12.5/16 pt Bembo Book MT Pro
Typeset by Jouve (UK), Milton Keynes
Printed and bound in Great Britain by Clays Ltd, Elcograf S.p.A.

The authorised representative in the EEA is Penguin Random House
Ireland, Morrison Chambers, 32 Nassau Street, Dublin D02 YH68

Penguin Random House is committed to a sustainable future
for our business, our readers and our planet. This book is
made from Forest Stewardship Council® certified paper.
www.greenpenguin.co.uk

To Jo

Prologue

We are on location, filming. Castle Howard in all its baroque splendour is our backdrop, the sky is blue and hopeful. There's always a buzz about filming days on one of Britain's best-loved, most enduring programmes. Thousands stand in line, cradling objects that they dream will be exceptional for one reason or another. Perhaps they'll turn out to be something that illuminates a tragic death, a lost love, a forgotten life, or a ground-breaking discovery. Or perhaps they have something that will just be identified as a masterpiece of unexpected value. The air is filled with promise.

I've worked on *Antiques Roadshow* for seven years and feel proud to play a part in it. It's a show that attracts regular audiences of more than five million viewers, and I think many see it as the TV equivalent of a warm bath, or a bowl of Sunday-night comfort food. Today is extra special: it's the programme's fortieth-anniversary show. Who knows what we might find?

At lunchtime, I've just finished talking to a lady about a collection of scarves. While she folds them away I look up to see Janet Gleeson, a specialist from the reception team, threading her way through the straggling lines towards the miscellaneous experts' tables where I sit. She is holding what looks like a cardboard shoe box. 'Where's Paul?' she asks. 'Or Hilary or Judith?', searching for my colleagues.

'I think they are at lunch, or maybe filming. What have you got? Is it something I could do?'

'It's a nice story – but probably not your thing,' she replies.

'Can I see, just in case?'

'Of course.' She comes to the table and puts down the box. I lift the lid off and see three glove puppets inside. 'The lady who's brought this in says her father was a prop-maker for Harry Corbett, the creator of Sooty and Sweep. Corbett gave them to her father after they were used in the shows in the fifties.'

A shiver runs through me. My stomach feels hollow. I take out Sooty, the little yellow bear, and examine him. There are signs of wear consistent with age. He isn't newly bought from Hamleys or Toys R Us. I put Sooty down and pick up Sweep, his floppy-eared dog companion. There are photos in the box too – some show Harry Corbett and Sooty and Sweep with audiences. It all fits together. I can feel my skin prickle and my pulse starts to race.

'It's a good story for someone to film,' Janet says.

There's a long pause. The truth is I'm having difficulty holding myself together. 'I would do anything to film these,' I say eventually, to cover an intense surge of emotion.

She gives me an uncertain look, maybe thinking I'm joking. 'Oh,' she says. 'Great – but I didn't think toys were your thing?'

But these aren't any toys, I want to say. It's what they represent. I compose myself and attempt an explanation. Janet and I have known each other for seven years. We joined the programme together and we get on well. I've told her a bit about my life as a DJ, a hairdresser, and an antiques dealer. But this is the first time I've revealed anything about my childhood to her. I see her initial surprise, questions stacking up behind her eyes, but with crowds milling and long queues to process there isn't time to say more. How can I say that I feel the puppets have come back to me, that by some strange fate they've found me?

I meet the owner of the puppets, a kind-eyed lady in her sixties who fleshes out the story. Her father had left an engineering job in Yorkshire to work for Harry Corbett. He did so for twenty years and the two men became close friends.

When I explain the significance of the puppets to Simon, the director, he needs no persuasion, grasping instantly that not only is this a moving personal story for the owner, it's special because it has direct relevance to me, a member of the team. Even if the filming schedule is now full, he promises he will find a slot.

The day is nearly over, and the crowds have thinned when the time comes. By then word has gone round the production team that this story is something out of the ordinary. Fiona Bruce says she wants to talk to me ahead of my interview with the owner. 'Ronnie, it must have been tough being in a children's home?' she says.

I always feel nervous before a recording, but this time my heart is pounding, my ribcage feels as if it's about to explode. 'It was an adventure,' I reply with fake nonchalance. 'I was well looked after.'

'You would say that,' she replies, unfazed.

I can't explain it in a soundbite: I can't say that to me the puppets represent my childish optimism, my happiness, the sorrow of loss. I can't say that I vividly remember the day Harry Corbett came. The innocent elation I felt. How my very best friend Anna and I rushed around till Sister Ida told us, 'Be good children, calm down and *just sit still*,' or she'd tell Mr Corbett and Sooty not to come, because Sooty only favoured good children with a visit. How we knew she would never carry out the threat, she was too kind, but we hated her being cross, and just in case she wasn't joking, we did as we were told. Instead, we wriggled about on our little plastic chairs and held hands at the table, looking at each other with round eyes, giggling. This isn't just about the puppets, it's about my childhood and it's about Anna.

Nor can I say that I also remember how a week later my life would come unmoored.

The filming goes seamlessly. 'Harry Corbett gave these to my father, for me, because he was getting new ones,' the owner explains as the cameras focus in and the watching crowd falls silent.

'When was that? How old were you?'

'It would have been 1955. I was about five years old,' she recalls.

I tell the owner, 'In 1955 I was in a National Children's Home and Harry Corbett came to visit. I had the privilege of him sitting next to me. He even let me play with his puppets. That is my fondest memory of my childhood. I think about it a lot.'

'My father was also in a National Children's Home. His friendship with Harry Corbett inspired Harry to visit many of them.'

'Really? I've got goosebumps,' I say. 'I'm not making it up.'

As soon as the filming is over and the owner has gone, I rush to the production tent and sob. Someone hugs me. I try to put the memory of Sooty and Sweep away, so that I don't have to think about my past and the people I've lost along the way. This has long been a coping strategy, but it doesn't work today. The truth is that for the past sixty years I have often wondered what happened to Anna.

Some months later, Janet gets in touch. She is writing a magazine article about the legacy of Empire and its impact on the art world we inhabit. She wants to interview me – we speak on the phone. How important are the objects that link us to our history? Ostensibly this has nothing to do with Sooty and Sweep, but in a way it does. Objects of every type have the power to transport us, to embody our past, to reveal hidden and forgotten truths. It is a subject that for me has personal resonance. I've spent much of my working life involved with cultural heritage – understanding history through the objects it has left behind, like a tide mark on the beach. Sometimes my colour has benefited me, sometimes not. My mother met my father in Sierra Leone. I have plenty of things to say.

'Terrible things happened which have to be acknowledged, but I think art is transcendent. Sometimes it's the phoenix that rises from the ashes of slavery and hatred, and sometimes it embodies passion, and love. You've got to look for the good, otherwise there would be no hope. We don't want to start book-burning and destroying. We must know the art's history and respect it. But change needs to happen.'

*

Afterwards I dwell on this more. As a rule I don't think about my colour unless it's brought to my attention. My mother was black and my father white, so I am mixed-race, although I often refer to myself as black because that's how the world normally views me. Still, I am conscious that becoming an antiques specialist on TV has brought me privilege. My passion for extraordinary objects and their stories allows me to connect with people. The things I see, handle, own and admire may not be conventional works of art – some have little monetary value – but as threads that bind us to history, they have a potency: to trigger memory, evoke understanding, and promote unity. I've always loved explaining how old objects open the door to our collective and individual past. How they recalibrate preconceptions and make history personal. But there aren't many black antique dealers, so in the past when I explained this, people often didn't listen. Now, thanks to the power of the TV, they do.

Remembering Sooty and Sweep leads me to reflect on the other objects that have defined my life. Some I still own, some I've lost or sold, some were never mine. But they are all intertwined in my life. At times the story is a painful one. There are episodes I've never before spoken of fully, even to close friends; recollections so freighted with sorrow I have deliberately tried to obliterate them. But the truth of the past is always there, even when you deny it. Maybe, after all this time, sharing my experiences would be helpful to others and cathartic for me. But how to make sense of a life as confused as mine?

Let me try.

I

A Baule Mask

We meet one Saturday at Portobello Road. He has a stand on the kerbside selling African art, and he catches my eye, thrusting a figure towards me as if he wants me to take it. I don't want to give offence, and I stop for a closer look. As I do so, in a strong African accent he tells me his name is Patrick and that he is from Congo. 'Patrick,' I repeat, unthinkingly. 'I had a half-brother with the same name, who I never met – he died in Sierra Leone from blackwater fever aged four, before I was born.'

Patrick shakes his head, sympathises, and tells me that he has a young family. A wife, a daughter aged twelve, and a new baby on the way. 'Family is everything to me,' he says. 'I sell these things to support them.'

I know about people like him – traders who buy works of art in Africa, ship them over to Europe and sell them on. Some are charlatans. Sometimes their stock is genuine; sometimes it's not deliberately fraudulent, just not what it seems. In certain African villages they've made the same objects for generations using traditional materials, then age them specifically for the tourist market. Then there are objects that have been illegally exported, some looted, around which, rightly, much controversy lies. I've learned the hard way that it pays to be wary, and I've always avoided objects with a questionable provenance for moral reasons, but nothing about Patrick alarms me, and after a cursory glance at his stock I'm increasingly intrigued.

Among the carvings laid out I recognise a Baule moon mask. It's better quality than anything I'd expected to see on a kerbside stall, and it appears to be genuinely old. 'Where did it come from?' I ask. He tells me that he has a contact in Congo who represents many serious collectors from North Africa, Belgium and France. Some of the collectors are old, and when they want to sell pieces from their collection, they use him. The mask I have picked up belonged to one of them. Under normal circumstances, I would be sceptical about a glib provenance like this. But the more I look at the mask the more I am struck by it, and the story rings true.

The Baule people originated in what is today Ghana, migrating west to Ivory Coast to escape the Asante three centuries ago. They are an agricultural, artistic people and to me this moon mask epitomises the refinement of their art. They used masks during rituals and dances, to symbolise a connection between nature and mankind – in a sense to show a link between the infinite and an idealised reality. The mask's aesthetic impact is as powerful as its meaning. The pared-down skull is an almost perfect circle, bordered by tiny, notched triangles. The domed forehead gleams with serenity and years of careful handling. The small, pursed mouth and half-closed eyes echo the circular form of the face. It all adds up to something as uncluttered and finely balanced as art can be. You hardly ever see pieces of this quality – or age. The patina and wear make me think it dates from the early twentieth or perhaps late nineteenth century.

I want to buy it, although in truth my interest in the mask has little to do with my African heritage, or Patrick's name, but my fascination in the evolution of modern Western art. Picasso, Matisse, Braque, Brancusi, Gris, Modigliani, Kandinsky and countless others were inspired by African tribal imagery, appreciating its dynamic simplicity, and echoed it in their own work. This is a subject close to my heart, on which I give lectures. We agree a price.

Afterwards I have no regrets. If anything, the mask seems to hold more personal relevance than I first realised. It strikes me that the man who made it more than a century ago inhabited a vastly different world from mine. His belief system told him that the moon and humankind could be symbolically fused through his craft. I may not share or fully comprehend this creed, but to me the mask also embodies something beyond its physical self. It represents a different synthesis: the connection between European and African culture, a link mirrored in my own heritage. My mother's family came from Sierra Leone, a West African country not far from where my mask was made. My British upbringing has shaped me. European art enthrals me, but Africa is part of the story.

My journey starts with my parents. My knowledge of their lives is incomplete, fragmented, perhaps nothing but myth, but I feel no desire to pick away and expose the truths and lies of either existence. Perhaps I'm a coward. Perhaps I'm afraid of what I might find. Perhaps I'd rather accept the slivers I've been handed as truth and move on.

This much I can tell you: my mother's name was Elizabeth Archer – but everyone called her Lizzie. Her grandmother was a freedwoman who had lived in Nova Scotia, in Canada, and returned to Freetown – Sierra Leone's capital city – in the nineteenth century. Her family probably feature in the *Book of Negroes*, a record of some 3,000 enslaved Africans who escaped to the British lines during the American Revolution, relocating to Nova Scotia as free people of colour.

My mother always told me that her family were wealthy, that she had studied in Paris, that her brother was knighted for services to medicine, and that for her sixteenth birthday she was given a house, a car and two pet chimpanzees – although whether any of that is true I have no idea.

She said my father was Ronald Morgan, a bridge-building British engineer of Welsh stock. He worked for the Ministry of Transport in the late 1940s when my mother met him in Sierra Leone. A photo I have shows a gentle-faced professional man, with regular features and a protective air, whom I have always thought bears a striking resemblance to Jack Warner as he looked in the TV police series *Dixon of Dock Green*. But that may be wishful thinking on my part.

Ronald was captivated by Lizzie. She was adventurous, headstrong and energetic. There was charisma and an air of Hollywood glamour in the way she carried herself. She loved music and dancing, she dressed stylishly, her face lit up when she smiled, and she was capable of great charm. There was also a less appealing side to her. When things didn't go her way, her temper was quick and could turn her into a tornado. She could be cruel and cold and would sulk for days. But that didn't happen often, and it didn't deter Ronald from pursuing her.

Lizzie's well-to-do family didn't comprehend the *coup de foudre* that had ignited the relationship between her and Ronald. In fact, they were outraged when Ronald appeared on the scene. After all, Lizzie was already married and had two sons, Gerald and Patrick, and divorce was shameful in the 1940s. But family opposition and threats did nothing to deter the lovers' determination. Lizzie divorced her first husband and abandoned her children for Ronald. As far as I know she was cut off from her parents for the rest of her life. Immigration records show that Elizabeth V. Archer Morgan, aged thirty-one, arrived in Liverpool on 18 July 1949, on board the MV *Apapa*. She may have already been pregnant. Was Ronald waiting to meet her? All I know for certain is that she gave her address as the Colonial Students' Hostel in Victoria, London.

I don't know whether they ever saw each other again but a few months later my father died in a car crash. By now, Lizzie definitely knew she was pregnant, and the catastrophic shock of Ronald's death, plus the estrangement from her family and her former world, the lack of friends, and her pregnancy were all too much. She plummeted into a deep depression and was eventually also diagnosed with schizophrenia. Anger is a common response to bereavement. Lizzie was probably furious with Ronald not just for dying, but for taking her away from her comfortable life, only to desert her, leaving her to carry a child without financial support.

When I was born in St Mary Abbot's Hospital, Kensington, on 10 April 1950, my mother was deemed unfit to care for me. I don't know how this came about, but I do know I was sent straight from the hospital to Ashwood, a National Children's Home for infants in Woking. I wonder if she held me before I was taken away. Somehow I doubt it, but she did name me Ronald, after the husband by whom she'd been abandoned.

Ashwood was built as an Arts and Crafts mansion. Three years earlier it had been established as a children's home to look after thirty-eight babies and toddlers and instil them with sound British Christian values, and it became the first home to me, a little black baby, in the heart of Home Counties Britain. A few vivid memories are all I have of my early life there: it's impossible to know how reliable they are, whether I have muddled them with other events or places I visited later, but this is what I recall.

The house had wood-panelled corridors, and shiny floors that smelled of beeswax polish, and French windows that looked over a big, sprawling lawn. In the middle of the lawn stood a huge cedar of Lebanon tree, and beyond its gnarled silvery trunk the grounds stretched as far as I could see.

I was an active child from an early age. I can see my small self, skating on the shiny floors indoors and careering down the grassy slope outside, and I remember the unexpected agony of falling in a patch of nettles. I recall planting apple seeds in the garden, then wondering why they hadn't grown into trees a week later. I remember making daisy-chain necklaces for my favourite carers, and picking lavender flowers, leaving them to soak in a jam-jar filled with water for several weeks in the hope of making lavender water. And I remember wondering why the result just smelled putrid.

For the first three years, I was as happy as a small child who has known no other life can be in such an institution. I became an adventurous toddler and a confident child. I was curious, precociously quick to learn, talkative and keen to be liked, but independent and unafraid to stand up for myself. I established a sort of status among the children and staff, being the first to reach several small developmental milestones: I could go to the toilet without anyone's help, I was able to pull up my trousers and braces, could do up my buttons and tie my own shoes, long before others of similar age. These were important achievements of which I felt extremely proud.

We slept in dormitories of eight or ten, each of us in small single beds. One night when we were playing pillow fights the light fused and everyone started crying. I told them all to be quiet – I would find the light switch and turn it back on. I fumbled my way around until I found it and pressed. Nothing happened and they all started wailing again. 'Shhh,' I reassured them. 'I know where your beds are. I'll help you get back to them.' In the darkness I located each whimpering child and led them to the safety of their bed. I was only about three or three and a half but I somehow sensed that I was different from the others; I had a quality which I would later identify as self-reliance.

The main thing I longed for and lacked was physical contact, cuddles, love. A limited supply came from one of the young girls who looked after me. She was probably just eighteen years old, and I think she may have been called Peggy. Sometimes at weekends, Peggy would take me home with her.

I loved these outings. Peggy's family would spoil me all weekend and I basked in her undivided attention. There would be games, treats and outings, and she would cuddle and kiss me, read me stories, and tightly tuck me into bed at night.

This was my first understanding of life in a normal family. I started to understand that the institution I lived in was not quite the same as a home, that love and demonstrations of physical affection were everyday occurrences and not rare treats. Best of all was the anticipation of the journey back by train on Sunday evening when I was exhausted. I'd sit on Peggy's lap and luxuriate in the feeling of arms enfolded around me, of her soft hand stroking my hair or holding my hand. But those occasional journeys also made me aware of what I lacked, and I hungered for more.

At Ashwood, I knew Peggy's routine. After breakfast I'd tear into one of the dining rooms where she was clearing up and we'd play a game where she would chase me around the table, catch hold of me, wrap me in a tablecloth and swing me round in the air while I squealed with delight.

One day when I ran down the corridor, she wasn't there. 'Where's Peggy?' I asked – only to be told she had left. There had been no warning or goodbye. I was bereft. I suppose it was against the rules for staff to tell the children when they were leaving but I haven't forgotten the sense of emptiness and abandonment I felt when I realised there would be no more weekend outings, no more cuddles, no more whirling tablecloth games.

Once or twice, I remember a black woman, a stranger, coming to visit. She was smart, yet brittle, and had a harshness in her manner very different from the carers. When she gazed at me it was with such fierce intensity that I shied away, my insides shrivelling as I stood in front of her. I sensed that she wanted something from me. I could see there was fury and displeasure in her eyes and I didn't know why or how to respond. They said this person was my mother and that I should call her Mummy. I wonder if she looked at me and saw my dead father, the architect of her misfortune. The small, frightened boy in front of her was all she had left of him. Neither of us knew what to say to each other and she'd soon leave. Afterwards I'd be fretful and anxious, until the memory of her faded.

My final recollection of Ashwood is 2 June 1953. Armed with Union Jack flags we were all taken into the street to watch the procession for the Queen's coronation. I was three – too old to stay in an infants' home any longer. Behind the scenes the authorities had probably already begun to make arrangements for the next stage of my childhood. A new institution awaited.

The only tangible thing I have left of those early Ashwood days is a small blurry black-and-white photograph that my sister gave me many years later. She found it in my mother's possessions after her death. I don't remember when it was taken, but in it I am very small and reaching up to give what looks like a posy of flowers to one of the carers. I like to imagine that it's Peggy.

2

The Light of the World

From Woking I was sent to Lancashire, to another National Children's Home called Westdene, a large redbrick Edwardian house in a suburban road in Southport. I must have gone to school, learned to read and count there, although I don't recall who taught me to do so. I do know that I settled in easily, made friends, and once again I felt as secure and happy as you can be in a children's home. Sister Ida, who was neither a nurse nor a nun, was my favourite carer. She was a long-limbed woman, with sandy hair, gentle pale eyes and a radiant smile. The other carers were kind too and I made friends with the other children. As I saw it, they were my family. We sometimes squabbled, I was scolded if I behaved badly, praised when I did well, but I felt safe within the organised structure of institutional life.

On weekends there was Sunday school and church, where I soaked up the Christian ideology I was taught. I loved every

Bible story: the Loaves and the Fishes, the Sermon on the Mount and, best of all, the Nativity. I could recite the Lord's Prayer and sing 'Now the Day Is Over' by Sabine Baring-Gould. I wanted to be good and to shine like the lamp in the picture in the hall at Westdene, so that God and Sister Ida would love me. I couldn't tear my eyes away from that picture. A figure of Christ, crowned and clad in a rich embroidered crimson cloak and a white robe, stood in an eerie half-light by a door overgrown with weeds, his hand raised to knock. In his other hand he clasped an ornate lantern, the light from which glazed his robe and highlighted the tangle of brambles and dead vegetation crowding the foreground.

I learned that this arresting composition was William Holman Hunt's *The Light of the World*, and it's the first picture I vividly recall. What did it mean? I wondered. Why did the door have no handle? What did the weeds signify? Why were they dead? Many years later I would discover that the painting was inspired by a line in Revelation, and represents Christ bringing enlightenment and salvation to a sinful world. I'd also learn that Hunt, one of the founding members of the Pre-Raphaelite Brotherhood, painted three versions of this subject. The largest version, completed in 1856, was bought by Charles Booth, a wealthy industrialist, and donated to St Paul's Cathedral.

A century later, when as a small child I was struck by its powerful Christian symbolism, it still ranked among the most popular paintings of all time, partly because, thanks to Booth, it had toured the British Empire, and been admired by around two million people, from Canada to Australia. Reproductions were to be found in countless Bibles and prayer books; they hung in churches, Sunday schools, nurseries and children's homes throughout the Empire, where many remain to this day. The large print that captured my attention was one of thousands. Even now, whenever I see one, memories of my early life return.

My best friend at Westdene was Anna. I can't remember our first meeting and don't know if we bonded because she was also mixed-race (her father was Jamaican, her mother British), but I do know that we loved playing together. Sometimes at weekends, we stayed with a foster family called the Phillipses. They would take us for walks on the beach or let us camp in the garden. I had my own bedroom in their house, a treat when dormitories were the norm, and the bed was excitingly different from institutional varieties – so high I felt I needed a ladder to get into it.

In winter, Anna and I spent hours making things out of bits of paper and old scraps of fabric, or sewing pictures on cards with brightly coloured wool, or painting and drawing. We were both creative and our interests were encouraged by the staff. There was a mongrel dog called Susie that we both loved. We were allowed to feed her and would stroke her and play games with her on the lawn, throwing the ball and trying to teach her to bring it back to us.

When we weren't lavishing love on Susie, dressing up was a favourite pastime. There was a laundry hamper, so big that you could climb into it, filled with a variety of unwanted clothes: flowery dresses, a cowboy outfit, a feather boa, jackets, shoes, hats, scarves. Anna would parade in long flowery dresses and twirl a Chinese parasol. There was a red tartan kilt that I loved and thought suited me perfectly, so I'd strut around in it whenever I could, feeling delighted. Perhaps this is where my enduring fondness for fashion started.

There was an old people's home next door to Westdene. Once a week, weather permitting, the elderly ladies would sit in a row in the front yard sewing and knitting. They loved to see the Westdene children, and we were encouraged to go and visit them. Everyone wanted to talk to me, stroke my hair and touch my face. I would go down the line and say hello and shake their hands and be as charming as I could, asking them questions about what they were doing, standing up straight, and smiling brightly. They loved the chirpy little boy and would give me a penny or a halfpenny and pat me on the head. I'd return to Westdene with a pocketful of money, basking in the extra attention they'd given me. I knew it wasn't just that I was well mannered, but because I was black, but that didn't make me uncomfortable. I felt I was being celebrated and encouraged, not condemned.

In summer, the staff would bring a table outside and we'd have lunch and races afterwards. Sport was my great passion. I was a very fast runner and highly competitive. One sports day, I won a race and was rather full of myself, so I was feeling confident of a second victory when I entered the wheelbarrow race. I asked my partner to hold my legs, because I knew I could go faster on my hands than he could. We shot off down the track straight into the lead, but I was going too fast for him to keep up and he stumbled and dropped my legs. We were disqualified on the spot. I stomped off, indignant at the injustice – we were way ahead: it wasn't fair. My eyes pricked with tears, but not wanting to be a 'sissy', I scurried off and found a secret hiding place in the shrubbery along the wall. I stood there sulking until Sister Ida came and found me sometime later. I was still shaking with fury and trying not to cry. She put her hand on my shoulder and asked me what I was doing. 'Nothing, nothing,' I mumbled, head down, unable to look at her.

'Games are games and you must be able to lose as graciously as you would be triumphant when you win. Nobody likes a bad sport,' she said, very firm but gentle.

Her disapproval was more than I could bear. I pulled myself together, partly because I felt ashamed and partly because I loved her so much. Ever since, I've always tried to be a good loser and hold my competitiveness in check.

Some afternoons at Westdene we could watch children's TV. *The Sooty Show* was my favourite programme. I could relate to the mischievous bear puppet with the black ears and thought his practical jokes and slapstick humour were hilarious. So my excitement was overwhelming when we were told we were in line for a great treat – Harry Corbett, Sooty's creator, was coming to visit, and Sooty would be coming too. Anna and I rushed around shouting Sooty's catchphrase 'Izzy, whizzy, let's get bizzy!' until even Sister Ida's patience was tested and she told us to calm down.

The table was arranged with Harry seated at one end, and all the children along the sides. Perhaps because I'd been good, or I was just lucky, I was chosen to sit next to him. My hero allowed me to put his puppets on my hands and play with them for a few minutes. This was heaven beyond expectation – Sooty and Harry Corbett right next to me. I felt that the world smiled on me, that anything was possible, that my wildest

dreams could become reality if I was good and worked hard —
and was a gracious loser when necessary. I remember that day,
even now, as the most euphoric of my childhood. I couldn't
possibly have envisaged what lay in store. Until this point
institutions and carers were all I'd known and the people who'd
looked after me had never given me reason for distrust. When
I behaved badly I had been fairly reprimanded; when I behaved
well I was praised. My world felt structured and reliable. But
in the months and years that followed, all that changed, and
at times danger and sorrow seemed overwhelming. Yet somehow amid the chaos Sooty and Sweep remained as constants —
a kind of promise that no matter how bad things got, magical
times might one day transform my existence once more.

Soon after Harry Corbett's visit, another less joyful surprise
awaited. My mother reappeared in my life. She had been busy
persuading the authorities that her mental health had recovered. She was fit to look after me and wanted me back.

No one warned me I was going to leave Westdene until the
morning of my departure when a small suitcase was packed
with my few belongings and I was ushered downstairs. Sitting
in the hallway was the black woman I remembered from Ashwood. She was stylishly dressed, her make-up was immaculate,
sweet perfume wafted around her, but there was no hug when
she saw me. No smile, no affectionate greeting, just a narrow-
eyed glance of recognition, dark, cherry-lipsticked mouth
pursed, as if she didn't much like what she saw. She rose from
her seat, clutching her handbag on an arm crooked like a
weapon. 'Ronnie. You're coming home with me. We'll have
to get a move on, or we'll miss the train.'

Just like that I was wrenched away from my familiar life and the people I loved most – the people I thought of as my family – Anna and Sister Ida. There was no chance to say goodbye to them. I didn't even know Anna's surname and she didn't know mine. For more than six decades we would be lost to each other.

I turned back to look over my shoulder as the door closed. The last image I recall is of a haloed Jesus surrounded by brambles, standing by a closed door, a look of concern in his eyes, a lantern in his hand.

3

The Organza Ball Dress

Walking into Portobello Road from Golborne Road towards the flyover, you see the whole of Portobello Road Market laid out like a map. It is a breezy sunny day, ideal for antique-hunting, and I am looking forward to a few hours scouring market stalls and shops for whatever takes my fancy, when some yards ahead a red transit van parked on the corner of the road catches my attention. Hanging on the side, visible from a distance, a dress of cobalt blue and white flutters like a flag. A vintage dress is not what I am looking for, but something about the brilliant contrast of colours draws me towards it. As I come closer, I see that the dress is every bit as striking as it was from afar. The bodice is strapless and covered with tightly pleated white organza. Beneath, a full skirt formed of tiers of vivid-blue, scallop-edged and trimmed in white, billows like a flower's petals. But as I rub the fabric between my fingers and examine the stitching closely, I shudder. There is more to this dress than its distinctive design and careful craftsmanship. I recognise it. I see my seven-year-old self, kneeling on the floor, tacking these same layers of fabric, under my mother's hyper-critical eye. This is my mother's ball dress – a dress that I helped her to make. It's an extraordinary coincidence but I'm certain.

I force myself to return to the present. 'Where did you buy this?' I ask the vendor. She tells me it came from Eastbourne – a seaside town that also played a significant role in my life. I nod and wonder how the dress made its way there.

Still bowled over at the strangeness of finding the dress again, I can't help myself from enquiring about the price. 'Two hundred pounds – but I can take £175,' the vendor tells me, waiting for me to make a counteroffer. I think for a minute, then I shake my head. 'Sorry, it's not for me,' I say. Before I walk away, I ask if she minds me photographing it. She agrees. Afterwards, I congratulate myself on having made the right decision. Had the price been lower, I might have been tempted to buy it. But the memories the dress conjures are ones I would rather forget. In a digital album, somewhere on my laptop, the photograph that I took of the dress remains. I haven't looked at it again, but neither have I deleted it.

When my mother came for me in Southport, we went straight to the station and took the train to London. The northern countryside flooded past the window. Unfamiliar fields yielded to scrubby wasteland, then, sporadically, unloved suburbs, cheerless houses, smoke-belching factories, gloomy tunnels, drab, rain-spattered stations all came and went. I scarcely saw them and I remember little, except that I cried uncontrollably all the way back to London, feeling deserted, anxious, desolate. My mother didn't try to calm or comfort me. Her eyes seemed unreadable as her gaze fell on me, and then away into the distance. I sensed my distress harden her, which compounded my fear.

As soon as we reached London, I was handed over to a babysitter called Susan. 'Be a good boy. Susan will look after you. I'm going to fetch Lynette.'

That was how I discovered I had a sister.

To pass the time Susan asked me to read the dates on coins. I was not quite six years old, but I wasn't stupid. I knew my numbers, although I had yet to learn to say the dates properly. If the date was 1945, I'd read, 'One, nine, four, five,' not 'Nineteen forty-five.' Every time I made a mistake Susan picked up a piece of wood and hit me hard across my knuckles. It was the first time I'd ever been unjustly punished. I was bewildered, frozen with disbelief. The adults I had known up to this point had always treated me fairly. Not knowing something I hadn't been taught didn't feel like a misdemeanour. What had happened? I would soon learn.

Lynette at four years old was fourteen months younger than me, a little girl with delicate features and an enchanting smile, who everyone, including my mother, adored. Her father, who we called Uncle Stan, hadn't married my mother, but he visited from time to time and provided some support, so Lynette's early childhood had been very different from mine. With Stan in the picture, my mother had been well enough to look after my sister when she was born – she hadn't been handed straight into care. As a result, they had bonded, and there was a closeness between them that I would never infiltrate.

We lived in a dingy first-floor flat at 10 Stanlake Road, Shepherd's Bush, very near Shepherd's Bush Market. There was one bedroom, a tiny kitchen area and a shared toilet. Wooden steps at the back led down to a neglected garden and the coal bunker. A zinc bath hung on the outside wall. To begin with, the three of us – Lynette, my mother and I – slept in one bed, but a year or so later we acquired a small adjoining sitting room and my mother bought bunkbeds for us, although we still all slept in one room.

We were very poor and my mother made ends meet by taking a variety of jobs: dressmaking, cooking, childminding, office work at London Transport, and as an administrator for *Reader's Digest*. But we always struggled and relied on family allowance to help us buy food and pay the rent. She was a proficient cook, often creating African dishes which were very spicy and contrasted violently with the bland institutional menu I'd been fed until then. There was no more shepherd's pie or rice pudding, instead I struggled with stewed-up pigs' trotters and chilli soup so hot I called it 'fire soup' and thought was torture to swallow. She despised me because I hated picking up her chicken drumsticks and wings and eating with my fingers. At Westdene I'd been taught this was bad manners. 'You're not a proper black man if you don't like picking up bones and eating them,' Mummy would yell.

Being the oldest child, from the age of six I was allocated a long list of household chores. I would be despatched to Shepherd's Bush Market to buy the groceries and return laden with heavy bags of provisions. It was my job to bring in the coal, do the washing-up and to launder our clothes in the sink and hang them to dry. I kept the flat clean and tidy, emptied the grate, laid the fire, swept the threadbare carpet with a stiff brush, mopped the cracked linoleum floor, made the beds, ensuring each corner was perfect, and I dusted the mantelpiece, replacing every ornament exactly in its place. But things were never right. Mummy had an eye for detail; she always noticed imperfections and corrected me, with a lengthy tirade and physical punishment so I'd do better next time.

Once a week on Friday, whatever the weather, I was sent to get the family allowance from the post office. In a December blizzard one day, I lost the cheque. I was terrified. I searched the windswept street for what seemed like hours, too scared to go home. I was only seven, but I still remember how relentlessly my mother beat me, to what felt was within an inch of my life, so I'd remember to be more careful in future. I have no idea how we managed for money that week, but I know I never, ever made that mistake again.

Mummy's punishments became the norm of daily life. She explained that she was only doing it for my own good, because she was a conscientious mother, and wanted to rectify my many inadequacies. 'Why haven't you cleaned your shoes? Why didn't you clear up that mess? Why aren't the dishes cleaned properly? Why is your shirt dirty?' she'd shout. And then she'd explain how ashamed she felt of me. How humiliating it was to have a son like me. 'You're just like your father,' she'd always conclude.

I still ask myself why she came for me in the first place, what made her want to take me back. Perhaps she felt it was her duty – maybe she wanted to prove she was as good as any other mother. Maybe she didn't realise the extent of her mental illness. Perhaps when she looked at me, she didn't see a little boy, she saw my father, the man who had abandoned her, the reason for the hardship of her life. She was still angry with him and, consciously or not, wanted to vent those feelings. Being my father's son did not endear me to her, but I provided an outlet for her bitterness.

For each catalogued misdemeanour there was a slap with a hand, or whacks with a stick or a shoe or chair leg, or a lash with a length of electric flex, or a home-made whip that made my calves bleed. 'You're a bad boy. I have to do this to make you better,' she'd say, and I believed her. She hit me because she cared about me. I'd mend my ways so that I wouldn't be punished. So that one day she would love me like she loved my sister, who was never beaten. So that I wouldn't be fixed with gorgon stares and forensic scrutiny, and scowls of disapproval. So that I would be regarded with warmth and indulgence, and kissed goodnight like Lynette was. The trouble was that no matter how hard I tried, it never worked, and the beatings accelerated as my mother's mental health ricocheted from crisis to crisis.

If I cried out during her assaults and she yelled back too loudly, the neighbours would summon the police. At the knock of the authorities, she could revert to normality and persuade them there was nothing amiss. 'It must be a mistake, officer,' or, 'My boy was having a bad dream,' she'd explain, and they would go away, convinced all was well. After a while, she took to stuffing a wet flannel down my throat so I couldn't make a noise. It was usually stained with blood when she pulled it out.

On Saturdays, we had our weekly bath. Mummy would

tell me to fetch the galvanised zinc tub that hung on the wall outside the kitchen and fill it with water boiled in kettles and pots on the stove. I dreaded this moment because, when my turn came for washing, something about my vulnerability or nakedness would trigger her fury. She would become agitated and grab me by the throat and hold my head under the water until I thought I would drown, then at the last moment release her grip and allow me to come spluttering and coughing to the surface. 'Why're you struggling so? You're a dirty boy, I need to clean you, Ronnie,' she'd say, with a strangely unfocused look in her eye.

Whenever I was being punished, my sister, understandably terrified, would try to placate our mother, saying, 'Mummy, I love you,' and kissing her, but Mummy wouldn't be distracted from the task in hand. She'd continue to batter me, shouting while she hit me: 'You're just like your father. I carried you for nine months and I hate you. He went away and left me with you. He's gone away building bridges.' This sowed a seed of doubt in my mind that would trouble me for years. Did my father die in a car crash or had he abandoned her?

Sometimes Mummy coerced my sister to join in the punishment, ordering Lynette to say I was bad, a useless, worthless liar, and to hit me too. I never blamed Lynette for that. I just thought, We're both terrified and doing what we can to survive: Lynette loves her mother and if she tells her to do something, she will. To this day, we have never really discussed what happened. It's possible my sister saw me as someone who caused disruption. Someone who upset the equilibrium. Witnessing my punishment was preferable to seeing me rewarded with my mother's love. She didn't want to share.

My mother believed it was important that I should understand that not only was my behaviour defective, my physical appearance was too. Her tongue was a weapon just as lethal as the flex or the chair leg she used, and she employed it unsparingly. The daily verbal dissection covered every inch of me. 'You're ugly,' she told me with withering glares every day. 'Your mouth is disgusting, your nose is horrible, your hair is a mess, your body is puny. When you grow up no one will like you and if anyone sees you naked, they'll shrink back in horror.'

I didn't doubt that she was telling the truth and became convinced that my physical appearance would revolt anyone who looked at me. It wasn't until many years later that I accepted that there was absolutely nothing physically wrong with me. At the age of nine, I took to wearing a hat to distract attention from my face. At school I'd never let anyone see me in the shower. After games I preferred to leave the pitch early and get into trouble, or hang around and be the last boy in so no one saw me undressed. Even in adulthood I shied away from mirrors, and years later, while working as a hairdresser, I still couldn't tolerate my own reflection. I wear a hat to this day. In fact, hats have become part of my professional persona. I tell myself this is because wearing them brings a sense of style, and I enjoy that feeling. But truthfully, in part it's because the shadows linger.

Respite from life in the flat came from a family called the Hoads. When Lynette was born, my mother had been able to put on a show of normality, and she loved her new child, but her mental health was still fragile. By the time Lynette was eighteen months old, my mother was struggling and was fearful of becoming more seriously derailed. But she couldn't bear the thought of her daughter going into institutional care as I had done. Deciding to look for a foster family privately, she placed an advertisement in *The Lady* magazine.

A woman called Molly Hoad responded. She was married to Roy, a tailor, worked as a chef at the Eastbourne Grand Hotel, and had six children of her own: Martin, Michael, Derek, Jackie, Christine and Lynette. Later a seventh was born, Gerald. The family lived in a large Victorian house near the coast in Eastbourne. What made the mother of six want to take in another child? The simple answer was Lynette's name, which Molly Hoad's youngest daughter shared and had made her notice and respond to my mother's advertisement. Perhaps it was fate.

To avoid confusion my sister was called Poppet when she went to live with the Hoads. My mother visited her every weekend, sometimes just for the day, sometimes staying overnight, and she too grew close to the family, especially to Molly, who never saw the darker side of her nature and was captivated by her refined manners and immaculate appearance. When Poppet came back to live with us in London, the Hoads continued to play a key part in our lives. My sister and I stayed with them for six weeks every summer, as well as Christmas and Easter holidays. We called the parents Mummy and Daddy Hoad and thought of their children as our foster brothers and sisters. To begin with I felt awkwardly aware that while Poppet was well established in their family, I wasn't and wouldn't have been there at all without her.

Over time that sense of being an interloper faded and I

learned much over the years from the Hoads. Martin, a high-flyer who went on to become area manager for Procter & Gamble in Scandinavia, was my role model. 'Always keep your shoes clean, wear a clean shirt, dress smartly, and smile when you greet people,' he told me. I followed his advice and always have. He would often take me on outings with his girlfriend, Ann, who later became his wife. We would go to the Long Man of Wilmington and climb it, or to the pub that Ann's parents owned at Beachy Head, or to the Tiger Inn in East Dean. I was an independent child and sometimes I would take Christine's bicycle and delicious sandwiches Mummy Hoad made for me and cycle up to the Downs, or I would trek on foot along the coast for miles. In the winter, Mummy Hoad wrapped my hands and feet with plastic bags and I spent hours alone tobogganing from dawn to dusk.

I shared a room with Michael, Martin's twin, who was in the RAF. Occasionally, if he was heading back to base at the same time I was returning to London, Michael accompanied me on the train, dressed in his uniform and greatcoat. He had an unusual penchant for knitting and often passed the journey with his needles, which astonished the others in the carriage. He was fascinated by Canada, where he would eventually settle, and there were books about the country and its culture scattered about his room. When I was about nine or ten, I began to take an interest in any books he'd left lying around on Native American history. The subject enthralled me and this was the origin of my long fascination with the plight of disenfranchised peoples.

Christine was about ten years older than me and took on a sisterly role, taking me boating in the park or dinghy-sailing on the coast. Sometimes Derek and his girlfriend, Doreen (whom he would later marry), took me on outings. Lynette, four years my senior though closest to me in age, was the family rebel, but I couldn't help myself from looking up to her. As time passed, she would take me to the cinema: I was small for my age but somehow she'd sneak me into teenage movies and rock'n'roll films starring Elvis Presley when I was underage. Afterwards she taught me to jive. I can still see her sitting in the bath wearing her jeans so they'd shrink to fit her as tightly as possible.

The more I stayed and the closer I grew to the Hoads, the more I realised how abnormal my London existence was. Their family became my benchmark for a happy home life. They gave me stability, warmth, normality. They provided a sanctuary. Most importantly, I learned from them how to love.

To begin with there was no TV in our one-bedroomed flat, but we had a record player and a collection of records. Mummy told me what to play, and I was rebuked if her order wasn't carried out correctly. She loved a wide variety of music: from big band and Vera Lynn, to Petula Clark and Spanish music. 'Get on my feet, Ronnie, and move along with me, that way you'll learn the steps,' she'd say, grasping me tightly on the shoulder and waist. It wasn't fun because if I fell off, I'd be ridiculed for my clumsiness and there would be trouble. Within a minute or two I'd get so nervous that I inevitably did.

Of the few friends who came to visit my mother, some were musicians. I saw a poster of a black woman recently and thought, Most people wouldn't know who that is, but I do, because she was a friend of my mother's – a pianist called Winifred Atwell.

Unsurprisingly, attractive men liked my mother, and, although she was very selective, occasionally she would bring one home. One boyfriend called Uncle John was kind and took an interest in us. Once he entertained us by showing us a gun he had. Later we learned that he had accidentally run someone over with his car and killed them, driving while he was drunk. He couldn't live with himself after that and before the case came to trial, he shot himself with the gun he had showed us.

Sometimes men would take my mother to dances. It was for one of these that I helped her make the ball dress – I watched her pin the folds of white organza on the bodice, passing the pins when she waved her hand. I held the bands of blue fabric while she gathered and attached them to the skirt, and I helped to tack them in place. When it was finished, she tried it on and twirled in front of us, posing by the mirror. In the gloomy surroundings she looked luminously lovely, yet somehow incongruous, as if she'd stepped out of a movie or the pages of a fashion magazine.

4

The Irish Elk

The Irish elk's antlers span twelve feet from tip to tip. I remember as a small boy, at the Natural History Museum, gazing up at them towering over me, enthralled by their incredible dimensions, trying to capture their undulating form in my sketchbook, and to picture the animal to which they belonged. I wanted to find out more about this incredible beast. What did it eat? Where did it live? What purpose did the antlers serve? From reading the labels and poring over books, I discovered that the Irish elk is the largest species of deer that ever lived, standing nearly seven feet tall at its shoulder, and that the animal dates back to the Pleistocene period, flourishing until 13,000 years ago. I also learned that its name is something of a misnomer. In its heyday, these great creatures weren't confined to Ireland, but roamed the plains and forests of modern Northern Europe, Siberia and North Africa. The name may have come from the many fossils which have been

35

found in the Irish peat bogs, or because the first scientific records of the animal were made in the late seventeenth century by Thomas Molyneux, an Irish physician. Molyneux examined large antlers found near Dublin but, like many scientists of the time, he didn't accept the possibility of extinction and was convinced instead that the animal still survived somewhere in the world. It wasn't until the following century that Georges Cuvier put forward the theory that the Irish elk along with the mammoth and other creatures were no longer living, and the concept of extinction began to pose further questions for the men and women of science, ultimately leading to Charles Darwin's theory of evolution.

With the benefit of hindsight, it seems to me now that this shifting interpretation of the Irish elk's significance also demonstrates that human understanding is subjective and limited. The same object viewed through a different prism in time can represent a different argument and underpin a different belief. Understanding is often shaped by time and cultural convention. But as a seven-year-old boy, it was neither the shifting social mores nor the puzzles of science that captivated me, but the sheer visual impact and scale of the antlers.

My amazement at the Irish elk was a catalyst for new interests. All around the museum, cases were full of displays of other animals that were equally revelatory: from hummingbirds to turtles, from herons to hippos, I looked and studied and learned and drew. Even today, whenever I see the fossils of the Irish elk, I am still awestruck, and if I see their distant cousins, the fallow deer, grazing in the park, I always think of them.

*

By the time I made the acquaintance of the Irish elk and its colleagues, I had been a pupil at Miles Coverdale Primary School for nearly two years. The school was five minutes from our flat. I would usually walk unaccompanied, crossing the busy Uxbridge Road. The playground backed on to the BBC Studios in Lime Grove, and while I waited for lessons to start, I often saw the newsreaders and presenters coming and going.

School offered an escape from home and I remember the excitement of my first day. The headmaster, Mr Pepper, welcomed me as a new pupil, and my teachers, Miss Sharp, Miss Dibell and Miss James, introduced themselves. When I was given some assessment tests, Miss Sharp and Miss Dibell were pleasantly surprised by my efforts. I'd spent most of my life in institutions but I could read all the *Janet and John* books and solve the maths questions quicker than most of the other pupils. Gradually, their assumptions about what I was capable of recalibrated and I was moved up a year, where I still often came top of the class.

Learning came naturally. I had a good memory and found every lesson interesting. I loved drawing and painting, and making models out of plasticine or balsa wood, or building Airfix models if I could get them. Reading was another passion. I read fairy tales and comics voraciously and fell in love with *The Little Bookroom* by Eleanor Farjeon. The story I liked best was 'San Fairy Ann' – a tale about an evacuee who goes to the countryside in Wiltshire. It strikes me now that there were parallels with my own life and the sanctuary that the Hoads gave me, but I didn't think of it at the time. Even now I keep a copy of the book by my bed and read it when I can't sleep. Not long ago I walked up Hampstead Hill and through a graveyard and came across the author's grave. Once again it felt as if the past was reaching out to me.

My earliest understanding of what racial prejudice was came about through my best schoolfriend, Kevin King. He was just as smart and quick as I was, and I remember being miserable when he told me he was emigrating to America with his family. On the morning of his last day, before school, my mother sent me to the local shop to buy some milk. Two ladies whom I knew and respected, because they sometimes minded my sister and me, were in the queue in front of me. They were discussing Irish immigrants, saying how much they disliked them because the children were dirty and uneducated, the men road workers, navvies, toilet cleaners and drunks, and the women lazy and immoral.

Later that afternoon, I walked home with Kevin for what I knew would be the last time. I felt subdued by the sadness of the occasion and as we headed towards the smarter end of the road near the park where he lived, I put my arm affectionately around his shoulders and decided I should give him the benefit of what I'd learned that morning. 'Watch out for the Irish when you get to America,' I said. 'Don't have anything to do with them. I've heard they're smelly, stupid people,' and I went on to parrot the women's conversation.

Kevin seemed to grow quiet and pulled away as we reached his house. On the threshold he turned round but instead of saying goodbye he said, 'Ronnie – *I'm* Irish.'

I stood frozen with confusion. Kevin was the total antithesis of what the women had described. His parents were professional, inspiring, clean, well dressed and clever. This could only mean one thing. What the women had said wasn't true.

It broke my heart to have repeated a lie to my best friend. I was filled with shame and I thought about it again and again over the following days. I decided then that I was never going to listen to generalisations about any group of people. I was always going to get to know them and make up my own mind. It was a painful way to learn about prejudice – but Kevin taught me a lesson I've never forgotten.

In those days at school there were far fewer black children than there are now. Racism was overt in wider adult society, but I don't recall ever thinking about the colour of my skin or feeling ostracised or disadvantaged because of it. I had lots of friends, both boys and girls, but only one was my colour, Earl Neash – though in truth, we were rivals rather than friends. We often raced each other in the playground. I was a very fast runner, and no one could beat me except him.

Naturally, I was teased in the playground, but if the colour of my skin came into it, it didn't feel any different from the teasing a ginger boy or a fat boy or a freckled boy would get. In any case, even though I was small, I was good at sticking up for myself. I was assertive and opinionated. If anyone called me names I would laugh at them and defuse the situation. If that didn't work, I'd fight.

The only racist incident I remember is when, about seven years old, I was in Frithville Gardens playing near the paddling pool, when a girl twice my size came up and asked if I was Japanese.

'No,' I said.

'You are.'

'Japanese people don't look anything like me.'

'Good, because I hate the Japanese, and if you were Japanese I'd beat you up.'

This was not long after the Kevin incident, so I'd worked out what racism was. Even if I didn't know what it was called I'd learned judging people in this way was wrong.

I was always well dressed, washed and well mannered, so the hell of my home life was hidden. When my mother came to school, I'd feel embarrassed because her arresting looks and dress sense made her stand out to my friends who said she looked like a film star. They didn't know the other side of her, and I wanted to keep it that way because I didn't want their pity. In any case, I benefited from my mother's head-turning allure – it gave me a status I didn't want demolished.

One day at school, a boy whose house backed on to ours said, 'I saw your mother chasing you round the room with a big stick.'

'You're lying,' I replied and pushed him hard.

'I'm not,' he said, recoiling.

I went to push him again, but someone said, 'Don't take any notice, Ronnie. He always makes things up.'

'Right,' I said, and threw him a contemptuous look instead.

But, of course, what he'd said was true.

At weekends, I couldn't wait to get out of the house, and from the age of seven I spent most of my free time at the Natural History Museum. I became a junior member there and they gave me a drawing board, a pad of paper with crayons, and a little folding stool so I could sit and draw the fossils, the taxidermy birds and animals, or whatever else took my fancy. There, I was cocooned in a parallel world to my own, a place where there were no beatings, and no admonishments. This was the beginning of my love of museums. On my own I'd also visit stately homes like Kenwood House, and my passion for art was growing. In the company of these dead animals or paintings I could lose myself and feel safe.

From the age of seven, I was allowed to travel unaccompanied with my sister to visit the Hoads in Eastbourne. We both loved these visits – an escape from the Shepherd's Bush madness. I could relax there, run around, ask questions, squabble with Lynette, stand up for myself, and if I behaved badly I wouldn't be hit or told I was ugly.

Sometimes, if I was noisy or cheeky, which I often was, Mummy Hoad would ask me, 'Why are you such a naughty boy when your mother is so wonderful? And Poppet is such a good girl – why aren't you like her?' I loved and trusted her, but she thought so highly of my mother. How could I ruin that by telling her the truth about the woman she admired? That at home, when Mummy's mental health was bad our lives fell into chaos? If I demolished her idea of who my mother was, would it change her view of me? Besides, my mother wouldn't thank me if she found out that I'd said anything to create trouble for her.

One weekend my mother came down to the Hoads' to take me back to London with her. Mummy Hoad had made peach flan, my favourite pudding, and she cut it into slices. 'Here you are, Ronnie, help yourself. I made it especially for you.' I could feel my mother's eyes on me as I chose a piece that was deliberately small so it wouldn't make her cross. 'Take the big piece,' Mummy Hoad insisted. Reluctantly, I did as she said.

My mother didn't say a word about it until we were on the train. I was sitting opposite her in a compartment when suddenly I felt a sharp kick in the shin. I cried out as she glared at me furiously. I looked away, terrified, but a few minutes later another kick hit me in the other shin. 'Ow, Mummy, you're hurting me.' She didn't reply. Every so often a sharp kick was directed at my shins, and by the time we arrived at Victoria station my legs were bleeding. 'Why, Mummy? Why?' I cried.

'You know,' she eventually responded. 'You made me ashamed at lunchtime with your greediness. Don't ever do that again.'

5

A Cartier Pillbox

I've always loved boxes of every shape and variety, and, perhaps because they are small, easily portable, and popular, pillboxes have always been one of the mainstays of my antique-dealing career. Over the years, I've bought and sold more of them than I can remember, but those made by Cartier are my favourites.

Ever since they were founded by Louis-François Cartier in Paris during the mid-nineteenth century, the company has been synonymous with high-status objects, and today they still rank as one of the world's most prestigious brands, selling to royalty and rock stars alike around the globe.

The boxes I like best usually date from the 1930s, 1940s and 1950s. They are designed like a little drum, decorated with a raised reeded pattern to resemble the rim of a milled coin with a tiny stirrup-shaped or half-circular handle that lifts from the centre of the lid. They're the size of an old halfpenny coin and are usually made in 9ct or 18ct gold. When I first started dealing, I would browse market stalls and junk shops on the lookout for them and sometimes I would spot them from yards away. I'd usually take the 18ct ones I bought to one of the fashionable Parisian jewellers on Rue de la Paix – a road that links the Place Vendôme with Opéra, an area long associated with shops specialising in luxury items – and sell them on at a reasonable profit.

I never thought much about the boxes' purpose, just that they were made for glamorous women to keep in their handbags or on their dressing tables to store their medication. Nor do I ever remember wondering whether my mother would have wanted to own such an object. But I do recall that she had a large number of pills to take every day to maintain her mental stability. Some were large, some small, some tinted in pastel hues, others shiny and sugar-coated. There were far too many to keep in a Cartier box, which in any case she could not have afforded. I also remember that sometimes, when the pills didn't work, she'd force me to share them with her.

Bottles and boxes of my mother's prescription medication were scattered around the flat. She drank very strong coffee constantly, which must have made her agitation worse. During episodes of mental disorder, her eyes would grow dark and unfocused. She'd hold long conversations with herself where one persona would ask a question and the other would answer. Sometimes she'd just speak nonsense. My sister and I didn't understand what was going on, but we knew this was weird and we'd exchange looks and point at our heads.

'I'm going to kill you,' she'd scream when she was seriously derailed, wild-eyed, face contorted with fury, and then she would grab a handful of her pills in one hand and my face in the other, ram her fingers between my lips to open them and force them into my mouth. 'I'll write to my sister to tell her what I've done and that it was all your fault for being a bad boy. Then I'll kill myself too.' To make her screaming stop I'd pretend to swallow the pills, then go to the toilet and spit them out.

If anything went wrong, my mother assumed I was guilty and therefore required severe punishment. As she saw it, physical correction was her maternal duty. The punishments were never sexual, but they seemed purposefully designed to humiliate me and make me feel degraded. Sometimes the punishments were so weirdly cruel that looking back I wonder how she ever dreamt them up. Had she been punished as a child? Or had she seen similar punishments administered within the family? One of the worst was to take a teaspoon of the hottest chilli powder imaginable and force it into my mouth. Then she'd take another teaspoon and force it into my behind. The pain was excruciating. The after-effects lasted for days afterwards. In adulthood, I discovered that children can be killed in this way, but I remember her doing this to me two or three times during my childhood.

One day Mummy was entertaining a few friends and had made some canapés. A piece of cheese was missing from one of them – perhaps it had fallen off, or perhaps she had missed putting the cheese on in the first place, but my mother had no doubts about who was to blame. From being a perfect hostess, wrath changed her in an instant. 'Ronnie – you are a thief! You steal from your own mother!'

I hadn't taken it of course – I wouldn't have dared – and I

defended myself. But Mummy knew better: I was a bad boy and a liar so I must also be the cheese thief. I was terrified that she was about to administer chilli powder to me, but instead she opted for another of her favourite methods of correction, which she called pin-picking. I was ordered to stand in the centre of the room with one foot in the air and just the tip of one finger touching the ground, and told to balance until she decided I had been punished enough. If I failed and lost my balance or put my foot down early, I'd be severely beaten. The guests stood around chatting and sipping their drinks witnessing what was happening. She told them I deserved punishment. I was a thief; she was a good mother. No one said a thing.

Even worse than this was one punishment so horrific that even now I find it impossible to recount in its entirety. It was my day to do the shopping at Shepherd's Bush Market. I was given a long list, with precise instructions about where each item was to be purchased. The list included a cos lettuce. 'Make sure it's a cos lettuce. I don't want anything else. You know the stall by the paper shop? That's where you buy it.'

'Yes, Mummy,' I replied, and I went to the stall as directed, but on that particular day it wasn't there. I visited other nearby stalls. There was no cos lettuce to be found. 'Take this,' one vendor said. 'It's nearly the same as a cos.' I did as she suggested and returned with the groceries.

My mother unpacked everything. When she saw the lettuce, she held it in her hand. 'This isn't what I told you to get,' she said.

'The stall wasn't there,' I nervously replied. 'I looked everywhere. That was the closest I could find.'

'That stall is always there. You're lying!' she said with a slap or two. 'Go back and find what I want.'

Terrified of the repercussions if I remonstrated further, I trudged off, but the stall hadn't materialised, and just as before, none of the others had cos lettuce. There was nothing for it but to return empty-handed, a feeling of dread gnawing in the pit of my stomach. 'You are a bad boy,' my mother said. 'Go outside and find a stick so I can punish you. And make it a good bendy one, or I will come outside and pick three sticks to hit you with at the same time.' I did as I was told, sobbing in fear at what was to come. I handed the makeshift cane to her which she examined closely and deemed acceptable. 'Turn around and face the wall,' she said quietly. I turned. She whipped my calves until they bled, while I cried for forgiveness. But I wasn't forgiven and this wasn't the end of it.

The next day she had invited friends to come round. Before they arrived I was ordered to sit in the middle of the living room, in a situation too unbearably humiliating to describe. All morning I was forced to remain there, a helpless exhibit, fully clothed but shamingly exposed, while friends and members of the extended family came and went. If anyone commented when they saw me, my mother explained that this was for my own good, to rectify a terrible misdemeanour I had committed the previous day. I was a bad boy, and she had a responsibility to do this as a good mother.

For me, the emotional torture that morning was beyond even the worst beatings she had ever administered. The people who made up my world, who I respected and whose approval I craved, were witness to my ignominious treatment. What would they think of me now, having seen me like this? How

could I ever look any of them in the eye again? The humiliation was so acute that to remember those hours fills me
with indescribable pain. I have never spoken about this incident since that day and writing about it now resurrects a
sense of degradation so overwhelming that it still moves me
to tears.

Auntie Sarah, a friend of my mother from Sierra Leone,
was the only person who spoke up on my behalf. She was a
beautiful Portuguese woman whose husband was the chief of
police in Freetown. I recall the look of shock on her face at
seeing me there and hearing her tell my mother, 'Lizzie, you
have to stop treating this boy like this. You're going to damage
his mind if you continue.'

'Ronnie deserves it, he's a bad person. He told me a lie. You
don't understand. I have to do this,' Mummy explained.

'You're not just punishing him, you are humiliating him.'

But my mother knew better and left me there for several
more hours. When my humiliation was eventually deemed
sufficient I was permitted to crawl away to a corner, wishing
I was invisible.

After that, Auntie Sarah stopped coming to visit. Still, in
a way she saved me. Hearing her protest against my mother
was a slender straw, but it was enough to keep me mentally
afloat. It told me that this punishment wasn't what I deserved.
It wasn't normal and it shouldn't have happened. I clung to
that reassurance. Without her, I think my mother would have
demolished me.

Around this time, when I was still only seven years old, my
mother's health deteriorated and she was bedridden for three
months. I can't remember what was wrong, but it must have

been serious because the authorities sanctioned me to take a month or two off school to care for her and my sister.

My list of chores increased. I washed her, bathed my sister, did the shopping, cleaned the flat, took my sister to school, prepared meals and carried out whatever other tasks she set me. Even then, I couldn't meet my mother's expectations. Everything was wrong, and from her bed the punishments continued. One day she told me to make her lunch. I opened a tin of baked beans, tipped them into a pan and put it on the stove to warm while I made toast and coffee for her. I was hungry and I liked baked beans, so I helped myself to one or two, and then a few more. I put the rest on her plate and took them to her. 'This isn't a full tin,' she said with beady-eyed certainty. 'What did you do with the rest?'

'It's a full tin, Mummy,' I replied, eyeing the chair leg she kept within reach on her bed.

'It isn't. You're lying again.'

'I'm not, Mummy, I promise.' I took a step back.

'Go and get the tin out of the bin. Wash it and bring it here.'

I did as I was told. She scraped the beans off her plate into the tin. They didn't quite fill it. There was a half-inch gap to the rim.

'Come here. Hold out your hands.' She reached for the chair leg and whacked it down hard across my knuckles. She repeated this, again and again and again. That night, just in case I forgot the important lesson, she ordered me to stand by her bedside and forbade me to sit down. By about four o'clock in the morning, my head was spinning with exhaustion and I could hardly stay upright. I watched her. Her eyes were closed, the soft rise and fall of her bedcovers showed her breathing was regular, Mummy was at last asleep. I bent my legs and lowered myself to a sitting position on the floor. A minute later the chair leg whacked down on my head. 'I told you to stand – get up,' she ordered. I staggered to my feet before she hit me again. Sleep deprivation became a regular punishment. She'd keep me up all night. To me it was worse than being beaten.

When my mother had recovered from her ailment, I was brought before some officials who congratulated me for my efforts. Mummy didn't offer any words of gratitude, nor did she moderate the punishments. As far as she was concerned, I was still a bad boy and needed correction.

There was a kindly old lady, Mrs Jones, who lived in an upstairs flat. I'd talk to her on the stairs and she'd always invite me to visit her in her flat. This became a regular occurrence, and once a week when I went, she would give me a couple of pennies that she kept on a tray in her hall as pocket money. One day I went up to see her. The door was unlocked but Mrs Jones wasn't there. It was pocket money day so I helped myself to the usual two pennies from the tray.

Later, Mummy found the coins in my pocket. 'Where did they come from?'

'Mrs Jones upstairs.'

'You stole them, didn't you?' Her brow furrowed, dark fury shone in her eyes. I knew what that meant and felt terror suffuse me.

'No, Mummy, I didn't. I didn't steal.'

'You're a liar. She's been out all day.'

'She always gives me two pennies pocket money on Saturdays. She won't mind, Mummy.' I backed towards the door.

My mother came towards me. I stood rigid and mute. 'I knew it. You're a thief and a liar,' she said. 'How could I have produced a child as bad as you? I'll show you what happens to bad boys.' Quick as a snake she grabbed me by the arm and hauled me into the kitchen to the corner where the gas stove stood. 'This is what happens to boys who steal and lie,' she said. She ignited the burner and holding my two hands in one of hers forced my palms over the flame until my pitiful cries convinced her I had been sufficiently corrected.

Afterwards, she realised my hands were so badly blistered they would arouse questions, so she bandaged them up. I couldn't sleep, dressing and undressing was agony, and I could barely hold anything or feed myself, but my mother was unrepentant. I deserved the punishment she'd meted out.

'What happened to you?' Miss Dibell said at school the following Monday.

'Nothing, miss.'

'What are the bandages for?'

'I burned myself with the kettle, making tea.'

The explanation didn't convince her, and she took me to the school nurse, who unwrapped my hands. At the sight of the mottled flesh beneath, they both recoiled.

'These burns are not from hot water,' one of them said. 'Tell us what really happened, and we can help you.' I was traumatised and in severe pain, but I wasn't going to let Mummy down. I stuck to my story. I'd inflicted my injuries by my own clumsiness.

Miss Dibell didn't give up. She'd seen suspicious cuts and bruises before and worried that something was amiss, but these injuries were too disturbing to ignore. She took me to Mr Pepper, the headmaster, and several governors were summoned. They all wore looks of concern and pressed me to tell them what had really happened. They'd be able to help me if I told the truth, they promised. It was all too much and I burst into tears, but I held to my story. The burns were my fault.

My reticence wasn't only inspired by loyalty or protectiveness towards my mother, but by the terror of what would happen if I told them. They would question Mummy, but leave me with her while they pondered a course of action. Then she would carry out the threat she'd so often made: she'd kill me.

Once my hands had healed my mother's programme of correction resumed. There was a local remand centre in Goldhawk Road. Mummy talked to the officials, and explained that I was a bad boy and needed to be taught what happened if I carried on in my bad ways. They locked me in a cell for several hours – a foretaste of what it was like to be in prison.

When I was nearly eight, we moved to a two-bedroom basement flat at 138 Lancaster Road, the last house before the crossroads with Ladbroke Grove, not far from Portobello Road. Now my sister and I shared a bedroom, my mother slept in another room, and we had the additional luxury of a separate living room in which, after a month or two, a TV was installed.

At Lancaster Road, in the summer of 1958, I witnessed the first major race riots London had seen. Notting Hill in those days was crammed with overcrowded dingy bedsits where many of the capital's West Indian families lived – a world away from the trendy area it is today. It was also close to the headquarters of far-right groups: Oswald Mosley's Union Movement and the White Defence League.

The trouble started late in August, when nine white youths went on what one called 'a n*****-hunting' expedition. Armed with iron bars, planks of wood and knives, they attacked a house where several black men lived, leaving three gravely injured. Tensions continued to mount, then the following week, on 29 August, the worst racial violence Britain had ever seen erupted. A Jamaican man and his white wife were arguing outside Latimer Road Tube station. A white crowd assembled to defend the woman and a scuffle broke out. By the next evening around 200 white people were rampaging through the streets, wielding weapons and chanting racist slogans. Eventually the West Indian community retaliated by throwing home-made incendiary bombs and giving chase with weapons of their own. This altercation is now seen as a watershed in British race relations: the moment when the black community of Ladbroke Grove realised the extent of racial intolerance and began to resist.

I understood none of this – as far as my eight-year-old self was concerned, race was something to do with running. I saw black and white people clubbing each other brutally with sticks and batons and heard the term 'race riot'. Why are rampaging men shouting and beating each other with pieces of wood? What's that got to do with racing? I wondered.

Our TV inspired my mother to come up with a new means of punishment. If there was something I wanted to watch and she felt I deserved correction I was forced to stand next to her, facing the wall with my arms crossed over my chest, my left hand holding my right ear, my right hand clutching the ear on the opposite side. I was then told to squat down to the ground and stand up repeatedly. If I slowed or didn't go low enough, a whack on the head with a chair leg was used to encourage me. Sometimes I was made to do this all evening until she judged I'd got the message. By the end my legs felt like jelly, hardly able to support me. I would be drenched in sweat, almost dead with exhaustion, and all I could long for was the sanctuary of my bed.

Bed had become a sanctuary now that I slept in a separate room from her. I'd developed a routine that became a compulsive ritual. I'd load my bed with my coat, my dressing gown, jumpers, towels, and whatever else I could find, so that when I was in bed I could feel as much weight as possible on top of me. Then, before I got in I tucked the top sheet right over the pillow, leaving just one small triangle untucked so that I could slip in. Once in bed I drew the sheet right up over my head and my pillow and tucked it under the mattress beneath, so that my face was entirely shrouded, and no one could see me. Why did I do this? Was I trying to make myself invisible? What was it about the feeling of weight that brought comfort? All I know is that whenever my mother discovered me like this she became enraged, but that didn't deter me. For as long as I lived under the same roof as her I felt compelled to hide myself in this way. Even years later I always weighed my bed down with blankets, and when I slept in a sleeping bag I always zipped it over my head.

★

With extra space at her disposal my mother started childminding babies for working black mothers during the school holidays. Every morning between eight o'clock and ten o'clock, mothers would drop off their infants at our basement flat. Carrycots, Moses baskets and playpens were scattered about the three-room flat, while my mother reassured the other mothers that their infants would be well cared for, fed and changed as required. As soon as all the babies had arrived, she left for her office job at London Transport. I was charged with caring for the eight or ten babies, feeding and changing them until my mother's return, which was carefully timed so that she could hand the children back to their mothers without them realising what was going on.

One morning, an hour after she had left for work, I was giving a little boy called Henry his bottle when he started spluttering and crying. I comforted him and tried to calm him, but it didn't do any good. Great chest-wracking spasms contorted his little body, and then I saw a trickle of bright red blood ooze from his mouth.

I recognised that this was an emergency. Unless something was done the child might die, but if I called an ambulance when my mother wasn't there she'd be in serious trouble, and then so would I. What would Mummy want me to do? I couldn't telephone because I didn't have her number. Nor could I ask for outside help.

My head was pounding as I formulated my plan and got to work. I made sure all the babies were comfortable, changed, fed and in their cots and baskets. Henry was still coughing up blood and crying but I cleaned him up and tucked him into his cot. Leaving them alone in the flat, I ran to Ladbroke Grove

Tube station. I had no money, but I dodged the barriers and ticket inspectors and jumped on the first train to Baker Street. I sat in the carriage vacantly watching the stops pass – Westbourne Park, Royal Oak, Paddington, Edgware Road – taut with mounting anxiety, each minute seemingly stretched to an eternity. Would Henry die before I could get help? If so, would it be my fault or Mummy's? Neither eventuality was in any way desirable because I would be blamed and punished severely either way.

These thoughts and the image of poor Henry and the trickling crimson blood haunted me with every jolt, sway and rattle of the train. By the time the train screeched to a halt and the doors hissed open at Baker Street I was in a state of complete turmoil. I knew my mother's office was somewhere in the station, although I'd never been there before. How would I locate her? Somehow, I managed to calm myself down sufficiently to ask an official where she was and I found her. 'Ronnie – what are you doing here?' she said, looking up in amazement.

'Something's happened, Mummy. I'm sorry,' I said, shaking with apprehension, holding back the tears.

She didn't want anyone to know what was going on at home, so she drew me to one side. Reassured by the fact her expression was one of concern rather than fury, I outlined what had happened to baby Henry. She saw the urgency of the situation, and, explaining that there was an emergency at home to her supervisor, we rushed home together. We could hear several of the babies wailing loudly even before she opened the door. Henry was half asleep, quiet, pale and feverish, but still alive. 'Go and see to the others, Ronnie,' she said.

She picked Henry up, cleaned the blood from his face, and swaddled him in a clean blanket. 'I'm taking him to the doctor.'

Mercifully, Henry recovered, but questions must have been asked, because after that there were no more babies to look after.

The following Christmas we didn't go to the Hoads'. My mother had decided we'd stay in London and celebrate in the Lancaster Road flat, inviting a few family members and friends round. She had bought some presents for me, but when the time came to hand them out, something I had done must have annoyed her and she needed to cut me down to size, so she gave the presents to my sister instead and enjoyed watching me while Lynette opened them.

It was a bitterly cold day with snow on the ground outside, and we had a coal fire to heat the living room. Just before lunch was served, my mother decided we needed more coal, and that I would have to go outside and stand in the front garden to wait for the coal lorry to come, because you couldn't see the traffic from the front room. Knowing better than to argue, I took up my position as directed, standing in the front garden, in the snow, while everyone else carried on enjoying themselves indoors and sat down to Christmas lunch. I watched my breath cloud the air in front of my face, I stamped my feet and rubbed my hands to try and keep warm. In the distance I could hear Christmas carols play on the radio. Of course the lorry was never going to come. It was Christmas Day.

For hours I remained there, freezing cold. Now and again I took my eyes off the street to turn to watch everyone inside in the warm, pulling crackers, wearing party hats, tucking in to their hot Christmas meal.

After lunch was over, I was summoned back in. By then my teeth were chattering, I was shivering uncontrollably and was scarcely able to walk because my feet had lost all sensation from the cold. Seeing the state I was in, Mummy frowned at me for a minute, then said, 'Don't worry, I know the cure for chilblains, go and get the pot.'

She instructed me to wee in the chamber pot, take off my shoes and socks, and sit on a chair, in the middle of the Christmas gathering, with my feet soaking in the pot of urine. Utterly humiliated, I swallowed the tears, did as I was told, and was rewarded with some leftovers of the Christmas meal.

One hot day in summer, I returned from school and walked into the living room. The first thing that struck me was the fetid stench in the room. Then I saw the feet sticking out from behind the sofa. Mummy lay sprawled unconscious on the floor. Her cotton dress was rucked up around her thighs, one of her shoes had fallen off, the other still clung to her foot like a man grasping a raft in a storm. All around, pills were scattered over the carpet like confetti. I worked it out quickly. She'd often threatened to take an overdose of pills. Now she'd carried out the threat, and in her unconscious state she had lost control of her bodily functions.

I squatted down beside her, not wanting to look, stomach heaving, uncertain what I should do. 'Mummy, Mummy, wake up. Please, Mummy, wake up,' I whispered. I was afraid to touch her, afraid to leave her, afraid she would wake up and hit me, afraid and repelled by the mess she was in. As far as I could see she wasn't breathing.

I had to decide what course of action to take. At the age of nine I had to be a man. I backed out into the sun-drenched street and sprinted down the road to the telephone box to call 999. Then I made my way back to the flat, pacing outside as I waited for the ambulance to arrive. I was too confused to re-enter the room, and numb from the shock of finding her like that. I don't remember if I felt relief or anguish at the certainty she was dead.

The ambulance siren notified the street that something unusual had happened and curious neighbours came out to gather around the front of our flat. I showed the emergency services where my mother was and slipped out into the street, trying to lose myself in the crowd. The thought of having to explain what had happened was more than I could face. I could scarcely work it out myself. I wanted to distance myself from the chaos. The ambulance men brought out my mother on a stretcher, completely covered with a red blanket. The colour seemed almost fluorescent in the bright sunlight, and to my watchful eye it was a signal. Had she been alive they wouldn't have covered her head – she was dead. The blanket confirmed it.

A boy I knew who lived nearby came up and looked at me hard. 'Isn't that the house where you live? What's going on? Who's dead?' he said.

I shook my head. 'No. That's not my place,' I said. 'I don't know who that is.' As soon as I spoke those words I was filled with a sense of self-loathing. I had just denied my own mother. What kind of person was I?

The police summoned social services. Lynette and I were comforted by carefully trained professionals who told us they were taking us to a National Children's Home in the East End of London while the situation was assessed. I sat in the back of a car as we were transported to safety, still filled with a sense of revulsion, not just at the scene I had witnessed, but at myself for not having acknowledged my own mother.

It was several days before we were given unexpected news: Mummy hadn't died. They'd pumped out her stomach and revived her. She was recovering in hospital.

We would go home as soon as she was better.

6

Ferragamo Rainbow Shoes

I often spend hours in Jermyn Street, gazing in the window of exclusive shops like John Lobb, Foster & Son or Henry Maxwell that sell bench-made shoes. When I was in my thirties, with money to spend, I had a row of Maxwell riding boots on display and regarded them as works of art. Ever since I was a child, shoes have represented a passage to other worlds – both glamorous and troubling.

Hollywood has long determined the way I dress. In the late sixties a group of friends and I regarded stars like Fred Astaire and Humphrey Bogart as the epitome of style and tried to imitate their way of dressing. We'd scour markets for vintage clothes, and we'd seek out men's outfitters in the East End of London, where the pristine stock sometimes dated from before the war. Once a week we would all dress up in our finds and go out on the town clubbing. We must have looked like a group of extras from a period film when we hit the dance floor, but we felt part of an elite and infinitely glamorous world.

Ladies' shoes have also long captivated me; not to wear, but because I love their sculptural qualities. The best designs can reshape the foot and simplify the form in astounding ways and, of course, they too connect to that imaginary universe of the movies. I started buying vintage ladies' shoes in the seventies, when I was also dealing in vintage luggage. In those days there was nowhere to sell luggage in London, but I discovered it was possible to sell it in Paris where the market was just beginning. Sometimes when I was looking for watches and jewellery, I'd come across top-quality bags, cases or trunks, which I would buy and take to the Champs-Elysées, where one woman dealt in the top brands such as Chanel, Hermès and the trunk-making king, Louis Vuitton. With the profits I would sometimes go to J. M. Weston – the best shoe company in France, where any Parisian man of worth gets his shoes – and buy myself a pair, or I'd buy vintage women's shoes as an investment.

Top of my list were shoes made by Salvatore Ferragamo, the shoemaker to the stars in Hollywood. His story is an inspiring one: born into an impoverished Italian family, one of fourteen children, Ferragamo emigrated to America where, as well as learning shoemaking, he studied anatomy, thus ensuring his shoes were comfortable as well as beautiful. From a modest start, he opened a shop in Los Angeles and built up an extraordinarily illustrious clientele. Some of his most elegant shoes were worn by stars such as Lauren Bacall, Sophia Loren, Greta Garbo, Audrey Hepburn and Marilyn Monroe (who had more than forty pairs). Ferragamo is also famous for his innovative designs and his use of experimental materials (kangaroo hide, fish skin, cork, metal and plastic), as well as for drawing on historic sources for the inspiration that propelled him to footwear stardom. In 1938, he designed the famous Rainbow sandals for Judy Garland, in homage to her iconic role as Dorothy in *The Wizard of Oz* and the signature song 'Somewhere Over the Rainbow'. They had a wedge platform, formed from layers of cork covered in suede of different hues, and gold straps. There's a pair of Rainbow sandals in the Salvatore Ferragamo Museum in Florence, and nothing says more about Hollywood fantasy than their ingenious design and multicoloured extravagance. Somewhere in a cupboard I still have three or four pairs of vintage Ferragamo shoes from the Golden Age of Hollywood.

Mummy shared my love of shoes. She had a pair of high-heeled beige leather court shoes that she always wore for smart occasions. As a child I was fascinated by how low they scooped down at the front so that you could see the top of her toes. She looked so elegant in them and they seemed to enhance whatever else she wore. But it is a different pair of my mother's shoes, stilettoes, that are etched into my memory. They profoundly altered my perception of who she was, and who I would become, but in a different, uglier way.

My mother remarried a year after her suicide attempt, to Edward Monday, a Yorkshireman who worked as a municipal gardener for the local authority. He was a boulder of a man, thick-necked and small-eyed, with hands the size of shovels, which he'd frequently use to punch me so hard that my feet left the ground. Monday lived in a house in Streatham and after their marriage we moved out of our Notting Hill flat and in with him. But the combination of his violent tendencies and Mummy's mental instability didn't make for marital harmony. Whatever it was that brought them together didn't last, and as the shine of their romance dimmed, he turned his fists on Mummy as well as on me.

School was my refuge from the violence. I felt safe in the classroom and the playground. If I worked hard and played hard it stopped me from thinking about the viciousness at home. My grades were good, though in the playground I got into fights almost every day, perhaps because physical sparring provided a release for what was happening to me.

My teachers said I was in line to pass my Eleven Plus and could go to grammar school but my mother was disparaging, twisting the teachers' praise into a failing. 'You know everything. You'll be a doctor one day,' she would say, in a dismissive tone to make clear that as she viewed it, my academic promise was nothing special. I agreed, to appease her and avoid a fight, but I knew that would never happen.

Ted Monday returned home one day with a stack of old literary classics. 'Read those if you think you're so clever,' he snarled. I knew he meant this to be a form of punishment, but I was delighted by his instructions and devoured *Black Beauty*, *Great Expectations*, *Oliver Twist*, *Little Women*, *Swallows and Amazons*, *The Adventures of Tom Sawyer*, *A Tale of Two Cities* and many more, often reading long into the night.

When the Eleven Plus came around, I sat it and, as predicted, passed. Grammar school places were offered, but I chose to go to a flagship co-ed comprehensive in Putney Hill called Elliott School that had opened four years earlier. Comprehensives were the new educational way. Elliott, one of the leading exponents of the system, had incredible facilities with buildings designed by the architects of the Royal Festival Hall. Being sports mad and keen on drama, I loved the fact that it had tennis courts, an Olympic-style gymnasium, an open-air theatre, an assembly hall modelled on the Festival Hall, and a playing area laid out with a path in the shape of an elephant's head that echoed the elephant on the school badge.

More importantly, I would discover, the most brilliant teachers worked there. Among them were Mary Berners-Lee, mother of Tim who invented the World Wide Web, Dr Forshaw, the head of maths, who used to ride his horse down the corridor, and Ken Jennings, the biology teacher, who brought his pet golden eagle to school. The physics teacher Bernard Beach was a favourite of mine. On one occasion some boys were caught in the lab filling condoms with helium and floating them out of the window. When the culprits were brought in front of him, he simply said, 'Don't be so bloody wasteful. Get out!' And then there was Huw Salisbury, the woodwork and metalwork teacher, awarded an OBE for his services to teaching, and the equally inspiring Jo Hawkey, an art teacher, who would later become Huw's wife, as well as a close friend and a surrogate big sister to me.

I'd settled into Elliott well when, six months later, I sauntered home, back an hour late from school. My mother and Ted Monday were there, standing in the front room, waiting for me. I was surprised to see them together. They'd argued a couple of days earlier and hadn't been speaking since, but my disappearance forced them to talk to each other, and neither were happy about it.

'Where have you been? What have you been doing?' my mother asked in a strained, high-pitched voice that signified danger.

I paused before replying. A couple of days earlier, when Ted was out at work, she'd seemed to re-evaluate her harshness towards me. 'Just tell me the truth when I ask you, and you won't be punished,' she'd promised. So rather than pretend I had been working late at school, I decided to come clean. 'I was playing football with some of the lads, and I forgot the time,' I said.

'You've been doing what? Playing football?' Monday snarled, as though this was a heinous crime. Before I could answer, a couple of vicious punches landed on each side of my head and one thrust went straight in my stomach. 'You're saying you've been mucking about playing football. And all the while, your mother's been worried sick.'

'I'm sorry, Mummy,' I managed to whisper, doubled up, head spinning.

The apology wasn't good enough and all hell broke loose. She removed her stiletto shoe and, with a look of concentration, came at me. Raising the shoe, she brought it down like a hatchet, striking my head with the heel. Again and again blows rained down on my temple. I cried out, begging her to stop because at some point she must have hit a blood vessel. Suddenly all I could see was dark red. It was as if a maroon curtain had fallen.

I yelled out: 'Stop it, Mummy! Please! Stop it, Mummy! Please! I'm blind, I'm blind!' I was more terrified than I'd ever been. It had always seemed to me that being blind was the worst thing that could happen to a person. And my mother, who had promised to protect me, who had assured me she would not punish me if I told her the truth, was inflicting this terrible injury on me and ignoring my distress.

'I don't care if you are blind. You deserve everything you're getting,' she responded. Intent on the task at hand, she continued until her fury was finally spent.

I couldn't see my hand if I held it to my face. I couldn't see the wall. The world had gone dark. There was nothing.

My sight returned the following day, but the incident marked a turning point. Until then I'd convinced myself that no matter how often my mother punished me, she was doing it for my own good. But her indifference to my distress called this assumption into question. She really can't love me if she just wants to hurt me, I thought. My trust didn't recover. I would never view her in the same light again.

After that I just wanted to escape. But I no longer bothered to answer back. I wasn't the chatty child I had been, I didn't ask questions. Feeling unsafe and unloved, apart from when I stayed with the Hoads, I became increasingly morose, embittered and introverted. And I couldn't bring myself to tell them what was happening.

The violence between Ted Monday and my mother escalated. One night a ferocious argument erupted during which he threw her down the stairs, grabbed a smouldering log from the fire, and began battering her face. My mother screamed out to me that I should take my sister and go to the police station to get help – her ribs were broken, she couldn't move. I didn't need asking twice. Holding Lynette by the hand, we sprinted for our lives the mile or so there.

We spent several hours at the police station while social services were notified. Eventually we were taken to a temporary care home called Earlsfield House while the authorities tried to untangle the truth of what was going on and decided what should be done with us long term. I was in turmoil. I desperately wanted to be put into permanent care where I would be safe. If I went back to live with my mother and Ted Monday again I wouldn't survive, mentally or physically. One way or another, they'd kill me. I was certain of it. But aged eleven, how could I bring this about?

Our case came to court. All I recall is that there were people everywhere and that I was deeply troubled. A police officer who had been on duty testified that we had arrived in a distressed state and raised the alarm. He also testified that he had never encountered such a well-mannered child – he couldn't have comprehended that this was the result of my mother's super-strict disciplinarian regime. The social services understood that my sister was terrified that Ted Monday would kill our mother, and they suspected that I was afraid he and my mother would kill me, although I hadn't been able to say as much. Shame is the worst part of abuse – the fact you have to let it happen, the shame of not running away, the shame of not reporting it, and not stopping it, even though as a child you can do nothing.

'Do you want to go back and live at home with your mother or stay in care?' one of the officials asked. I was an articulate child, but too petrified to speak out. More than anything I longed to escape my mother, but I was somehow conscious of the prevailing wisdom that it is best to keep families together if possible, even if they were dysfunctional. Didn't they know what would happen if I said I desperately wanted to stay in care, and they decided to send me back to my mother anyway? Couldn't they see she'd kill me for publicly shaming her? What could I do? The dilemma was unbearable. Gagged by terror and confusion I sobbed uncontrollably. But somebody must have understood. They reached a decision: my sister and I would be put in permanent care. We never went home again.

We remained in Earlsfield House for several months, while a permanent home with room for us both was sought. Slowly my body mended. The cuts and grazes disappeared, but the memory of the trauma hadn't faded and my head was more messed up than I realised. April came and with it my twelfth birthday, but I told no one. I had no expectations. My birthday wasn't something my mother had felt required celebration.

At Earlsfield House, there was a weekly ritual where we'd all gather in the hall by a locked cupboard. One of the members of staff would unlock the cupboard and hand out presents to the children who had been sent them over the last few days. My birthday, 10 April 1962, happened to fall on present-giving day. The staff member in charge opened the cupboard with a ceremonial clanking of keys. She reached for the packages, examined the labels and began handing them out. 'This one's for Tom.' Pause. 'This one's for Jill.' Pause. 'This is for . . . Michael,' and so it went on. I stood there witnessing the generosity of other families and friends and the good fortune of the recipients. But as I took in their delight and eyed the presents being handed out, I asked myself, What have they done to deserve a gift? *It's not their birthday*.

Uncontrollable emotion began to well. I tried to hold myself in check, not wanting to cry. I was twelve years old now, too old for tears. Pull yourself together, Ronnie, I told myself, but then involuntary tears started, and they rapidly became a waterfall. Now I was shaking and sobbing, hyperventilating, yet confusingly ashamed of my weakness and the torrential emotion I couldn't control.

In my head conflicting thoughts wrestled. There was something fundamentally unjust in this ceremony. For the last six years the world had swallowed me up and battered me around and it still wasn't over. Everyone else had a present and it wasn't their birthday – and their looks of pleasure seemed to be deliberate taunts directed at me. Yet at the same time I loathed myself for thinking this way. I was behaving as if I was a spoiled brat. I had to get a grip.

My sobs brought present distribution to a halt. Everyone looked at me aghast. 'What's the matter, Ronnie? What's the matter?' I couldn't bring myself to speak. I hated myself for what was swirling in my head. 'What is it, Ronnie? What's the matter?' they repeated. No response from me. There was no way I'd reveal my weakness and there was no one more expert than me at keeping mute.

The house supervisor was sent for, and coaxed me to explain. Between my sobs I lied, saying I didn't know why I was upset, but I couldn't stop howling. In desperation they led me to the residential manager's office. I was still inconsolable.

'We have to know what the problem is,' the residential manager said, not unkindly, examining me with shrewd eyes from behind his large shiny desk. 'We can't have children in our care so distressed and not understand the reason.' I refused to speak; the tears continued unabated. Eventually, his patience wore thin and he threatened punishment.

This terrified me. 'It's my birthday,' I blurted out, detesting myself as I heard the words spill from my lips. 'I haven't got any presents.'

I don't recall what he said next, only that half an hour later a present was handed to me: a model castle with numbers on it, a chart showing what colours to paint it, and all the paints I needed to decorate it.

Thank you, Earlsfield House. That was the best present you could have given me. As I unwrapped and appreciated the gift in all its glory, I began to imagine myself constructing it. A piece of my fractured soul was mended.

There was a youth club at Earlsfield House, and a highpoint of the week was disco night. I was good at dancing, I won competitions, and the older girls often wanted me to be their partner. I remember dancing to Sam Cooke's 'Twistin' the Night Away' with a sense of abandoned ecstasy. I was dancing because I was free. No one was going to blind me or burn me or abuse me or drown me or stuff pills in my mouth. I wouldn't be told I was ugly every day. Dancing exorcised the past and the pain. It was sustenance and inspiration. I twisted and twirled and twisted, as if I were possessed. I don't remember what shoes I wore, they were probably borrowed from or swapped with a friend, or they came from the cupboard of donated items. All that mattered was that shoes were on my feet for dancing and that they weren't weapons any more.

7

A Dunhill Smoking Compendium

A few years ago, I was filming *Antiques Roadshow* at Audley End in Hertfordshire when a casually dressed young man handed me a slender gold box and asked me what I thought of it. I recognised instantly that it was the pinnacle of all smoking accessories, a compendium made by Dunhill, one of the most prestigious twentieth-century luxury brands. I opened the box to examine its ingeniously fitted interior and to my delight found it still complete with all its original components. Beneath a mirror-lined lid lay a cigarette lighter, a powder compact and a lipstick holder. When you pushed a catch on one corner, a rectangular watch popped out, and carefully hidden in the side was a small pencil. The marks told me that all of these, as well as the case, were made from 9ct gold and dated from 1933, a time when cigarette smoking and sophistication were synonymous.

I asked the owner how he'd come by such an object and he

explained that it had belonged to his father, who had wanted to sell it for scrap a few years earlier. His son had taken it to Hatton Garden where it was weighed and valued, but at the last minute he couldn't part with it – he felt it was too beautiful to destroy. However, his father needed the cash, and so his son had given him £2,500 for it and kept it himself. His father had since passed away, and although he now regarded it as a family memento, he wanted to know if his decision was wise.

'That's quite a lot of money,' I said, before giving him my reassuring verdict. 'Would it surprise you to know that not only is the compendium now worth around three or four times what you paid for it, but you have saved a precious work of art. Dunhill compendiums like this are rare and highly collectable today, and one, in 1932, won the gold prize at the Goldsmiths' Hall, and it was said to be an "ingenious assemblage of engineering".' He'd done the right thing.

For me, though, this wasn't just a good story but a déjà vu moment, one that transported me back to the 1970s, when accessories made by Dunhill, Cartier and Hermès were my stock in trade, and the Alfred Dunhill Museum was among my clients. In those days I worked with a business partner called Rick, who was an ex-model and looked like Clint Eastwood. When Rick wasn't busy filming, we would scour the markets of London and the South East on the lookout for exactly such luxurious trinkets. I was heavily into smoking and kept a stylish vintage lighter to hand, often finding new clients by offering them a light. I'd taken up smoking at the age of twelve when I was sent to a new permanent care home, and as I recall, even in my teenage years I was drawn to all kinds of vintage designs, although my earliest experience of smoking was far from an enjoyable one.

The permanent residential home found for us was Beechholme, in Banstead, Surrey. It was an experimental institution, founded in the nineteenth century to look after poor children from the slums of Kensington and Chelsea in a pseudo-village community. Children lodged in one of twenty-three large detached houses set on either side of a long tree-lined avenue. Each house was named after a tree or shrub and operated as an autonomous family unit, with house parents looking after around eighteen children. Strung along the leafy thoroughfare were playing fields, administrative buildings, workshops, a church, a shop, a school, a swimming pool and a youth club, where I'd be in heaven dancing to songs like 'He's a Rebel' by the Crystals.

To begin with, Lynette and I were sent to Kerria House. I'm not sure how we ended up there since it was renowned for housing the toughest and most disruptive juvenile offenders. Perhaps it was the only house that had space for us together. Uncle Bob Green, the house father, a huge man with a rugby forward's build, greeted me on the first day. As he tendered his huge hand to me, I smiled and shook it. 'You've got a bright smile, son,' he said. 'Use it whenever you can. It's a great asset.' I nodded and said I would, and I tried to keep to my word. Later on, I came to realise that a smile deflected people from my inner anguish. It became a form of armour, a shield against monstrous memory, a way to counter my conviction that people wouldn't like looking at me. I couldn't help my face, I decided, but I could alter its expression by thinking pleasant thoughts. It's a strategy that I still consciously employ. Even so, life at Kerria demanded more than a smile – it could be a terrifying environment, where swearing, smoking and keeping in with Colin Woodford were the keys to survival.

It helped that I'd already met Colin while staying in Earlsfield House. At fourteen, he was a boy mountain, with fists the size of my head. I remember once seeing him fight off two male carers and winning. Before I could become a member of his gang, I had to pass an initiation ceremony. It was winter and snowy outside. Colin Woodford left a handful of pennies on the windowsill overnight. The following morning a couple of his mates held me facedown on the bed while the frozen coins were placed on my bare back and left there till they warmed up. The sensation was almost unbearable.

Having survived this ordeal, Colin made it plain he didn't mind me hanging around with him. I was good at swearing and quick thinking, which made me useful when it came to the planning of escapades. But my small size was against me – he wasn't having a pipsqueak who looked about nine damaging his hard-man reputation. The only way around this obstacle, he announced one day, was to toughen up my image. To do this I'd have to take up smoking.

'I really don't wanna fucking smoke, Colin. I hate it, it makes me cough.'

'Who the fuck do you think you're talking to?'

Ignoring my protests, he demanded that I gave him my pocket money. I knew he wasn't joking and handed over a shilling. He marched me down to the village shop where he bought five Player's Weights, non-tipped.

'Right, we are going to the woods and you are going to fucking smoke every single one of these, you little jerk.'

'Leave it out, Colin. I really don't fuckin' want to.'

'You're fuckin' gonna, 'cos you'll get my fist if you don't – and you know what that's like!'

In a secluded clearing he stopped, laughed and tore open the packet. He lit the first cigarette, drawing deeply on it so that the tip went red like a warning signal, then thrust it at me. I put it gingerly to my lips and inhaled. The taste was worse than I'd anticipated. I blew the smoke out speedily.

'Do it properly, you arsehole. Hold it in,' he ordered.

I took another puff, deeper this time. It was disgusting. I spluttered, my stomach heaved, my eyes were smarting.

'Again, arsehole.' And he watched me smoke it right down to the end, admonishing me if he thought I was shirking. By then my eyes were streaming, but he didn't waver from his aim. He lit the next.

'Now this, you wanker.'

I coughed, heaved, retched. He was utterly unmoved.

By the time I got to the fifth cigarette I wasn't coughing any more.

He looked at me, his face impassive. I could have choked to death and he wouldn't have flinched.

'Now you can smoke, you stupid bastard. So whenever you're with me, get a fag out and light it.' He dropped a massive arm on my shoulder in a gesture of brotherly solidarity. I felt as if I'd been awarded a medal.

Being part of Colin's gang and passing his smoking initiation test didn't stop him from turning on me when the mood took him. Once we were washing up together, when I saw a dark look come across him. There was a big skillet frying pan, thick with bacon fat mixed with a small amount of water forming a horrible greasy mess. He picked it up.

'Look at this. It's fucking revolting and I've got to put it in the bin. But I want to rub your stupid fucking face in it.'

I tried to conceal my alarm. 'Piss off, Colin. I really don't want you to rub my face in that.'

'Don't you fucking tell me to piss off, wanker. For that I'm gonna give you two choices. Either I rub your face in it or I punch you in the face.'

'For fuck's sake, Colin,' I pleaded. 'I don't want either.'

I woke up in the sick bay, my face bruised and swollen – and revoltingly larded with bacon fat.

I can see now that Colin wasn't mentally stable but at the time I was used to violence and thought his behaviour was normal. I didn't know any different. I learned to look after myself because of him and we often had a laugh. During the time I spent at Kerria he was the closest thing I had to a best friend.

We entertained ourselves by zooming around and terrorising the neighbourhood on bikes we'd made ourselves, using our pocket money to buy parts – a frame or wheel from someone, a saddle and handlebars from somewhere else. Anywhere we could find trouble our gang invariably would be, although I was always the strategist, and being small and quick I rarely got caught.

Sometimes I'd suggest we should go on a midnight walk for a laugh. We'd get out of our beds, get dressed, and ramble around the neighbourhood shouting and swearing. When it snowed, we'd have nocturnal snowball fights in the fields in our bare feet, dressed only in pyjamas. Sometimes we'd go down to the Driftbridge pub in Epsom on the nights when the rockers congregated there, because Colin liked to 'sort them out'.

'You fucking calling my mate names?' he'd say before throwing the first punch.

One evening Colin got into an altercation with a puny-looking rocker. He had him by the neck of his shirt so he couldn't move, then brought his fist full back, his body stretched, preparing to land the punch straight at his face.

'If you do that, you'll fucking kill him,' I said, holding on to his fist with both hands, but barely able to restrain him. 'You've already shut him up, now leave him, for fuck's sake. He won't mess with you again.' He calmed down as quickly as he'd flared up. I think I saved that boy's life.

I'd learned how to protect myself (and others) partly because from the age of twelve, at Earlsfield House and then at Kerria, boys of all ages would learn boxing. We took part in proper competitive bouts in a ring in front of spectators. I was quite good for my age group and on one occasion I punched an opponent hard in the face. Blood and mucus gushed from his nose and he crashed to the ground, crying. The onlookers all cheered. 'Finish him off! Finish him off!' they chanted.

'Don't hurt me. Please don't hit me again, Ronnie. I can't take any more,' the boy begged, staggering to his feet.

'Get on with it! Finish him!' the other boys roared. I was upset that I'd hurt him so badly and ignored them.

'Sorry, mate,' I said, taking off my gloves. I don't know

what disgusted me more – myself or the bloodthirsty onlook-ers. I told everyone that I refused to punch him any more. Although I was often encouraged to do so, I never put a pair of gloves on again.

Elliott School was more than an hour and a half's journey from Banstead, but because I'd settled in well, and was in the gram-mar stream, the authorities took the unusual decision to let me stay there rather than move me to the school on site at Beechholme which all the other children attended. The teach-ers were notified about the change in my circumstances and the events that had led to my sister and me being taken into care. They responded by providing extra pastoral care, and several members of staff became personal friends with whom I stayed in contact for years afterwards.

To get to school on time, I'd leave two hours early, walk a mile through the woods to Banstead station, take the train to Wimbledon, then take a bus along Wimbledon Common to school. In winter it would be dark when I left and dark when I returned. If it was snowy the trees would be laden down like a tunnel of white. On foggy days I could barely see two yards in front, but I was committed to my education and relieved to be allowed to stay at Elliott. In time others would join me, and the journey became less arduous.

One day, when it was just me, I was going home from school and I'd taken the 93 bus from the Green Man pub on Putney Heath to Wimbledon station. I liked sitting at the back on the little single seat, so that people couldn't sit next to you and you could see out of the back window. On the other side at the back, two children, aged about nine or ten, were sitting with their mother. They turned and looked at me and started making faces, putting their tongues out, rolling their bottom lips down, making *brrr* noises and muttering, 'Rubber lips.'

Here we go, I thought, wondering when their mother would intervene and tell them to behave. Then one started chanting a racist slogan.

'W** a matter? N***** mind – you'll be all white tomorrow.'

They kept on and on and on, chanting it loudly, repeating it over and over and over, until my temples were pounding and I thought my head would explode.

'W** a matter? N***** mind – you'll be all white tomorrow.'

Far from reprimanding them, their mother egged them on. There was no one to protect me. What could I do? What should I have done? The bus was very full, and before long everyone was looking round to see who they were aiming this at. No one told the boys to stop. They just stared and muttered to one another without thought for the target of their cruelty, a small boy at the back of the bus. I felt as if I was on stage with nowhere to go or hide, held hostage to racial abuse, undefended, all the way to Wimbledon station.

When the authorities were confident neither my sister nor I had violent tendencies, they moved us out of Kerria to the more peaceful Jasmine House just down the road. I stayed close to Colin and his mates but I made new friends too. Ambrosine, Betty and Jeff Bernard lived in the house next door. Their parents were of black Caribbean heritage. Jeff and I were the same age and had a similar small wiry build. Like me he was strong and tough, and we loved pitting ourselves against each other, pushing, shoving and scuffling, then rolling on the grass in friendly, bonding wrestling matches, as we laughed and exchanged banter, before breaking off to puff on a cigarette.

Like Colin, Jeff could flare up, and he was expelled from school at fifteen for beating up a teacher. He stayed on at Beechholme but found a job as a builder. He said he didn't miss school and that he liked having extra cash to spend. The rest of us felt slightly envious of his new independence. It seemed to give him an air of authority, and although it didn't put a stop to our scuffling play fights, something about him changed. I suppose we were moving apart.

A couple of months after he'd started at the building site, Jeff didn't return home one evening. When he still hadn't turned up after supper, we asked the staff where he was. Maureen, the housemother, gave us the bad news. There'd been an accident at the site. A crane had dropped its load on Jeff. He'd been killed instantly. We could barely absorb the information. We asked her question after question, heads reeling with the dawning realisation that Jeff was gone. I wouldn't be play wrestling with him any more. He wouldn't be flirting and dancing with the girls. Within a year, Ambrosine, Jeff's younger sister, would have tragically passed away too. There had been complications when she had surgery to remove her tonsils and she died in hospital. We were young, we thought we were invincible, but we weren't.

8

A Carved Wood-and-Polychrome Figure
of St Benedict of Palermo

Religious figures have always intrigued me, and I have bought and sold many over the years, but one I found on a stall in Covent Garden a few years ago filled me with special excitement. It depicted a young male saint, about ten inches tall, made from carved wood that was gessoed (covered in a white chalky layer), painted and gilded. His arms were raised, and a patterned cloth was draped over them. In the middle of the cloth there was an old pin, a signal that something had come detached. I scrutinised the figure more closely. The face was finely carved, and the eyes were made from glass. The painted robe was damaged, and possibly repainted, but it was richly adorned with gilding. The figure looked as if he might be Spanish, or Portuguese or Italian possibly, and date from the late eighteenth century. But to me what was most exciting about him was that his face, hands and bare feet were clearly black. I had found a black saint – or had he found me?

Black religious figures are extremely rare in Western art, so although I didn't know who the saint was, I brought him home, meaning to find out. But despite my intentions, my black saint remained with me, unresearched but admired, watching serenely over me on a shelf as the months passed, until a chance conversation over Christmas reminded me of him. I decided the time had come to find out more. By the miracle of the internet, it didn't take long to find out that my figure depicted St Benedict the Moor of Palermo.

St Benedict's life was an inspirational one, I learned. Born in the early sixteenth century to enslaved Africans in Sicily, as a child Benedict was granted his freedom and worked as a shepherd, giving his earnings to the poor. When subjected to racial abuse, Benedict responded with such dignity that he was invited to join a community of hermits. He was illiterate and served as a cook to begin with, but rose to become the group's leader. The community later joined the Franciscan friary of Palermo, where Benedict again progressed. He was appointed guardian of the friary and established a reputation as a healer, and thus is often depicted holding a sick child. This was probably the missing element once held by the pin on my carved figure. After his death in 1589, Benedict was interred in the friary at Palermo, and his body is still there on display in a glass coffin. Every year on his feast day, 4 April, it is paraded around the town. His restraint when confronted with prejudice made Benedict's fame spread. He was venerated as the patron saint of African Americans and there are several

Catholic churches in the US in black communities bearing his name.

Miss Bulmer, the RE teacher (and a dead ringer for the actress Liv Ullmann in my eyes), cast me in the school nativity play when I was thirteen. Like many of the boys, I was a little in love with her, so this was an important moment for me. Naturally, I was to be Balthazar, the black king.

Knowing that it was a long journey back to Beechholme, Miss Bulmer kindly told me that on the night of the performance she would take me out to dinner before the play. I was excited at this prospect. I saw it as the perfect opportunity to make her see me in a different – romantic – light, not as a pupil but a suitor. I would gain an advantage on the other boys and make her fall in love with me.

There was one obstacle to this strategy, as I saw it. Beechholme rules compelled me to go to school in short trousers, and no woman as beautiful as Miss Bulmer could possibly find a suitor in shorts attractive. I tried to deal with the issue. I asked Auntie Meira, my housemother, if I could be allowed dispensation just for that occasion. No, she said, rules could not be altered on a whim. I pleaded with her. I would go without pocket money for a month if she relented just this once, I offered in desperation. But no, she wouldn't yield – you had to be fifteen to wear long trousers to school: I had two more long years to wait.

I tried not to think about my short trousers when the much-anticipated evening arrived. Miss Bulmer took me to a little bistro in Putney. We sat at a tiny table in the corner. It was lovely, and I prayed she hadn't noticed what I was wearing. I looked at the menu and asked for bangers and mash with gravy – I'd decided I would order the cheapest thing so that she would think I was considerate. But while I was in heaven, I was also in a fever of anxiety. I put down my knife and fork – the knife slipped. I grabbed it and knocked my glass. Water spilled all over the table and all over her. That's it – I've blown it, I thought.

I doubt that the drenching had anything to do with Miss Bulmer's subsequent decision to marry Mr Beach, the cool physics teacher. I remember my delight on hearing that my two favourite teachers had got together. It almost made up for my disappointment. Although she overlooked me as a potential suitor, Miss Bulmer was destined to remain a significant figure in my life. She tutored me at her home, and after her marriage she regularly invited me for dinner at her flat in Twickenham. She and Mr Beach introduced me to Mose Allison's music. Their living room was filled with studio pottery and paintings by artist teacher friends, and helped formulate my own taste for simple, good, modern design. In later years, after her husband died, our friendship continued, and in a way I looked after her, visiting her in Bristol, taking her on trips in England and the South of France.

At Beechholme, I became friends with a likeable young tearaway, Alex. Alex was the same colour as me and said his family had originally come from Brazil. 'I've got a surprise to show you guys,' he boasted to me and another friend, James, one afternoon after school. He led us down the road to the woods, then along a narrow track to some undergrowth near the station. He pointed to a mound of torn-down branches. 'Look,' he said. 'What d'you guys reckon?'

We kicked away a few branches. There, concealed from view, was a stolen scooter. 'Great, isn't it?'

He uncovered the scooter and propped it up on its stand for us to appreciate. 'Let's go for a ride,' James said.

'Not sure there's much petrol in it.'

I intervened. 'I'll check.'

I lifted the seat and unscrewed the cap to peer inside. No liquid was visible but it was dark and difficult to be sure. I struck a match and held it to the open mouth of the tank to see more clearly. As I did so I heard a scuffle behind me and half turned to see Alex and James diving for the bushes. I looked back at the tank – a small flame had ignited and was now flickering around the mouth of the opening. To extinguish it, I lowered my head and blew. That only made things worse and the flames started to take hold, circling the open tank. I started to panic. Alex would kill me if the scooter blew up after he'd so cleverly stolen it. I had to do something – fast. I took off my jacket and patted at the flames. I managed to extinguish them, but the jacket always reeked of fuel after that.

'Yeah, there's petrol in it,' I announced nonchalantly to the two cowering in the bushes.

Gale Boone was one of the few female members of our gang. There was something wild about her. She looked a bit like Chrissie Hynde from the Pretenders, androgynous looking, with a heart-shaped face, white-skinned, dark-haired, with pale blue eyes. She was incredibly belligerent and rough – she'd fight boys and often beat them – but she was funny and brave and posturing. I liked her, and I felt a bit honoured that she liked me too. We'd talk long after the gang had dispersed.

Sometimes we'd lie in the grass with our bikes beside us, like cowboys lounging next to their horses, smoking and talking, mostly about music. We loved music, and it was a source of endless frustration that the radio in our house didn't work reliably – because it was so abused. Whenever it failed, knives and forks would be hurled across the room at it to make it work.

One day, when we were still getting to know one another, Gale and I met up. 'D'you fancy a snout?' she mumbled. 'Where can we go?'

I gestured towards some sheds near the main buildings. We wandered over and slipped behind into a small enclosed yard – a favourite smoking sanctuary. All was clear so we lit up, but two or three puffs in, we heard footsteps.

Wordlessly we looked at each other and cuffed our cigarettes. This dangerous strategy involved holding the lit fag in your pocket, cradled by your hand, so it was invisible and didn't burn a hole in your trousers. The footsteps came closer and a figure materialised. Mr Dicker, the deputy superintendent, a man we both knew to be strict and swift to punish any infringement. He seemed surprised to find us standing there quietly, not involved in any obvious misdemeanour. 'Hello. What are you two up to?' he asked suspiciously.

Gale turned away and looked at her feet.

'Morning, sir,' I greeted him with bravado. 'Gale and I are just having a quiet chat.'

He fixed us with a penetrating gaze, then, after what seemed an eternity, nodded. 'I can't believe it! You two – you're not swearing, or shouting, or rampaging round the neighbourhood. This is something I never thought I'd see.'

If he doesn't leave soon, I thought, either he'll smell the smoke or we'll do ourselves serious injury.

I nodded. 'Thank you, sir . . . It's something quite important.'

'Don't worry, I'll leave you to it. But good to see you've both turned a corner.'

'Thank you, sir.'

Gale grunted something unintelligible.

Mr Dicker disappeared.

Gale wasn't easily impressed, but my performance hit the mark.

'God, you were cool, Ronnie,' she said, forgetting her usual monosyllabic way of talking in her relief. 'I seriously thought I was going to burn myself if he stayed.' Then she added, unthinking, 'Before I met you, I thought—' She suddenly realised what she was saying and stopped.

'What? What did you think?'

'No, I can't say it.'

'Yes, you can. Tell me.'

'No.'

Back and forth this went, until, eventually, she relented. 'I thought all black people were horrible. But I don't think that now I know you. Now I've said it, forget it – but that's what I thought.'

Her words shook me. 'Gale, that's a really nice thing to say,' I said as I mulled them over. I thought deeply about them more over the next few days. Gale wasn't someone to reveal thoughts of any kind, let alone her prejudices and feelings. She was the toughest girl I knew, and I'd changed her mind about a whole race. All I'd done was hang out with her, and we'd shared an experience together.

Upton Sinclair, the US writer and campaigner for social justice, said, 'It's difficult to get a man to understand something when his salary depends upon his not understanding it.' I would alter that and say you can't change the mind of a person whose belief system depends on his mind not being changed. But you *can* change by example – if bigoted people see that you are just like them, that you risk what they risk, that you have the aspirations that they have, and you are as good as they are, prejudice will be overcome. And Gale's words, and the realisation that came from them, have been something, quite consciously, I have held in my mind ever since. I call it Gale's Law.

As it turned out, my friendship with Gale was short-lived. Not long after that incident she was removed from Beechholme for disruptive behaviour and sent to a series of ever more secure institutions. In Holloway prison she encountered heroin addicts, who introduced her to hard drugs the night she was released. She spiralled into addiction and died from an overdose at the age of nineteen. Her wasted life became the focus of an award-winning BBC documentary called *Gale Is Dead*.*

Our friendships at Beechholme were close, but we never really discussed our families or why we were there. I was no different from the rest in that I didn't talk about my mother or what had brought me and my sister there. I was probably suffering from post-traumatic stress and couldn't bear to remember my

* In the documentary she was called Gale Parsons.

earlier life. In any case, I couldn't have articulated my distress if I'd wanted to. My emotions had gone underground. I was descending into crisis but all I wanted was to shut the past away and not talk about it.

Perhaps this explains why my memories of my mother at this time are so vague and confused. I was aware of her in the background, maintaining contact with my sister, but I always tried to avoid spending any time with her when she visited by concocting something I had to do. I sensed that my absence was as much a relief for her as it was for me. There must have been shame and guilt on her side, which she found hard if not impossible to confront. I do remember being asked what I wanted for Christmas one year and saying I wanted a jacket with a fake-fur collar that I'd seen in a C&A catalogue. She gave it to me, and I wore it, but it didn't change anything or make me forgive her. I just remember thinking, This is too little too late.

The Hoads remained a constant in our lives. On one visit, Molly grew furious with our housemother because she had given my sister and me some clothes that had disappeared into the Beechholme laundry system, never to be seen again. I don't think she ever knew the full extent of the abuse my mother had inflicted upon me, but she did realise I was becoming increasingly morose and withdrawn, and was enraged by my inadequate childcare officer, who she believed was just going through the motions, doing the bare minimum. Perhaps as a result, I was placed under the supervision of a new childcare officer, Ann Barraball. Miss Barraball quickly understood that I was on a downward spiral. My unresolved issues were poisoning me and were turning into implacable hatred for my mother. This emotional cancer would destroy me if it wasn't sensitively addressed.

She took it upon herself to do so, explaining that my mother was ill, and that she had tried to exorcise the pain she had suffered through me. 'She didn't hate you, Ronnie, she was sick. It was the illness she hated. She didn't ever want to harm you.'

At some point I must have told her I had lost all sense of who I was, that my mother had even made me doubt the reason for my father's absence. Had he died, as she'd sometimes said, or had he abandoned us, as she'd also claimed? She listened to me and took me to the Public Record Office and together we found the records of my father's death in a car accident. All of this helped, and knowing my mother had been ill when she abused me gave me a coping strategy. Without Miss Barraball who knows how low I would have sunk, although the memories of the torture I'd endured were too dreadful to reconcile entirely. In the end, I decided it was easier not to discuss it but to keep myself as busy as I could and, in this way, try to deal with what had happened to me.

I wasn't alone. Everyone at Beechholme found their family situations hard to articulate. No one admitted that they'd been mistreated or abused, just that their parents had lost their jobs or were short of cash, and they'd be going home in a few months. It was seriously uncool to say that you liked being there. In my case, the truth was I actually loved being at Beechholme. I felt safe, I had some good friends there and plenty to distract me from the nightmares of the past. Looking back, I still see the four years I spent there as a great adventure. But I was conscious of the unwritten rules – I had to pretend I hated the children's home if I was to be accepted by my peers. And as part of my subterfuge, when I was fifteen years old, I decided I'd lead a great escape.

9

A Welsh Walking Stick

Wielded by kings, aristocrats, clergymen and members of the military, as well as country folk and travellers, walking sticks fulfil numerous functions. They can be symbols of power and status, practical supports, or fashionable accessories. They can be used to ward off marauders or wild dogs, or as tools of correction, or to provide a place to conceal a hidden sword, a secret letter, poison – or even live creatures: it's said that silkworms were first smuggled from China to Italy concealed inside the cavity of a walking stick.

With a history that reaches back through the millennia (Howard Carter found them in Tutankhamun's tomb), they are a vast collecting area, and another of my many miscellaneous passions. Part of their appeal lies in the myriad inventive forms they take and the various materials they incorporate. There are sticks with heads carved in the form of dogs and donkeys, there are beaked birds, horses, dragons, crocodiles and snakes. Some sticks are knotty and gnarled, some smooth and elegant. Some are whittled from a branch pruned from a hedgerow, some fashioned from exotic imported woods and embellished with mother of pearl, ivory, silver, gold, amber and gems.

We were filming at Plas Newydd House in Anglesey a few years ago, when a walking cane dating from the mid-nineteenth century was brought to my table. Walking sticks aren't rare on the show, but what made this example especially interesting for me were the beautifully incised views that decorated the shaft, showing the nearby Menai Suspension Bridge as it looked soon after completion in 1826. The engineer Thomas Telford had decided that because of the fast-flowing water and shifting sands of the seabed, a suspension bridge, built high enough to allow shipping to pass underneath, with towers set on the solid ground on either side of the strait, was the answer.

When the bridge opened to great fanfare, it was the world's first major suspension bridge and provided the first permanent link between the mainland of Wales and the island of Anglesey. Prior to this, people crossed the treacherous stretch of water by ferry, and farmers wanting to take their cattle to market on the mainland had to swim the animals across, often with the result that they were swept away and lost.

Half a century earlier, when I was about fifteen years old, I made my own trip to North Wales. I'd escaped from my children's home and was on the run nearby, but when I saw the bridge I decided I'd wandered far enough and headed in the opposite direction.

Earlier that summer I, along with others from Beechholme, was taken on a camping holiday to the Brecon Beacons.

The sun shone, and we all thought it was paradise. So, in early September, as school term started again, I proposed that we run away to visit Abergele and Rhyl, because the penny arcades there were meant to be incredible. I nominated myself as leader of the escape because I knew how the train system worked, and everyone else agreed.

About a dozen of us banded together including Alex, James and Sarah, who was James's girlfriend but who I wished was mine. We had hardly any money, but we made our way to Victoria, then across London to Euston, where we boarded a train heading north. I knew how to bunk on the trains. In those days they had carriages with corridors, so we piled into two compartments and drew down the blinds. When the guard came, we said our teacher had our tickets and was in another compartment further up the train. This strategy worked until we got to Rugby, when the guard realised what was going on, herded us off the train and summoned the police. While we waited, we were corralled onto a disused section of the platform and left under the supervision of just one guard. We looked at each other and thought, There's no way that one guard is going to be able to keep *us* prisoner.

A section of wall along one side of the platform was undergoing repair and had been partially demolished, leaving a wide gap with a pole across. I signalled to everyone and counted down on my fingers. 'Three, two, one, go!' One by one everyone vaulted the bar and jumped into the side road leading to the main shopping street beyond. I went last because I was the fastest runner and felt cockily confident no one would catch me. As the guard realised what was happening, he blew his whistle and several more guards appeared from every direction.

I cleared the bar easily and saw the others disappearing towards a shopping street and take a right turn. The guards were close behind.

I'm going to get caught, I thought. I'm too conspicuous, and I'm in the wrong place. There's only one way out of this.

I took the corner at full tilt and stopped in a doorway, then stripped off my jacket, turned it inside out, put it over my arm, and walked nonchalantly back in the direction I'd come. The guards, focused on a running quarry, raced past without registering me, and I sauntered on my way.

I headed to the nearest park, where we'd agreed to meet by the swings. I waited. After an hour or so, three others turned up – Sarah, Alex and James. Everyone else had been apprehended. We decided we'd change tack; from here on we'd split into two groups, avoid trains and hitchhike. The plan was to meet up in Rhyl in North Wales in four days' time. I went with Sarah, who I fancied but was trusted to look after. Alex and James teamed up together.

Sarah and I slept rough and lived on apples scrumped from orchards, and milk, bread and biscuits that we stole from milk carts. As we walked along the road waiting for the next lift, we sang 'Here Comes the Night' by Them at the tops of our voices. When drivers picked us up and asked questions, we would spin a yarn. We were on our way to see our parents, we'd say. No one ever asked why we were travelling alone when we should have been at school.

As night drew in, we would search for a place to sleep that was warm and dry. Barns were a favourite refuge. I remember climbing up the stacked bales to the top and opening out a couple of bales to make a bed that was prickly but comfortable, apart from the insects. When dawn came, we would sneak away before we were discovered.

In Rhyl we rendezvoused with James and Alex as arranged and swapped partners. I went with Alex and we agreed to meet up with the others the next day in Abergele. Alex and I made it there but Sarah and James didn't turn up. Eventually, we decided to explore Wales further and headed west. We saw the Menai Suspension Bridge with its great limestone towers and chain cables supporting the vast span in the distance but decided against crossing it. By now the allure of living rough in Wales was beginning to wane. The weather was wet and getting worse by the day, nights were uncomfortably cold. We felt hungry all the time and longed for a hot meal, and all the attractions were closing. Without much of a plan about what to do next, we turned back for England.

We found our way to Chester. By this time, it was beginning to get dark and we hadn't thought about shelter for the night. Finding somewhere to hide overnight is less easy in a town than in the countryside, and two bedraggled young black boys wandering the streets soon attracted attention. Before we could find anywhere to hide, two policemen stopped us.

They took us to the police station where we had to confess what we were doing. Calls were made to Beechholme, but before we were returned, accompanied by a social worker, they made us wash thoroughly with carbolic soap. We thought we'd maintained reasonable standards of hygiene by washing in public toilets, but we were still wearing the clothes we'd left in, and the authorities were probably right: we looked and stank like vagrants.

We'd been on the run for a fortnight – longer than anyone

from Beechholme ever had before. James and Sarah had been apprehended four days earlier. In my heart of hearts, I wasn't sorry to get back to a warm bed, dry clothes and hot food, although I didn't say so. Still, the authorities threw the book at us. We were caned, pocket money was suspended, and we were barred from going out for a month. But they couldn't alter the fact we'd broken the record – it was all worth it. Within the Beechholme family, we were heroes.

The more established I felt at Beechholme, the more my priorities changed. By 1964, the year I turned fourteen, school seemed less important. Study wasn't the refuge it once had been. I wasn't obsessed with my survival any longer. I still enjoyed Elliott, but my thirst for life and my growing desire to be part of the cool scene of music and fashion were increasingly distracting. I did my homework on the bus, so when I got back I'd be free to roam around on my bike with the gang. No one checked to see if I'd done the work anyway.

With the money from my paper round and various weekend jobs I bought new clothes and hung around meeting places in Epsom, Sutton and Banstead that the local mods frequented. I loved the way people in the mod movement were dressing. We struck up conversations. They would often compliment me on my clothes and from there we'd progress to chat about their music. Much of what they listened to was by black artists such as Tommy Tucker, Marvin Gaye, Little Stevie Wonder, Otis Redding, Booker T. & the M.G.'s, Prince Buster, the Jamaican bluebeat and ska musician, and many other black singers on US record labels. The mods' love of black music, plus the fact that there weren't many black mods in those days, and the way I dressed made me stand out, may have been why they took an interest in me. Hanging out with them one spring day I learned that on Easter Sunday a mod rally to the south-east coast was being planned, and a retinue of mods from my area were going. Why didn't I join them and ride pillion with the head rider, someone suggested. Seeing this invitation as a great honour, I agreed without hesitation.

I wanted to do justice to the occasion, so I dressed with care. It's one of the few times from those days that I can remember exactly what I wore: a French Navy collarless Beatle-type jacket, a red Fred Perry polo shirt, light grey perfectly pressed slacks, and cool Ravel slip-ons in black textured leather. I finished off the stylish ensemble with a pair of Ray-Ban-style sunglasses. It was my finest mod outfit and people said I looked like Stevie Wonder, the height of cool at that time.

All the way to Clacton, I rode pillion on the back of the coolest Vespa GS imaginable, feeling like a prince. The scooter had the shiniest chrome panels, the most lights mounted on a chrome frame on the front of the scooter, and the longest aerial with the most foxtails on it, fluttering in the wind as we drove. We were part of a cavalcade of around forty scooters and heads turned in every town or village we drove through. In Clacton we met up with thousands of other mods from all over the country, all riding on customised Vespas and Lambrettas. Many were wearing army-surplus military parkas over cool tonic mohair suits of all colours, or sports jackets with Fred Perry shirts and Levi jeans or Levi Sta-Prest trousers.* It

---

* Intended to be pronounced 'stay-pressed', they were a new non-iron crease-resistant brand of trousers.

was a spectacular and historic moment in British social history, one I'm proud to have been part of and shall never forget.

At weekends, I tried to supplement my pocket money so that I could feed my appetite for clothes and music. My first job was for the vicar, a mirthless man who paid me two shillings and sixpence for working without a break from 8 a.m. to 8 p.m. I moved pew benches, waxed floors and swept paths without a word of encouragement, let alone a cup of tea. Even my housemother said I was being exploited and told me to quit. I wanted the money, but I questioned Christianity for a bit after that, and eventually found a Saturday job at Sainsbury's in East Sheen, breaking down boxes and cutting cheese in an airless basement room.

With my new-found wealth I'd go to Carnaby Street to look at the current fashions, to Brick Lane and Petticoat Lane to buy cheap fabric, and then to John Lewis, where I'd buy standard patterns and adapt them. I'd learned to sew at Elliott. On the curriculum you had to choose between woodwork, metalwork and technical drawing, all taught by Mr Salisbury, and sewing – not taught by him, and generally viewed as a subject for girls. Mr Salisbury was a great teacher and I enjoyed woodwork and metalwork a lot, but after a year, I opted for the sewing course and dared anybody to laugh at me. It was so I could be with the girls, I said. They didn't laugh; in fact three of the unruliest boys thought it was a great idea and joined me in the class.

Using my freshly acquired skills I was able to make trousers, jackets, coats, suits and shirts. I would cut off the waistband on trousers to make hipsters, put patch pockets on my trousers, make them flared instead of straight, and choose colours like maroon or pink or apple-green that I'd seen in Carnaby Street. I was still shadowed by my mother's criticisms of my appearance, but cool clothes gave me confidence and appealed to my aesthetic sensibility. I'd always enjoyed wearing something a bit different from everyone else, ever since the kilt I put on when I played dressing up with Anna at Westdene.

For a fifteen-year-old mixed-race boy in 1960s London, shopping in the West End wasn't always an enjoyable experience. I remember once going to a knitwear shop near Bond Street Tube station and South Molton Street. I saw a chocolate-brown sweater in the window that I liked and went into the shop to look at it. The shop was packed, but I waited my turn and an attractive fair-haired woman in her mid-thirties asked me what I was looking for. 'There's a brown sweater in the window – could I have a look at it, please?'

She gave me a strange look. 'What, the n*****-brown one?'

'No, the dark brown one,' I replied.

'That's what I said. The n*****-brown one.' She said the word again and again, becoming louder and louder, repeating the offensive term about ten times, and each time she uttered the word it felt like a stabbing. I was cringing inwardly. The whole shop stopped and looked at me. Even in those days the word was regarded as being unacceptable. She must have been saying it to cause distress, and I didn't know how to respond. It was one of the first public humiliations I received just because of my colour. Afterwards, I resolved that from then on, I would be small and inconspicuous to minimise the chance of attracting racial hostility.

The fear of racism never stopped me dressing up for evenings out though. Cool clothes were too important. On Friday or Saturday nights at Beechholme, aged fifteen, I'd pretend to go to bed, then get dressed, go downstairs and sneak out to go to the West End or to Brixton to a club. I'd usually go with Alex and Sandra, who was a really good dancer. We loved the Ram Jam Club in Brixton, an iconic venue where Jimi Hendrix and Ben E. King and Cream performed. The Roaring Twenties* in Carnaby Street, an amazing place, where they played bluebeat, ska, soul, rhythm and blues and jazz, or Tiles in Oxford Street were also favourite night-time destinations. For me the chief draw of the clubs wasn't the people but the music. I'd let it take over my body and lose myself in dancing. I've never forgotten the atmosphere of those days. It was music that was all new, that you wouldn't hear anywhere else, so powerful that you felt as if it was coming from inside you.

Some of the clubs were frequented by Jamaicans, who usually assumed I was one of them and would speak to me in Jamaican Patois. I couldn't understand a word, but to integrate I pretended I did, and tried to reply in similar dialect, which those who knew me thought was hilarious.

One night we slipped out of the toilet window at Beechholme and went down to the Ram Jam Club. There were a few of us, including Sandra. I wore some maroon patch-pocket low hipster trousers, with a thick white roll-neck woollen sweater, tucked neatly into the trousers, and a black-and-white leather belt, which I'd saved up for and bought in Carnaby Street. In the youth club at Beechholme, Sandra and I had

* Which we always called the Twenties.

practised a dance routine to 'Shotgun Wedding' by Roy 'C'. The record came on that night and we took to the dance floor. A group of West Indian guys, amazing dancers, started to gather round us and clap us on. Eventually the whole club was watching. In my thick roll-neck I was so hot I thought I was going to melt. I really suffered to look the way I wanted to in those days. But it was worth it for the buzz of the music and feeling part of the scene.

Soon after that, at the Streatham Locarno, I was wearing a new suit that I'd had made out of tonic mohair. Perhaps I looked too conspicuous and that caused irritation, because one of a group of about ten guys came up and kept pushing me with his finger and asking if I 'wanted bother'.

'I don't want any trouble, man,' I said, but he kept on provoking me and prodding me, each prod annoying me more. Eventually I snapped and threw a punch. He was on the floor and I didn't even remember hitting him. Then about eight or nine more guys were on me. I'd been set up, I realised, and new suit or not, I'd have to fight my way out of it. I punched for my life, picking up chairs, hurling them at my attackers – it became a real brawl. Two friends, one white and one black, pitched in to help me before the bouncers joined the fray. One of the bouncers eventually knocked me out cold and carried me to a side room where I recovered consciousness.

Afterwards, word spread and I was the hero of South London. 'I didn't know you were like that,' people kept saying. They didn't understand that having had Colin Woodford as a teacher, I could look after myself. But I was banned from the Streatham Locarno for life.

★

Going to clubs made me aware that the police weren't like the officers on TV shows. They often stopped and searched me, wrongly assuming I was carrying drugs or stolen property. A few times, when a crime had been committed, not content with quickly frisking me in the street, they'd take me to the station, prod me, slap me, and try to coerce me to confess to doing something they clearly knew I hadn't done. Their aggression and targeting of black people shocked me initially, although I quickly learned to expect it. But I was aware that some of the black people in the clubs I frequented were becoming distrustful of white people in general, as a result of the heavy-handedness of the predominantly white police. I'd had so many positive experiences with white people – friends, teachers, social workers – who had enriched my life, which made my perspective different. I didn't think about my colour, unless forced to do so.

By the time my sixteenth birthday approached, I felt ready to embrace an independent life and I decided to leave Beechholme. One of my favourite Bob Dylan songs at the time, 'Mr. Tambourine Man', included a line about dancing beneath a diamond sky that seemed to speak to me directly. I'd got to a stage where the rules seemed overly restrictive. I wanted to enjoy life and I didn't want to become institutionalised. If I stayed on another year, I would run the risk of ending up like Kevin Shepherd. At eighteen, he was the oldest boy in Beechholme, and I respected him, but he was so used to conforming to rules he would never be able to comfortably live without them. I explained all this to Ann Barraball, my childcare officer, reminding her that I'd looked after myself and my mother and sister from the age of six. She was surprised by my logic, but she agreed. She would help me find a bedsit close enough to Elliott to continue my A levels. After that I'd be on my own.

It wasn't easy to find permanent accommodation because landladies weren't keen on young lodgers. But Miss Barraball could see I was desperate to go, and a couple of days after my sixteenth birthday I was temporarily set up in a students' hostel in Wimbledon. I shared a room with a boy named Anthony and a couple of other privileged public-school boys from King's College. My life and theirs had little in common, but we got on well and I ended up going hitchhiking round Britain with Anthony that summer.

Several mature Persian students were also staying in the hostel, and at weekends, they passed the time playing poker. Sometimes I would join in their games, playing from Friday to Monday, with no sleep, using my weekly allowance as stake. When my cash ran out, I'd persuade them to give me credit. I hadn't told them my circumstances, and they must have assumed my father was a well-heeled diplomat. Sometimes I would be down £100 – a terrifying fortune at the time, especially since I was certain they'd lynch me if I couldn't pay them – but I'd manage to blag it out and occasionally I'd win £100 and have enough money to go to Carnaby Street and treat myself to some new clothes. At school on Monday I'd turn up kitted out in crocodile shoes and smart tailored jackets.

Eventually Miss Barraball found me a bedsit in Twickenham, a three-minute walk from the train station, close to the rugby ground. On match days the streets seethed with people and the roaring crowd made you feel as though you were in the stands. But their cheers didn't stop the unexpected sense of isolation that took hold of me. This was a move I had elected to make, but transitioning to an independent life at sixteen wasn't seamless. I had a home of my own but very few possessions; a kettle and some bedding and a few knives and forks were about it. All my life I'd lived in institutions or cramped flats with my mother and sister, never on my own. Instead of the liberation I'd expected to feel, the novelty of having my own space gave way to overwhelming loneliness that pitched me into depression. I felt unmoored and uncertain of who I was, where I was going, or what I'd become. I tried to focus on my studies, but I struggled to concentrate. I remained estranged from my mother; the ache of childhood wounds still disturbed me. I couldn't forget what she'd done to me, but nor could I talk about it. Going to clubs offered an instant remedy, a way of escaping solitude, of forgetting the past, and just losing myself in a world I loved.

One September day, I was alone in the bedsit, feeling rootless and miserable. I had a pile of work to do but couldn't motivate myself. Had I been right to leave Beechholme? Where did I belong now? What was the point of staying on at school?

There was a knock at the door. I opened it to see Jo Hawkey, one of the art teachers at Elliott, standing there with a russet-coloured rug under her arm. 'I thought you might like this,' she said, thrusting it at me with a smile that lit up her face.

'Thanks. Would you like to come in?' I said.

I watched her gaze flicker over the blank walls, the grimy, curtainless window, the grey lino floor, the spartan furnishing. It was a sunny day outside, but the light filtering through the dingy panes made the room feel cold. She turned back to me. 'I overheard Marjory Lee mention your name in the staff-room last week. She said she'd been to see you and was worried because you didn't have anything for the floor. I told her I had a spare rug, and she suggested I drop it in to you. It looks like you could do with a bit more than a rug, Ronnie.'

It was a statement not a question. I didn't know what to say. I'd seen her around the school but had never spoken to her before, and I didn't want her to think I was pathetic or weak. She flicked on the kettle, walked over to a chair, and plonked herself down while she waited for it to boil. 'From now on I will be your big sister,' she announced.

What she was really saying was that from then on, she'd be my best friend. Someone who would always be there, always watch my back, encourage me, cajole me, pick me up and save me when I needed saving.

'Thanks,' I said. How else could I respond? Suddenly my life didn't seem quite so forlorn. Jo was in it with me.

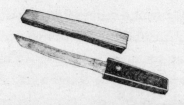

10

A Japanese Fan Tanto

What is it? I'm always drawn to objects that are unfamiliar, and that's what makes me take note of an object I spot lying among various items of bric-a-brac on a market stall. At first I think it's a fan. I pick it up and examine the striations of leaves on the sides of the handle. Above the handle there's a sheath-like cover that splays outward slightly to accommodate the leaves within, and it's decorated with a sophisticated design – a trellis of delicate prunus blossom and flying birds that signal its Japanese origin. But a closer inspection shows me that part of this is in fact just window dressing – nothing but a clever disguise.

I remove the sheath and realise that what I have in my hand is actually a knife concealed within a fan-like cover. There it is, exposed to view: a blade that appears dull grey against the warm glow of the brass handle. I feel no sense of disappointment at this discovery – quite the reverse. Fans are all very well, but knives are something that have always fascinated me. As a small boy I remember the Hoads giving me a Swiss Army knife: I liked using it to cut wood and carve balsa models. When I went on my escapades at Beechholme, a pocket knife was a handy implement for living rough. As time went on, I began to appreciate and learn about the craftsmanship that went into making them, so I'm intrigued by this knife masquerading as a fan and I take a closer look.

Japanese knives are mostly single-bladed, but this one is double-bladed, and it's constructed from top-quality folded steel, similar to a Samurai sword. I think it could be Meiji (nineteenth century) or maybe earlier, but either way I decide the knife is too interesting to pass over, so I buy it and take it home with me to do some research.

I discover that the knife belongs to a group of Japanese weapons known as tantos, a form of dagger originally carried by warring Samurai. The one I discovered is probably a *kaiken*, the smaller female version. It would have been concealed in a lady's robe or *obi* (sash) and used as a means of self-defence. In the late nineteenth and twentieth centuries some were also made for the tourist market, but the quality of this one suggests it was made for a high-status Japanese woman. Since discovering this, whenever I look at my *kaiken*, I like to imagine a silk-robed geisha wearing it tucked away in her sash to keep herself safe when she entertained her clients in the time-honoured tradition. Perhaps it protected her as she went about the dark streets and saved her from robbery or worse. But all of this can't obscure another aspect of its purpose, any more than the beautifully decorated scabbard can expunge the presence of the blade within. In the wrong hands, knives are not just practical tools, or means of self-defence, but weapons of aggression.

I met my first proper girlfriend, Rose Harding, not long after I'd moved into my bedsit. We got together in the Twenties. She had gone to the club with three old schoolfriends, while I was with Alex and his girlfriend. Rose was wearing a pink angora minidress and shiny white boots. She stood out because she was different, quietly attractive, with dark wavy hair and a shy expression, unlike most of the flamboyant girls there. We started talking and immediately hit it off. 'Rock Steady' by Alton Ellis was playing, then 'Thread the Needle' by Clarence Carter came on. We danced a bit and then, over a cigarette afterwards, she told me she was eighteen, a year older than me. She lived with her parents in Lutyens House on the Churchill Gardens Estate in Pimlico, and worked as a secretary in Westminster. There was no way I could bring myself to tell her that I was seventeen and still at school or she wouldn't have taken me seriously, so I said I was an architect's assistant, which must have done the trick because she agreed to go out with me. I thought she was brave to do so. It wasn't easy for a white girl to go out with a black guy in those days.

Rose's parents were clearly not happy about their daughter's new boyfriend. Her father was frosty and made it abundantly clear that, architect's assistant or not, I wasn't good enough for his daughter. I knew Rose felt uncomfortable, torn between loyalty to her parents and love for me, so I went to her flat as little as possible.

One night at the Twenties, a tall, heavily built man asked Rose to dance with him. I could see from her body language that she didn't want to, and I sidled closer. Realising I was with her, the man asked me if he could dance with Rose. 'If she wants to dance with you. It's up to her,' I replied.

'No, thanks,' Rose responded.

He didn't take her rejection kindly and blamed it on me. Pushing back the crowd to make space, he challenged me to a fight. I could hear from his accent that he was Irish. The Twenties was a club where you hardly ever saw a white man's face. It was a rough place for white people in those days, but he must have felt safe; no one would dare challenge someone of his stature.

Fearing I'd never be able to get into the club again if I backed down, I faced him. 'Come on then.'

He was so tall his head was almost touching the low ceiling. When he made a fist, it seemed gut-meltingly vast. There was a long pause while I waited for his first punch to connect with my head. I noticed that my six-foot friend Alex had slipped into the crowd and hidden himself away, leaving me alone to confront this titan. I was trembling to the point where I thought I was going to collapse with fear. But then he looked down at me, and just said, 'Nah. What a fucking waste of time,' and walked off. Clearly, there was no glory in Goliath flooring a midget David.

Jo could see that my heart was no longer in studying for my A levels. I was seventeen years old now, with a beautiful girlfriend, and I wanted to get on with my life. I told her I was thinking about leaving Elliott but didn't know what I could do. The opportunities for a boy like me seemed extremely limited. Jo disagreed; she said I could do anything I wanted if

I believed in myself. She didn't set any store by limitations and nor should I. She asked advice from the other teachers who knew me. Huw Salisbury, my woodwork and metalwork teacher, said there was a good job as a technical draughtsman and modelmaker at Imperial College London. Among my O levels, I had woodwork, metalwork and technical drawing, which was all I needed. It was a field that interested me and it sounded like the perfect job – the only problem was the other 2,000 applicants. Still, I shouldn't let that deter me. It was worth a try, Jo encouraged. Huw wrote a glowing reference and both he and Jo helped me with the application form. I was called for an interview and my enthusiasm must have won them round. A week later a letter arrived from Imperial. I'd landed my first proper job.

With my new role came financial independence. For the first time in my life I could choose to live where I liked. I couldn't wait to escape the solitude of my Twickenham bedsit, and when the offer arose to flat-share with three girls I knew, I jumped at it and moved to a flat in Brixton.

Margaret, Amanda and Angela were schoolfriends of Rose. Margaret and I trusted one another instantly, and I got on well with her boyfriend, Luke, an easy-going East End scaffolder with a dependable manner. By contrast, Angela and Amanda were party girls. They backcombed and lacquered their hair into crusty beehive coiffures, completing the look with false eyelashes and lashings of black eyeliner and pale lipstick that combined to give them a slightly predatory vampy look. Neither had regular boyfriends, and a variety of men who they had met in pubs or clubs regularly came back to the flat with them to smoke, listen to music and sometimes to stay the night. This didn't bother me, until one Friday night about a fortnight after I'd moved in.

Around midnight Margaret and I were in my room listening to Tommy McCook & the Supersonics' amazing instrumental 'Real Cool', a new favourite of mine. Above the music we heard the girls return from a club. From the sound of it, they had company with them: a couple of guys they must have picked up during the evening. Next thing we knew there was raucous shouting outside, thumping on the door and the clatter of ten or more of their boyfriends' friends bursting in. We heard shouting and swearing in thick Jamaican accents, boots thundering up the stairs, followed by more shouts, thuds and crashes as doors were kicked in and furniture overturned. Amanda and Angela yelled at them to stop, someone shouted a string of expletives, and then there was an unintelligible jumble of raised voices.

Sensing danger, Margaret and I locked ourselves in my room and turned off the music. Instinctively she backed to the far side of the room by the window. Whether the girls told them about us I never discovered, but we heard footsteps leaving the sitting room and marching down the corridor towards my room. The doorknob rattled but the door didn't yield. Then a couple of hefty kicks were aimed and it burst open without further resistance.

A group of seven or so young Jamaicans stood there. The one in front was particularly tall and well built, and wielding a large kitchen knife. Margaret retreated as far as possible from him, standing with her back pressed against the window, eyes round as marbles, visibly trembling. As the man with the knife advanced into the room she let out a loud involuntary exhalation. I didn't say anything.

'Hi there, guys, you're missing the party,' said the first intruder with an unpleasant sneer. 'Brian, look what we got here.'

'Let me see, Reggie,' Brian said. Behind him five more men stood poised to attack if signalled.

I stood in the middle of the room, trying to create a barrier between the intruders and Margaret. My mind raced as I tried to work out our limited options.

'What do you want?' I tried to say. But the words didn't come out because Reggie grabbed hold of me by the collar and hurled me back against the wall. Holding the point of his blade to my throat, he started slapping me around the face with his free hand.

'What you gonna do now? Hit me, man. Go on, you know you fucking wanna hit me,' he goaded.

I could feel the cold metal of the blade flat against my skin. His eyes were bloodshot, open unnaturally wide. His mouth was slack, saliva glistened on his lower lip. Behind him, the others were standing by, waiting to attack me. Meanwhile Brian was flicking through my record collection, glancing back over his shoulder at what was going on. In the silence, every sound and sensation seemed amplified. I could hear my breath and my blood pulsing in my head, the coldness of the blade on my neck, and the slap of the record sleeves.

'I don't want to hit you,' I said evenly. 'I'm not stupid. Why would I do that? So you can fucking stab me?'

'Yeh, man, go on. Hit me.' He slapped the right side of my face.

'No, I'm not going to hit you.'

He slapped the left side. 'You like us to get friendly with your woman first?' He slapped me again, hard, on each side. 'Go on,' he taunted, half smiling, nostrils flaring.

Margaret was crying quietly now. Between sobs she interjected, 'I'm not his woman. I'm nothing to do with him.'

'Brian — tell her to shut the fuck up, man,' said Reggie, turning his head.

'If you let her go, she will,' I suggested, putting Margaret's betrayal down to terror. 'She's a friend of the other girls. You don't want to hurt her, we're all friends here, man.'

'Did I ask for advice?' said Reggie, narrowing his eyes and pressing the knife harder and now at a slight angle. It felt as though the tip had just pierced my skin.

'Go easy, man,' said Brian. 'We don't want the pigs to come and make more fucking trouble.'

Margaret screamed, span round and yanked at the window. It didn't open. 'Help! Help me!' she shrieked, thumping the glass. 'They're trying to kill us!'

'Shh, girl,' said Brian, yanking her back by an arm. 'No need for that — we won't hurt you, if you do what we say.'

'Get off! Get away from me, get away!' she shouted, shrugging him off before letting out a series of penetrating screams.

Brian put his hand over her mouth. She gurgled resistance, then went silent.

'Look, guys,' I said, holding up my hands in a gesture of surrender, 'I don't know what you want, but whatever it is you can have it — just let the girl go. We're your friends. No need to hurt us. Let me take her away. She's got nothing — and once she's gone, I swear on my life I'll come back and give you whatever you want.'

'No way, man,' said Reggie.

'I give you my word. I don't lie,' I said calmly.

'Sure you fucking do.'

'I swear, I'll keep my word.'

This went on until eventually Brian capitulated. 'He's got a point. Let them go, Reggie. They're in the way. We don't want them.'

Visibly reluctant, Reggie stepped back. I rubbed my neck, glanced at Margaret, and jerked my head towards the door. 'I'll be back in an hour,' I said. 'Just promise me one thing. Don't wreck the place while I'm gone, will you?'

They grunted a reply and we dashed down the corridor towards the stairs. From behind the closed living-room door, a babble of deep male voices was audible – but we didn't go in. We left by the front door, closing it behind us. At the end of the road, I hailed a cab, pushed Margaret in, and jumped in beside her. Neither of us knew what to say and we sat as far apart as possible, in fidgety silence. When we reached her parents' flat in Pimlico twenty minutes later, she left without a goodbye. I put this down to the trauma of what had happened and told the driver to take me back to Brixton. I had given my word and it didn't occur to me to notify the police about what was going on.

The front door was open again when I got back to the flat. I shouted up the stairs – no answer, no noise. The place was apparently deserted, but then I heard what sounded like gushing water. With a sense of mounting unease, I bolted upstairs and peered into the bathroom. The taps had been left on in the bath and the sink. The plugs were in and the water had overflowed and was now cascading over the floor. I turned them off, but I could still hear water flowing. In the kitchen I discovered they had done the same thing – plug in the sink, both taps left on – and the flood had spread into the living room and soaked the carpet, which was littered with broken glass, overflowing ashtrays and overturned furniture.

I returned to my room, heavy with dread, to discover my worst fears realised. The room had been ransacked: emptied drawers scattered on the bed; the cupboard cleared; every piece of clothing gone; my record player, all the records I had kept there had disappeared; the papers I possessed, including drawings and designs, had either vanished or lay in crumpled shreds on the floor. I absorbed the scene of devastation, and a strange sense of disbelief came over me. I felt as though I had fallen into a nightmarish vortex. In a single night, almost everything I owned, everything I'd worked for, everything I'd created, had disappeared – like a bad magic trick. I had nothing now except for the clothes I was wearing, a coat hanging on the back of the door that presumably they had overlooked, plus the few records I had stored at Jo's for safekeeping. I wanted to wake up, to rewind the evening and discover it hadn't happened. But there was no awakening, no relief at the discovery I'd dreamt it up. I was horribly awake; it was all horribly real.

I notified the police, but they said there was nothing they could do. The unspoken reality was that I was a black man reporting a crime by a black gang. They weren't interested. To add to my woes, after this, Margaret refused to speak to me. She spread the word among her friends that I'd been a coward for not fighting Reggie and Brian, not bothering to explain that my strategy had saved her, without the need for any violence.

I realise now how fortunate we were to have escaped

unharmed. Reggie stabbed his girlfriend a few years later. He was sentenced to life imprisonment for murder.

I telephoned Jo and told her what had happened. 'Don't worry,' she said. 'There's a bed for you here. And we'll find some spare clothes until you're able to get some more.'

I stayed with her until I found a new place of my own: a bedsit in a pretty street off Wandsworth Common. I shared the flat with Alan, a schoolfriend. The house belonged to the mother of another schoolfriend who lived in the flat below. For nearly a year, all went well there and I worked hard to replace the possessions I'd lost in Brixton. Then one day a pleasant-looking man came round and told us that he had just bought the house. He was planning to renovate the property so he was giving us the statutory three months' notice, but if we were able to leave earlier that would be much appreciated. He seemed polite and plausible. Keen to oblige, I said I'd move out sooner, if he didn't mind storing my belongings in his basement. I would come back for them before the three months were up, I promised. The man smiled, shook my hand and agreed. I asked Jo's brother-in-law, Sem, who had recently separated from her sister, if I could sleep on his floor. 'That's fine, Ronnie,' he said.

I took a bag of belongings with me and moved a cabinet, books, records and the rest of my clothes into the basement. As agreed, I came back with a car to collect my stored possessions a few weeks later. I knocked. The door eventually opened a crack.

'Yes?' said the man, whose expression now seemed a lot less amiable than when we'd last spoken.

'I've come to pick up my things in the basement,' I said.

He squinted at me with open hostility. 'What things? I don't know who you are or what you're talking about,' he said.

'It's Ronnie. We agreed I could leave my things in the—' but before I could say more, the door slammed shut in my face.

After the robbery at Brixton, I could scarcely believe it. I knocked again. No reply. I stood rigid on the pavement for a few minutes, then, sick to the core, climbed back into my friend's car. Once again I had lost my belongings, once again I could see no recourse to justice. What proof did I have that my possessions had been stored in the basement? It would come down to my word against his. He was white. Who would the police believe?

Things weren't going so well with Rose. She wanted to mould me into a suitable husband. I'd look good in a white shirt, she said. This wasn't what I wanted to hear. I was eighteen and hated anything conventional. In my view, boring guys wore white shirts. I saw myself in T-shirts and polo-necks under well-cut jackets, looking cutting-edge, not remotely corporate. I was in love with Rose, but I was more in love with life. Jo was in the wings, encouraging me to travel, to stretch myself, to find out who I was. I'd never been abroad, and I longed to see Europe and have fun. Settling down wasn't on the agenda. It frightened me.

I knew Rose and I would have to split up, but I didn't know how to bring things to a graceful close. One night we arranged to go to the cinema. I wanted to tell her beforehand, but I couldn't bring myself to say it. Normally we'd hold hands during the film but that night we didn't. All I could think about was that I had to end it and I hated myself for the hurt I was about to inflict. 'What's wrong?' she asked as we walked away from the cinema. I couldn't bear to look her in the eye and say it. In the distance a bus was approaching, slowing as it reached the stop. 'I'm sorry but I don't want to see you any more,' I blurted out, and sprinted towards the departing bus, abandoning poor Rose in the street. Filled with self-loathing I sat on the back seat and stared vacantly into the darkness. I was a coward. It was an unchivalrous way to behave. I still feel really sorry about it. But I wasn't ready to settle down.

II

Michelangelo's *Pietà*

How easy it is to let go, to lose all sense of reality, to be taken to another place, another age, when you contemplate art. I don't think I have ever felt that sensation more powerfully than when I stood in front of Michelangelo's *Pietà*. To call it one of the most beautiful pieces of sculpture in the world seems inadequate. Giorgio Vasari, the sixteenth-century art historian, said it embodied 'divine beauty' and I agree. There is something so transcendent about it that makes you forget the physical reality of the subject and lose yourself in the emotion it conveys.

The *Pietà* was commissioned in 1497 by the French cardinal Jean de Bilhères, for his tomb, which he wanted adorned with the most beautiful marble sculpture in Rome. Michelangelo, aged only twenty-two, accepted the challenge and created his masterpiece from a single block of Carrara marble that he claimed was the most perfect he had ever seen. He also said that he could see the figures in the block, and all he had to do was chisel away the excess stone to release them.

The naturalism and classical beauty that characterise his interpretation of the subject marked a departure from medieval tradition and encapsulated the ideals of the Renaissance.

For me, however, what struck a chord was Mary's expression of tenderness, serenity and acceptance. As I looked on, I didn't think about my own life. I forgot who I was, touched the hem of her beautifully carved robes, and felt a profound sense of peace. I had arrived here, in Vatican City, like a pilgrim, with this mission in my heart, and the experience was all I'd hoped for and more. After some time, I turned and left, pausing at a vendor's stall in the piazza outside. I bought a postcard of the *Pietà* and addressed it to Jo. 'I made it,' I wrote. 'Thank you for believing I would.'

A fortnight earlier, in London, I'd packed my small holdall with everything I'd need for a month or two abroad. I held it tight and turned to say my goodbyes to Jo. She gave me an affectionate hug and a bright-eyed grin. 'Goodbye, Ronnie. Take care of yourself, and promise you'll write!'

'I will,' I said. 'It's going to be great – don't worry about me. Look after yourself.' Her smile remained etched in my mind as I walked along the drizzle-splashed London streets.

I'd always longed to travel. France, Italy, Spain, Africa, America, Russia. I wanted to see them all. But my resources were limited, and I had to begin somewhere, so I set my sights on Italy. I lined up some travelling companions, but as the departure date approached, one by one they all pulled out. Jo told me not to be disheartened: to stick to the original plan.

'Growing up is about getting away,' she said. 'Breaking free. Experiencing new things. Spend the summer hitchhiking in Italy. You'll be fine on your own – a change of scene will be good for you.'

Art had become my new focus because after a year of working at Imperial, I'd acknowledged to myself that I hated it there and had handed in my notice. Mr Rewald, my superior at the college, had given me a bumpy ride. An authoritarian, old-school type, he was dismissive of my technical qualifications, because despite his senior rank he didn't have them, and resented the fact I was asked to make drawings and models he couldn't. To begin with I'd ignored his hostility, working as hard as I could, with the aim of winning him round. My models and drawings were accurate to a couple of millimetres. I came in early, I stayed late. But the strategy didn't work. My diligence seemed to increase his annoyance.

A few months in, he began to sabotage my work. I'd leave a model overnight and return to find pieces broken and missing. In design meetings his head jutted forward on its reptilian neck, and he peered at me through his thick metal-rimmed spectacles. 'You think that will work, do you?' he'd say. 'Let's hope you're right. Because you weren't last time, were you?'

After the robbery in Brixton and then getting ripped off in Wandsworth, my perspective had shifted. I faced the fact that this working environment was toxic, and no matter how hard I worked there was no way my career would advance with Mr Rewald at the helm of the department. I didn't take his dislike personally; he manifested the same antipathy towards everyone. But with my future in his hands, I was at an impasse.

I'd also realised that the work wasn't stretching me, and my creative interests were starved. I was a civil servant, the job wasn't stimulating. I dreaded going to work. Why was I wasting my time doing something I no longer enjoyed? 'You're good at art,' Jo said, when I confided my frustrations. 'Why don't you go to art school? What about Hornsey?'

'Why Hornsey?' I asked.

'It's the only art college where you can get a degree.'

I wasn't convinced. 'I don't have any A levels, let alone a portfolio. Would they take me?'

'You've done a year at Imperial. You've got work to show from your time there. They'll be interested. But not if you don't try,' she urged. 'And don't forget this – your creative masterpiece.' She waved her arm at the wall of her living room. 'It's incredible. I'll bet you could get in with that on its own.'

The long wall at which she was gesticulating was filled with a wooden wall unit. I'd created it for her over the weeks I'd stayed. It was my way of thanking her for taking me in after the robbery and letting me lodge rent-free when I had nothing and nowhere else to go. I'd designed it to suit her lifestyle, incorporating shelves for her books, a work desk, a place for the TV, sections for pieces of sculpture and pottery, and spaces for paintings to be displayed.

'I can't take that,' I laughed. 'It's massive.'

'No, but you can take photos of it,' she retorted.

I took her advice and applied to do a foundation year at Hornsey. The admissions board were impressed by my photos of the wall unit. When I went for an interview they barely looked at the other pieces in my portfolio.

'The inventiveness and craftsmanship this demonstrates is

commendable,' they said, when I explained how I'd set about designing and making it. They sent me a letter a fortnight later: they'd waived their usual requirements and offered me a place starting at the end of September.

Before term started, I planned to hitchhike my way to Rome, down through France then stopping to see a friend who had invited me to stay with him and his family in a small northern Italian town called Canelli. I would fund the trip with £24 raised by selling drawings I'd made of Notting Hill.

I'd formulated a strategy before I left. Instead of the usual hitchhiker's garb of jeans, T-shirts and trainers, I would dress smartly – in French-made Newman orange velvet jeans, matching fine velvety stretch polo shirts, and chocolate-brown tassel loafers. In place of a rucksack, I would carry a leather holdall.

The plan worked well and I thought I was fortunate when, near Lille, a car going all the way to Italy stopped to give me a lift. The driver, Luigi, insisted on stopping off at every church that we passed on the road, so progress was slow. I was happy to go along with him, until we got to Nancy, where Luigi's intentions became clear and we parted company. Running the gauntlet of predatory people became something I would learn to anticipate and deal with in the weeks to come. But it was a relief when a driver stopped and gave me a lift over the San Bernardino pass. Sophia was an Italian furniture designer, she told me, and she was travelling to Turin. Being driven by a woman with flawless olive skin and long glossy hair was an enjoyable contrast to Luigi. I remember when we stopped at a service station I went to the gents' cloakroom and smartened myself up for her. She didn't notice.

In Turin, Sophia recommended a small hotel, tucked down

a side street. They had a room on the fourth floor where she left me. I threw open the shutters to flood the room with evening light, drinking in views across the city's terracotta rooftops. It was the first time I'd ever stayed in a hotel – excitement enough – and I was at last free to explore. It had been a long day but the opportunity to see the nightlife and to taste the food in the arcades of Turin was one I couldn't miss. I walked a short distance, then, suddenly ravenous from the delicious smells wafting down the street, stopped in a small osteria and ordered my first pizza and Campari. Afterwards I walked and walked, drinking in Turin's nocturnal sights and sounds.

By midnight fatigue caught up with me and I decided it was time to go back to the hotel. What was it called? What was the name of the street? In my excitement to explore I'd forgotten to make a note of its name and location. Even worse, I had left my key at the reception desk, so I had no record of it. All my belongings were at the hotel. I was desperate to sleep, but my only option was to go on walking and try to work out where it was.

I asked a couple of policemen but all I could say was, 'I've lost my hotel,' and they pointed to hotels, thinking I wanted one. Eventually, at about 6 a.m., when I was almost delirious with tiredness, by sheer accident I recognised the end of the road where I'd stopped to eat my pizza. Half walking, half running, I retraced my route to the hotel. The receptionist was smoking a cigarette and sipping a coffee, when I asked her for my key. '*Buongiorno, signor,*' she said, handing it to me. '*Va tutto bene?*'

I nodded. '*Bene – grazie.*' I dragged myself up the four flights of stairs; each one felt as though I were scaling a mountain. I found my room and crawled into bed.

★

I made my way to Canelli, a small town in the Piedmont region, which clings to a gentle hillside, surrounded by vineyards. I'd arranged to meet up with Gino Bistanignio, a friend who'd invited me to stay for a few days. Gino was an architecture student, studying in Canada. We'd met and become friends a few months earlier, when he was visiting London on his way home for the summer vacation. Gino's family had been millers for generations, and the family home was an old stone watermill just outside the old town walls, where flour was ground for pasta. When I look back on the days I spent with Gino, I think of warmth and the generosity of his family, of the scent of pale pink earth and of the olive trees and vines that surrounded his house. I think of the shiny terracotta floors inside it that always felt cool even in the baking summer heat, and I remember the shady terrace where there was a long wooden table, at which the family would congregate for meals that lasted all afternoon. My bedroom was over the mill wheel. I can still hear the sound of water gushing beneath my open window in the velvet night, and how it soothed and excited me at the same time.

In the local bar, Gino introduced me to his friends in the village. I was greeted with friendly curiosity and during the evening somebody approached Gino to ask if I'd like to take part in the procession due to take place in the nearby city of Asti in a few days' time. I knew the conversation involved me but couldn't follow it until Gino translated. He explained the Palio di Asti is a traditional ceremony, the oldest in Italy, dating back to the thirteenth century, and similar to the famous Palio at Siena. It ends with a bareback horserace in the triangular piazza at the heart of the medieval city, after a procession of hundreds of horses, riders and footmen through the ancient gates to the square. 'My friend invites you to walk at the head of the procession and lead the horse on which the lady of the city is seated.'

Maybe the Campari I'd drunk made me more impulsive than usual, but without thinking too deeply I said yes. I didn't know then that I would be outfitted in medieval costume: a bottle-green velvet doublet and hose with great pointed turned-up shoes and a floppy velvet beret with an orange plume in it. But when the time came and I was handed my costume, it only added more to the sense of occasion. Dressed in my medieval finery, I took my place. The lady of the city was seated side-saddle, her robe fanned out over the horse's flanks. She nodded and smiled; I grasped the horse's bridle and at the signal set off. Flag-waving crowds lined the way, and at the gates a great cheer rose up. As we progressed, the crowd became more densely packed, with hundreds of spectators lined up behind barricades. They were evidently astonished and delighted to see a black person at the head of the procession. To them I resembled a black page from a Renaissance painting. I vividly recall the shouts that rang out as they saw me: 'Nero! Nero! Bello nero!' and how the cameras flashed. My appearance had never been celebrated in this way before and I felt both embarrassed and exhilarated. I recognised the honour I'd been given and I couldn't help smiling broadly and waving encouragement to the crowd.

Back in Canelli, the celebrations continued. Crates of Asti Spumante were produced, bottles were shaken and opened and sprayed over me until I was utterly drenched. Later there was a disco at the home of a wealthy friend of Gino. During the evening James Brown's 'Papa's Got a Brand New Bag' came on, and Gino's friends started urging me to dance: 'Ronnie, dance! Ronnie, do your shake!' When I started dancing they cheered, clapping me on, and I lost myself in the joy of the music and the day. I know some people today might see this experience differently, as though I was being objectified, taken advantage of or exploited in some way. But I still don't see it like that. I loved the experience. I was a medieval page, a celebrated guest, Gino's friend, welcomed by his big-hearted family. Life was ripe with opportunity, there for the taking. Jo was right, anything was possible with self-belief.

The highs of my visit to Canelli hadn't made me lose sight of my mission to get to Rome. A couple of days later, Gino and a couple of his friends walked with me towards the road leading out of the village. As usual, I dressed with care: orange Newman cords, a matching shirt, a chocolate-brown leather belt and chocolate-brown loafers. This wasn't how most young men in Canelli dressed first thing in the morning, and when I walked through the village, a passing man on a bicycle did a double take, his head whipping round in such astonishment that he drove straight into the back of a stationary lorry and tumbled off his bike. Gino and his friends erupted with laughter.

I said goodbye to them and walked along the slip road not far from the junction with the autostrada. Minutes later a car stopped. The driver was a modest-looking man in his forties. 'Where are you going?' he asked in Italian.

'South – to Rome,' I said in English.

'Me too, get in,' he responded in English.

His English was fluent enough, though strongly accented. He asked me my name and what I did. I told him I was Ronnie and that I'd been working at Imperial College as a technical draughtsman. 'What do *you* do?' I asked in return.

'I'm involved in photography,' he said.

'What kind of photography?'

'Film-making.'

'What films?'

'I direct and make low-budget avant-garde movies.'

'Which ones?'

'You won't have heard of them. They are too specialist,' he said.

'I'm a member of the National Film Theatre and a couple of other film clubs. Try me,' I urged.

'A film called *Oedipus Rex*.'

'I know that. What others have you made?'

'A film called *Theorem*.'

'I've heard of that too. What's your name?'

'Pier.'

'What's your family name?'

'Pasolini.'

The celebrated film director was my driver, I realised. We chatted easily about films he'd made and things I'd seen, all the way from northern Italy to Rome. As we approached the city, several hours later, he asked me where I was staying. Gino had told me to go to the railway station to find cheap accommodation. 'Oh no, that's not a good area for *pensioni*. It's very dangerous. A lot of dodgy people hang around those areas and they prey on young men like you. There's a nice place near the Colosseum – I know the woman that runs it and if she's got a room, it's a better place for you to stay. But first, would you like to see the sights?'

I said yes, and Pasolini drove me all round Rome, pointing out the main sights. Afterwards he dropped me by the Colosseum where his friend did have a room, and we said goodbye.

Tragically, six years later Pasolini made international news headlines. He had been brutally battered to death, after picking up a rent boy in his car near Rome's Termini station, where he had warned me not to stay.

I found my way on foot to Vatican City the next day, crossing the vast piazza to enter St Peter's Basilica, the largest church in the world. I had seen photos and read books about the basilica, but nothing prepared me for the blast of opulence and the theatricality of the interior: the height and span of the dome, the lavish marble covering the surfaces of floor and walls, the sculpted reliefs, the gilding, the bronzes, the baldachin with its contorted columns. There was so much – too much – to absorb. The magnificence of it all swamped me.

I found the *Pietà* without difficulty to the right of the main door and approached the most beautiful sculpture I've ever seen. In contrast to the opulence all around, it was simple and tender, one of the most poignant images of motherhood and love I'd ever seen. Michelangelo had depicted Mary as a young mother, not the middle-aged woman that was the fifteenth-century norm. How had human hands turned solid stone into this soft, beautiful, tender yet powerful piece of sculpture, I marvelled, as I touched the hem of Mary's robe.

I was fortunate to be able to have that physical connection. Three years later, in May 1972, a delusional Hungarian geologist called Laszlo Toth attacked the *Pietà* with a hammer, severing an arm, breaking Mary's nose, and chipping her eyelid.

The restoration took ten months and ever since, the sculpture has been preserved behind a bulletproof Perspex screen.

From Rome I went to Pompei and then back north to Florence. I was expert in the rules of hitchhiking by then. First, start early – the later in the day you begin the more competition there will be with other people on the road. Second, wait on the slip road to the autostrada. Don't attempt to walk on the side of the autostrada – I'd learned that lesson the hard way. The *carabinieri* came zooming up on motorbikes and pressed me against the central reservation with their rifles in my chest and told me firmly to climb over the embankment, walk across the fields and find another road to hitchhike on.

On a fine late-September morning, I was stood on the slip road, dressed in my red velvet cords and matching red polo shirt, clutching my leather holdall. I was first there, so I would be first to get a lift, I thought. But no cars stopped and three-quarters of an hour later another couple appeared. Still no lifts. Ten minutes later another couple turned up. Within an hour and a half there were at least twenty groups of people waiting for lifts heading north and I was feeling despondent. There is just no way I can get this lift north, I thought. At nine o'clock, about three hours after I'd arrived, a car stopped. Everybody surged forward, charging towards the vehicle. Seeing the approaching stampede, the vehicle pulled away, stopped a bit further on, and a woman half stepped out from the passenger side. She waved the crowd back and pointed in my direction. A person standing next to me started walking forward. She shook her head, waved them away and pointed at me – out of all those people, she wanted me to have the lift. I walked towards the vehicle, conscious that everyone was looking daggers at me. Had my Italian been better I might have pointed out that I'd been there first, but I didn't want to push my luck. I leapt into the car, thanked them, and asked why they'd chosen me. 'You looked the most interesting,' the woman replied.

When it was time to head back to London, I got a lift as far as Geneva with a man who ran a club and wanted me to stay and work as his disc jockey. 'I have to go home, I'm starting college,' I said. 'And I need to be in Calais the day after tomorrow.'

'You're crazy – you'll never make it in time, and you can't go at night,' he warned.

'I have to go,' I repeated. He gave me dinner in his club and then offered to drop me at the foot of the Jura Mountains. We followed the signs out of town then took a road that wound up to the foothills until he stopped. 'I can't take you any further, I need to get back to the club, but follow this road, and it will take you into France,' he told me.

I got out of his warm car, thanked him for his kindness, and set off with a determination I didn't feel. The temperature was much colder here up in the mountains than I had been expecting, and my summer clothes weren't suited to a nocturnal mountain excursion. But telling myself that walking would soon warm me, I trudged on, up and up and up, on a single-track road that wound its way up over the Jura and down into south-eastern France. It was dark, and getting colder and colder as the hours passed and I climbed and climbed. The mountains were black angular shadows, the stars brilliant pinpricks of light in the night sky. I don't know how many degrees of frost there were by one or two in the morning, but I remember that I wasn't wearing any socks – so my feet were numb with cold, as well as increasingly sore and swollen. Eventually they hurt so much I decided I'd stop for a while. I sat on a rock on the side of the road, removed my loafers, and rubbed my poor toes and heels, then tried to get my shoes back on. But my feet had swollen so much they would no longer fit.

If I sat there for too long, I would succumb to exposure, I realised. So I did the only thing I could think of and set off barefoot. Soon I was freezing cold, my feet cut and bleeding. On the left of me as I walked, the moon illuminated the tops of the fir trees like a wall of jagged spears. To the right their dark roots contorted over the mountain boulders. Now and again I heard the eerie call of wild animals echoing in the dark, but I trudged on, trying not to wince as yet another stone pierced my feet, or think about the danger I was in. Two hours later I spotted the headlights of a car making its way up the pass. The car came closer, slowed, passed me, and drew to a halt. I galvanised what little energy I had left, and sprinted towards it. But I must have looked like a scary desperado and the driver had second thoughts. Before I could open his door he zoomed off.

I walked on and on, until I came to a shepherd's refuge. The door was bolted closed but there was a bench outside. I sat down, took a towel out of my holdall, and wrapped it around me for warmth. I told myself not to fall asleep, fearing I'd die of exposure if I did. I was shivering violently, but I made no attempt to prevent myself from doing so because I thought that if I stopped shivering it would mean my body had given up. The night seemed vast, unfriendly and endless. I felt dwarfed by the landscape that surrounded me, but I wasn't ready for death.

★

Dawn was just breaking when I heard the faint hum of a distant car winding along the road. I staggered to my feet, remembering the lesson I'd learned from the last vehicle I'd seen, trying not to look too mad, desperate or excited. The car approached, saw me, and pulled to a halt. The driver wound his window down and in French asked where I was going. 'Anywhere north,' I responded, trying to control my desperation. 'I'm heading for Calais.'

He made some exclamation about the state of me. I don't know what I said in reply, but it must have done the trick because he said, 'Get in. You just need to sleep. Put the seat right back and don't talk. I'm driving as far as Lyon.' He asked no more questions, and I gladly did as he'd instructed. When I next opened my eyes, we were approaching Lyon, and I'd recovered enough to continue. I sometimes wonder if I'd have survived without that lift. Probably not.

I eventually got myself to the northern plains near Ypres. I worked out I had half an hour to get a lift to Calais or the boat would leave without me. I walked along the roadside, chilled to the bone, thinking of the soldiers in the trenches. After the highs of Italy, this was hell on earth. A short distance away I could see a gigantic crucifix with a corpus looming out of the bleak, featureless landscape. I stood there staring towards it then back along the empty road, scouring the grey ribbon of tarmac for cars. Across the open terrain there wasn't a vehicle to be seen. Even Christ had forsaken me, I thought, as desolation got the better of me. I glared at the figure of Christ on his cross. 'You bastard!' I shouted.

As soon as I'd uttered those words I saw the distant pinprick of light – a car was coming. This car has to give me a lift, I thought. The road was fast, open, and three lanes wide. The vehicle was travelling at such speed, I thought it wasn't going to stop. As it closed in on me, I jumped out in the road directly in front of it. I knew it was foolhardy to do this, but danger didn't seem to matter. The car screeched to a slow. The driver could have swerved around me and driven off, and I half expected him to do so, but instead he ground to a halt within a couple of feet of me. The door opened. 'You must be desperate or mad to do that,' the driver said. 'Where are you going?'

'Calais,' I responded. 'And thank you for stopping.'

He drove me all the way there and I caught the ferry.

Fifteen years later, in the 1980s, I went in search of redemption. I retraced that route in my own car. I found the road I'd climbed barefoot in the Jura, then I drove back through France and located the crucifix that I'd blasphemed. I stood beneath it, head bent, and apologised.

My trip to Italy had given me a taste for travel and nine months later, in 1970, when I was twenty, I set off again. By then I knew Hornsey wasn't for me, even though I'd begun there full of hope, enrolling in courses I'd always longed to study: graphic design, fashion design, life drawing and sculpture. I drew at every opportunity. Jo's sister, Christine, a doctor of zoology at London Zoo, arranged for me to have access to the zoo's famous resident, Guy the gorilla, and I spent hours sketching him while he contemplated me. I drew my friends and the world around me. I drew trees in Hyde Park, I went back to the Natural History Museum in South Kensington and made studies there. I was determined to immerse myself in art – at least I thought I was. But I was a mature student, and less compliant than those who came straight from school. A few weeks in, the novelty of the course dimmed. The teaching was too prescriptive, not what I'd expected – or thought it ought to be. I didn't want to follow the usual time-trodden routes of learning to paint, draw, sculpt, design by copying others. I had ideas and I wanted to explore them, rather than retracing established traditions and techniques.

I became disillusioned by the sense that whenever I came up with radical concepts, I was discouraged from developing them. I wanted to make a huge sculpture in bright colours from fibreglass but I was told the idea was unworkable. In fashion classes I just wanted to cut to the chase and make things. I couldn't accept that I had to follow directions, research, write an evaluation before cutting and stitching my brilliant creations. I was impatient – for life, for novelty, for instant gratification. This isn't what art should be about, I told myself: it's nonsensical. They've got it all wrong. They should be encouraging me to expand on my ideas, not suppressing them.

Apathy took hold. Instead of working hard, I came in late, missed classes, spending hours in the common room playing table football and smoking. Meanwhile, my grant disappeared on clubbing, which offered a far more compelling way of passing the time than writing an essay or making a series of scaled-down line-drawing studies.

Only one subject unexpectedly captured my imagination: art history, as taught by Margaret (Maggie) Knight – an inspiring woman and a brilliant teacher. She taught me how to *really* look at a painting, to understand its heritage, to recognise its innovations. It is her whom I credit with kindling a passion that has never faded.

To make ends meet while I decided what to do next, I found a job selling clothes in All Kinds, a trendy men's boutique on the King's Road. The owner, Fenton Conway, watched me helping people, and could see I had an eye for fashion. He owned a company called Petronius that made clothes for various brands including Take 6, a men's high-street fashion chain. 'You're talented at this, Ronnie – I love what you do here,' he said. 'Would you like to join my design team?'

'I'd love to,' I replied, grinning. I imagined myself in a fancy design studio, with a huge white desk and white walls and my drawings stuck on boards as exquisite models wafted in and out. I pictured myself styling catwalk shows, as photographers filmed and the fashionable glitterati watched admiringly.

It wasn't quite like that.

The workshop was in a dingy warehouse in the East End. I worked with a team of elderly men, cutting patterns, to put together a range of denim jackets and trousers. There was no white desk, no beautiful models, no catwalk glamour. As soon as I got there I missed the buzz of the King's Road and wanted to leave.

At that time, I had two close girl friends called Helen and Linda whom I'd met in a club. Both were cool rock-chick hippy types and the three of us loved smoking and listening to the music of Dylan and Hendrix, going to concerts and clubs, daydreaming about travelling and what we would do in the future. Helen was Scottish with reddish-blonde hair and pale eyes. Linda was dark and I was more than a little in love with her. On Sundays we'd often meet up at the Eros statue in Piccadilly to listen to the buskers. There was always a crowd of young people around and on one occasion I started talking to a good-looking guy dressed in an embroidered waistcoat and tight velvet trousers, who looked like a mixed-race Jim Morrison. His name was Jacko. He was a musician in a band and had lots of friends in the music world, he told me.

'Cool waistcoat,' I said.

'Yeh, man, Jimi Hendrix gave it to me. You fancy a smoke?'

We drifted away from the crowd for a drink somewhere and arranged to meet again in a few days' time. I introduced Jacko to Helen and Linda. He liked them and they liked him, so we'd often go out clubbing together or to listen to bands. A few weeks into our friendship, Jacko announced he was in love with Helen. I didn't mind because I'd set my heart on Linda, although there was no sign that she thought of me as anything other than a friend. By then I'd begun to suspect that Jacko's claim to be a musician was an exaggeration, and he was mostly just scraping by on the dole, bumming odd jobs here and there wherever he could. Whenever I asked where his next gig was and if we could come along, he'd say, 'Sure, man, I'll let you know. It would be good to see you in the green room.' But details were never forthcoming, and then he'd say, 'We did a great gig last night, you should've been there.'

I didn't think about this much. We were all young and he was a handsome, likeable guy, and if Helen or Linda had suspicions there was anything untoward about him they didn't voice them. I introduced him to Jo and to other friends, who were also captivated by his charm and sincere manner. So what if he was a bit of a fantasist? He wasn't harming anyone, was he?

One day in early May we were all together in the park. 'Have you heard the news, Ronnie?' said Helen, holding her face towards the sun. 'Linda and I are leaving next weekend. We're hitchhiking to Greece, then island-hopping around the Cyclades – Mykonos, Paros, Santorini, Naxos – they're meant to be fantastic. Why don't you come too? It'll be a laugh.'

'I need to work, we haven't finished the clothing range,' I replied, taking a drag of my cigarette, thinking miserably of the dark workshop and the hunched old men with whom I spent my working hours.

'I've got a gig,' said Jacko, looking at his sleeve. 'Mott the Hoople at Earls Court – you should come.'

'Great,' I said. 'When?'

'I'll let you know, man. We're fixing the dates this week.'

Helen and Linda went off on their travels. 'Maybe I'll come and find you,' I joked as I kissed Linda on the cheek and hugged her goodbye.

I missed them more than I'd expected. After they'd gone the job in the East End seemed to get me down even more, and a fortnight later I'd had enough.

'I want to go travelling for a few months,' I told Fenton one rainy Friday afternoon in May, when he came to see how we were getting on. 'I'd like to leave at the end of next week. The range is pretty well sorted now.'

If he was surprised by my sudden departure he didn't show it. He shrugged his shoulders. 'I'm sorry to lose you, Ronnie. Come back and see me if you need work when you're back and I'll see what I can do.'

'OK. Thanks, Fenton,' I said, amazed at the surge of relief

I felt. 'But not in the design team. It's not my thing. I'm better at sales.'

'I reckon you're right,' he said.

I was now officially renting a room in Sem's flat in Richmond. I wanted to keep the room, so that I'd have a place to come back to, so I paid the rent for three months in advance. I must have mentioned this to Jacko. 'That's cool, man, because, get this: I need a place to crash. So I could stay at yours and keep an eye on everything for you?'

'I'll have to ask Sem and see if he agrees,' I said, taken aback. It was the first time he'd mentioned he was looking for somewhere to stay. He'd only brought it up when I said I'd paid the rent. But still, he was a friend. I trusted him and felt I had no choice. 'If Sem's OK with it, that's cool,' I said.

Sem was happy with the arrangement when I introduced them, on the understanding that Jacko would move out as soon as I returned.

'Thanks, mate. Sounds good,' said Jacko, putting his arm around Sem in a brotherly gesture.

A few days later I was on my way. Hitchhiking to Dover, I crossed on the ferry then worked my way south through France, Italy, across to Yugoslavia and onward. To help my chances of securing lifts, I was smartly dressed once again, in a waisted leather jacket with rounded lapels, long boots under velvet flares, and a cowboy hat. I carried a few extra clothes and a sleeping bag rolled up in my leather holdall. I'd had my ear pierced before I left, and I thought that, all in all, I looked like a rock star. In retrospect, the outfit wasn't suited to Greece in the height of summer, but I had to get there first, and I was willing to suffer for fashion.

Yugoslavia was still under Tito's communist rule, and Albania was a no-go area. Not wanting to take any chances, I steered clear, instead following the route the Serbian Army took when they retreated in the First World War. At night, I slept rough in woods or in deserted buildings, wherever I could find shelter. Yugoslavia bore little resemblance to the tourist-friendly place the area is today. In the south, in what is now Macedonia, the people I encountered were unexpectedly wild and hostile. I remember mountain villages where men with a Middle Eastern appearance, a legacy of their Ottoman heritage, carried knives between their teeth, and there were often dead, bloated animals left decaying on the roadside.

I wasn't far from the Greek border near Thessaloniki when a farmer and his son in an open-backed farm truck stopped to give me a lift. I climbed into the back and found a perch on a wooden crate, next to some dangerous-looking farm implements. The truck wound its way down through dramatic mountainous terrain with craggy grey outcrops, rivers snaking through steep-sided ravines, then up gentle hillsides covered in long-needled pines, oak and walnut trees, across plains on which livestock grazed and over rickety medieval bridges. Then, with the engine revving alarmingly, we mounted another steep climb.

It was around midday when they dropped me near the turning to their farm at a junction near the border and indicated the direction I should follow. I walked a mile or so before I came to a Greek village. As soon as the first houses came into view people appeared in doorways, and as I drew closer they stared and waved at me – amiably, but as if I were some bizarre curiosity. I waved back and nodded, and when I passed by they emerged from their houses and followed a few yards behind me. By the time I reached the centre of the village's one main street, my entourage had grown, and I was being shadowed by what seemed like most of the village. Some of them were calling out, '*Mavro! Mavro!*' (which I later learned means 'black'), and gesticulating at me. I didn't feel threatened, they still seemed friendly enough, but it was as if I'd turned into the Pied Piper.

I entered the village shop, in search of bread and cheese. The stream of people didn't wait outside, they poured in after me, their voices raised, as if that would help me to understand what they were saying. There were so many of them that I found myself pressed uncomfortably against the counter. The shopkeeper gazed blankly at me, unable to hear what I was saying, let alone understand what I meant. In the middle of the chaos, a uniformed soldier broke through the throng and entered into a rapid exchange with the crowd and the shopkeeper, gesticulating towards me as he did so. The crowd gradually grew quiet and retreated to the open door.

The man turned to me. 'These people don't want to hurt you,' he explained in a commanding manner. 'They are interested in you because they have never seen a black person before. The shopkeeper is honoured you have chosen to visit his shop and says you may take whatever you need free of charge. If you wish to stay the night I will find a room for you.'

I thanked him and said I wouldn't stay as I was heading for Thessaloniki and then to Athens and the Cyclades.

'As you wish. But take care on the road, make sure you aren't out at night. There are wolves in the mountains around here,' he warned.

I reassured him I could take care of myself and traced the road that snaked through the hills towards Thessaloniki. No vehicles came by that afternoon, and when nightfall came I had to sleep rough in a wood by the roadside. I ate some bread and cheese before I fell fitfully asleep. I heard wolves baying, but I woke unharmed, so perhaps I was dreaming.

I had no way of contacting Helen and Linda, but they had mentioned Mykonos as one of their destinations, and when I reached Piraeus there was a boat leaving for Mykonos in a couple of hours, so I felt that fate decided I would start my search for them there. By 1970, Mykonos had earned a reputation for a relaxed, cosmopolitan vibe that drew celebrities along with affluent tourists, artists and musicians, not to mention impoverished hitchhikers like me. There weren't many black tourists, but many of the island's eclectic visitors headed for the 9 Muses. Converted from an old warehouse, it stood on the waterfront, and was said to be the best club on the island, so I headed there on my first night.

I'd paid for five days' accommodation in advance, but my holiday funds would soon be exhausted and I needed to find a way of making money fast. In the club several people admired my earring – in those days few men had pierced ears – and that gave me an idea. The next day I went to a local jewellery store and bought some gold sleepers, and a needle and some surgical spirit and cottonwool from the pharmacy. Then I paraded up and down the beach, offering an ear-piercing service.

Within two days I had made about £125, enough to last until I found regular work.

To celebrate I went back to the 9 Muses. That night 'Ball of Confusion' by the Temptations came on. It's a difficult song to dance to, but I'd been taking dance classes in London, and took to the floor and gave it my best. People in the club quickly noticed me and stood back and watched as I moved effortlessly to the beat. I was in my element, conscious of being watched, yet so lost in the music and a sense of elation that I didn't feel uncomfortable.

Afterwards an attractive dark-haired girl came over and we started chatting. She told me her name was Cynthia, and she'd seen me on the beach piercing ears. She lived in New York but her family were Greek and a cousin had a business in Mykonos. She liked black guys and had lots of black friends in New York. Did I have a girlfriend? What was I doing here?

'Yes, I have a girlfriend,' I lied. 'But she's in London. I've been studying art and working in a boutique on the King's Road in Chelsea, selling and designing. I'm here for a change of scene.' I didn't say in so many words that I was looking for work, but she must have guessed as much, having seen me on the beach.

'So, Ronnie, you should come and talk to my cousin, Kimon Kouros. He owns a boutique here. Maybe you can help each other.'

Kimon told me he was looking for someone to run his boutique now that the summer season was getting underway. 'With your experience I think you would be ideal.'

'I'm not sure,' I replied. 'I'm not looking for permanent work. I'm planning to meet up with friends. And I speak French and some Italian, but I don't speak Greek.'

'Our customers are mainly tourists, and you'll pick up the

Greek you need,' he replied undeterred. 'By the way, I should mention – the job comes with a house and I will need you to go to Athens once a week to pick up new stock. There's a house where you can stay there too. I have many friends I'll introduce you to. You'll enjoy it.'

The house, salary and travel all seemed too good to turn down. I accepted – after all Helen and Linda didn't even know I'd left England. And if they turned up I would be able to offer them a place to stay.

As the season got underway, Kimon introduced me to Bobby Porter, a US designer friend of his, and together we staged fashion shows in the street in which exotically outfitted men in togas and kilts strutted around with women clad in skimpy swimwear. I found myself helping women choose crocheted bikinis. I made friends among the glamorous clientele and the designers who supplied us. During the long hours of the lunchtime siesta, I would go down to the salon in the basement where Kimon had an endless supply of ouzo for his friends and clients.

In the evening I'd often go to the 9 Muses, and I learned Greek dancing and to sing Greek songs, and sometimes joined in a display for the visitors. Other nights we would all sit around in someone's house smoking hash, dancing, talking and listening to music

The Mykonos season was winding down by late September. Crochet bikinis weren't selling as fast, the 9 Muses was half empty, and Kimon said our next show would be the last. 'I can keep the shop open and you can stay on at the house if you want,' he said, 'but we'll have to cut down on the hours.'

I thought it over. Many of my friends had left. After the buzz of the summer season, Mykonos in winter wouldn't be much fun. The time had come for me to return to reality.

By late October I returned to my flat in Richmond after an arduous journey. 'Where's Jacko?' I asked Sem, surprised that there was no trace of him to be seen.

'I had to ask him to leave.' He explained that as soon as I'd left Jacko started spreading malicious rumours and telling disparaging stories about me. Sem refused to tell me what precisely he'd said. He didn't want to upset me, he said. But I gathered that Jacko had also started pilfering things from the flat, and eventually Sem confronted him and told him to go. He hadn't stopped there. Helen and Linda had returned from Greece earlier than I had, and when I tried to contact them, they refused to speak to me. Jacko had ingratiated himself into my life and defamed me to my closest friends. It wasn't just Helen and Linda: I discovered he'd tried the same with Jo and with others. Most hadn't believed him when he described whatever heinous crime I'd supposedly committed. But Helen and Linda fell for it. I never saw either of them again.

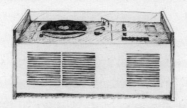

12

A Braun Dieter Rams SK4 Audio System

Sometimes I feel overwhelmed by everything I've accumulated over the years. The floor bows with vinyl records, thousands of books on myriad subjects fill shelves and overflow on tables. A multitude of disparate objects that I'm in the process of restoring or researching, for one reason or another, surround me. Shoes, a Japanese knife, an Inuit carving, a headless wooden Madonna, a piece of broken ancient glass, a cracked Wedgwood vase, paintings, prints, photos, beadwork, textiles – they inhabit drawers, they fill chests and lie folded and wrapped in storage boxes ready to take to my lockup.

When I have an overloaded moment, I take myself to my imaginary house where there's no clutter at all, and every object is perfectly displayed. It's a longstanding dream, one that's never wavered, and it was for this reason that in the 1980s I bought a Braun Dieter Rams SK4 audio system. Four decades on, I haven't come any closer to realising the ideal house fantasy, nor have I decluttered. The sound system has stayed where I put it the day I brought it home: in the attic, bubble-wrapped. An iconic object waiting for the moment when it will be the perfect centrepiece of the music room in my perfect home.

If he could see it there, swathed in plastic, unused, Dieter Rams would probably be appalled. He was a designer who trained as an architect and served as a carpentry apprentice before he became Braun's chief designer in the 1950s. His style emerged from the Bauhaus tradition, and one of his key design principles, that less is better, and that good design enhances function, are dictums that have always been close to my heart, even if I struggle to achieve them. When it was launched in 1956, the SK4's pared-down form was sometimes known as Snow White's Coffin, for self-evident reasons. Its design may look retro today, but in 1950s Britain it was revolutionary. Rams had effectively transformed the appearance of an everyday electrical appliance into something that was undeniably innovative, austere, modern and aesthetically pleasing.

Thirty-plus years ago, when I saw the sound system on a dealer's stand at Newark Antiques Fair and brought it home with me, music had become more than just a recreational pleasure – it was central to my working life. At this time, postwar design hadn't attracted the attention of many collectors. People said I was mad to try and deal in it, and the only buyers were Italians. Now all that has changed. Mid-century modern design is the pinnacle of fashionable taste. But fashion has nothing to do with my desire to keep my SK4. The fact is I can't reconcile the dream with reality, but I can't give up on my dream either, so it's one of a few things that I've bought, never used, never had on display, and have no intention of selling. Just knowing it's there brings me solace.

My first gig as a DJ was in 1971, at the Marquee Club in Wardour Street. I think it came about thanks to contacts I'd made at Contempo Records, my favourite record shop in Hanway Street, where I'd been hanging out since my teens. Writing those words now I have to pinch myself. Most people's first attempts at DJing are in the village hall, if not in their bedroom. The Marquee Club was the other end of the spectrum. When I worked there, it was already established as what *Melody Maker* magazine called 'the most important venue in the history of pop music'. Yet it wasn't what you might expect. Not plush or luxurious like the Café de Paris or the Embassy Club, it was a cavernous place, shabby when the lights went up, yet a magnet for anyone serious about music. This was where musicians and record company moguls mixed and where, in the early 1970s, the Faces, Queen, Status Quo and David Bowie sometimes took to the stage. In between whatever band was on, a DJ would entertain the audience. And that was where I came in.

I arrived at the Wardour Street door laden down with my box of records and a feeling of incredulity. Was I really about to entertain their illustrious clientele, when I'd never done such a professional gig before?

I wandered through the club to the DJ area, where two decks with a mixer in between were set up on a podium. I plugged in my headphones, so I could switch from one deck to another. As one record played I'd line up the next, listening to it on my headphones. The skill came in knowing when to fade out one and merge it into the following one. Usually, I didn't start right at the beginning, I'd wait for the bass to come in, or a beat that linked in with the one that was ending, so it was important to know each record really well.

I'd brought all my own records filed in an aluminium box. I'd made the box while I was working at Imperial, using their sheet metal guillotine and riveting machine, and in it I stored home-made colour-coded cardboard sleeves so that I could flick through and easily find what I wanted from each musical genre: blue for soul, red for reggae and so on. The box of records had survived the robbery because I'd left it at Jo's for safekeeping.

I was determined I wasn't going to follow the norm – I would do things differently. I wouldn't talk over the music the way club DJs did back then – I would be the silent DJ, with minimal chat, introducing clubgoers to music they'd never heard: I'd be a musical educator.

I hadn't planned my set, because I wanted to play according to the vibe. If a song went down well I would play something similar, if not I'd go for something different, until I found something they responded to, and I'd blend it all together. What I wasn't going to do, if I could possibly avoid it, was play the Beatles or the Who or any other mainstream tracks. I'd become serious about music and had virtually stopped listening to the radio. Along with barely talking, I was adamant I didn't want my sets to be influenced by fashion or what was in the charts.

Things didn't go entirely to plan. People came up and requested music they knew from the charts. 'You're in the wrong club,' I responded in frustration, although I could see that I would have to compromise and play *some* music people recognised. As the evening wore on I found myself synched into the mood of the crowd – in the zone, I'd call it. It was an exhilarating feeling, and afterwards, when it was all over, my head was buzzing for a few hours, and then I was utterly exhausted.

I'm not sure my approach was quite what the Marquee wanted, and I wasn't invited to work there regularly. But that night was enough to convince me of one thing: DJing was something I could do. It made me feel alive in a way that other occupations hadn't. I was hungry for more.

I was getting by selling jeans in Kensington Market, looking for other DJ work, when I became friends with Cool Jay, a good-looking black American man in his thirties. We had interests in common – music and fashion – and he was soon saying he would help me find gigs. He also told me that he and his girlfriend, Melanie, were starting up a fashion company specialising in suede clothes: could I help them with that?

One evening in La Valbonne club in Kingly Street, Cool Jay introduced me to some of his friends. Among them was a striking woman with dark hair and intense blue eyes, who reminded me of Vivien Leigh. Her name was Catherine. She worked in the Playboy Club as a Playboy Bunny and as an extra in films. She wasn't my usual type – I was usually drawn to women less overtly striking – but Catherine was interested in music and films and art. We talked all night and arranged to meet in a couple of days' time, and soon we were going out on a regular basis. I knew I was lucky. Heads turned wherever we went. But I wasn't happy. I was several years younger than Catherine and didn't have a secure job or source of income. I felt out of my depth and I didn't understand what she saw in me.

I confided my anxiety to Cool Jay, who shrugged his shoulders. 'Don't tell her you don't have a job. Just make something up, man. She won't know.' I started lying to her, exaggerating my one night as a DJ into a career, saying I was a professional dancer, which I certainly wasn't. I hated myself for doing it, but once I'd started it was hard to backtrack and I kept on for a month or two.

My dishonesty increasingly appalled me. It kept me awake at night and troubled me during the day. Eventually I couldn't stand it any longer and confessed. 'I know,' she said, laughing. 'But I don't mind, Ronnie. It's you I love, not your job.' She didn't try to make me feel bad, but this only made things worse. I wanted her to be furious, to storm and shout at me for my deception. The fact that she did none of this just made me feel small, like a child caught stealing sweets. After a week or so my turmoil became intolerable. The only way out I could see was to finish with her.

I wasn't sure how Cool Jay earned his living. He didn't have a market stand, as far as I knew, although he spent a lot of time there. He told me he had a flat in Knightsbridge, above the Midnight Shop almost opposite Brompton Oratory, and he wanted someone to share with him. Would I like to move in? I didn't need long to think about it. It was a great location, and it would spare me from the commute in from Richmond. I moved in.

Not long after I finished going out with Catherine, Cool Jay introduced me to a black friend of his called Cecil, and Charlotte, his white girlfriend. Charlotte wasn't like any women I'd encountered so far: she was the daughter of a lord and owned a flat nearby in Cadogan Square. She told me she had a huge circle of friends who'd love to meet me. I was swept up by her world. My Knightsbridge life was suddenly full of promise, and the memory of the devastation I'd felt after the two robberies began to fade. One night Cecil said he'd be able to offer me work. I was a friend of Cool Jay's and I was at clubs most nights so there'd be 'golden opportunities'. He was vague about what exactly those golden opportunities entailed and skirted my questions. Gradually it dawned on me that something here wasn't right. But I pushed it away, not wanting to confront the unsavoury truth.

One evening Cool Jay took out two wallets, several watches, a gold necklace and a silver lighter and asked me what I thought about them: I couldn't ignore reality any longer. Cecil was involved in organised petty crime. That was partly how Cool Jay made his living. They wanted me to join their circle, pickpocketing in clubs. Cecil would sell on anything I offered him. We'd split the proceeds between us.

This Oliver Twist lifestyle didn't chime with my idea of what I wanted my Knightsbridge existence to be, nor did it seem a wise career move. I'd seen what happened to those who got on the wrong side of the law, plus I'd twice experienced robbery first-hand. I had no intention of being responsible for someone else suffering the sense of desolation that comes with losing treasured possessions. But neither did I want to give offence. 'I'll be working as a DJ – that doesn't give me much time to mingle with the clubgoers,' I explained, as politely as I could, wondering if I should think about moving.

Cool Jay accepted my reluctance to join his venture. He had various other dodgy-looking friends who'd hang out in the flat sometimes, smoking weed and listening to music until the early hours. Presumably they were part of his entourage and were less fastidious than me, but I turned a blind eye to what was going on. That was my big mistake.

I came back from working in Kensington Market one day to find the front door kicked in. I stood in the street, looking at the splintered wood, unable to believe the evidence of my own eyes. Eventually I stepped inside and called out.

'Hello? Anyone there?' My voice was croaky with fear, pulses of anxiety coursed through my veins. No reply. I mounted the stairs, flinching at every creak, treading softly so that I would hear any sound of intruders before they heard me. I had no desire to repeat the Brixton experience of having a knife at my throat.

I needn't have worried. The flat had been ransacked but no one was there. My head pounded as I registered that once again all my belongings had disappeared. Clothes, books and some records were gone. So was everything Cool Jay owned. I blundered downstairs to the shop below and asked if anyone had seen anything. The shopkeeper must have seen how upset I was, but he was briskly matter-of-fact. He had spotted a white gang coming and going, disappearing with armloads of things, laughing as they did so. Why didn't he call the police? I am not sure I even asked the question. I felt hollow yet swamped with helplessness. What could I do? Experience had taught me to be wary of the police. If I reported the crime

My first home was Ashwood, a National Children's Home for infants in Woking. My memories are muddled from those years, but I like to imagine this is Peggy, a young care worker who was the first to show me love.

At Westdene National Children's Home I made my first friend, Anna. Our favourite pastime was dressing up with clothes we found in the huge laundry hamper. Perhaps this is where my lifelong appreciation for fashion began.

My father, Ronald, after whom I was named, worked as a bridge-building engineer. His work at the Ministry for Transport in the late 1940s took him to Sierra Leone, where he met my mother. This is the only photo of him I own.

My mother, Lizzie (here with Patrick), was born in Sierra Leone to a well-to-do family. They were outraged when she fell for Ronald, and couldn't understand her decision to join him in London.

The lovely Sister Ida, photographed here a few years after I left Westdene. She was the first to teach me real values which continue to shape my life today.

After my mother collected me from Westdene, my sister and I lived with her in a dingy first-floor flat in Shepherd's Bush, very near the market.

Mummy loved to go dancing, wearing beautiful dresses that made her look like a movie star. Extraordinarily, I found this dress in Portobello Road Market. Fate must have brought me here: fifty-odd years earlier, at seven years old, I had helped make it.

Respite from home life came from the Hoads, who quickly became a second family to me, my sister, and my mother (clockwise from top-left: Michael, Mummy, Daddy, Martin, Derek, Jackie, Lynette and Christine).

Me, aged fourteen, with my sister and Jackie Hoad and her son Jonathan.

Darling Jo, to whom I owe so much, and probably without whom
this book would never have been written.

Dearest Mummy Hoad and me underneath the
Algarrobo outside her house in Santa Eulalia.

Me in 1979. I always did hate having my photo taken . . .

Hairdressing satisfied my creative needs and brought me into the heart of the 1970s London fashion scene. And it didn't hurt that I could sell watches to my clients on the side!

Me in my riding gear, with Keith from Smile (left) and his friend.

One of the few photographs of me spinning tunes.
I remember Vivienne Westwood being at this gig.

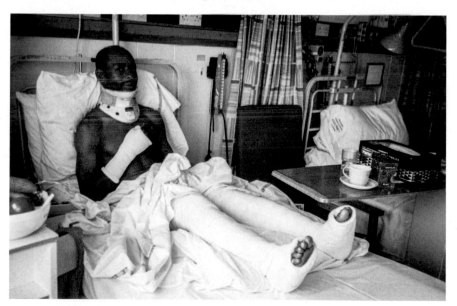

Thursday, 17 August 1995 was a turning point in my life. What started as an evening with friends ended with a broken neck, two broken legs and a broken arm. In the end, it was the most unlikely of objects that gave me the drive to pull myself through. This photo was taken by my good friend, Romas.

Working on *Antiques Roadshow* has been one of the greatest joys of my life. It is a privilege to handle people's treasures, and to be the bearer of good news to an unsuspecting owner is one of the show's greatest pleasures. So it was all the more special to experience this first-hand, and to reconnect with Anna (and Sooty) after all those years.

I knew they wouldn't help. For a third time nearly all my belongings, everything I'd worked for, had gone, and there was nothing to be done apart from accept it and move on. Looking back I think part of the reason for my triple misfortune was my naiveté. I was living a nocturnal existence, rubbing shoulders with dubious characters not of my choice and disregarding my own personal security. Yet by a strange quirk of fate, my coat, the only possession that had survived the Brixton robbery, was again still hanging on the back of the door.

I couldn't be certain that it was one of Cool Jay's acquaintances who had been responsible for the break-in, but it seemed probable. Cool Jay was upset but resigned. 'Shit happens, man,' he said, and then, like my possessions, he too disappeared from my life.

I found a four-bedroom flat nearby in Cromwell Road. I would be sharing with Chris Moss, whose stall I shared selling jeans in Kensington Market. A couple called Sue and Jane would be our new flatmates. My domestic arrangements would now be less perilous than with Cool Jay and his entourage. At least I hoped so.

One of the coolest women I've ever known entered my life around this time. Pat King was Barbadian and worked as a personal assistant to Ossie Clark, Celia Birtwell and Alice Pollock. I loved hanging out with her, hearing about the fashion world in which she worked, and in the evening we often went to clubs together. Pat always wore striking outfits she had made herself and arranged her hair in avant-garde styles, but underneath she was self-effacing and uneasy with the attention she attracted. This was something I could relate to and it made me feel there was a special bond between us.

It was through Pat that I met Ronnie Williams, a regular DJ at Ronnie Scott's clubnight, Upstairs at Ronnie's, one of my favourite clubs at the time. Ronnie Williams was a very bright black guy, with a borderline obsession about music. 'Don't waste your time on popular music,' he'd say. 'Look at where it comes from, and you can find the originator of most of the sounds that are being watered down today.'

He and Pat and I would sit around talking music for hours. He shared my taste for underground artists and tunes, like Jesse James's 'Believe in Me Baby', Rodger Collins's 'She's Looking Good' and 'Foxy Girls in Oakland', and singers such as Aaron Neville, Arthur Alexander, Johnny Otis and Willie Tee whose amazing song 'Thank You John' was Pat's favourite.

'D'you wanna take over DJing at Ronnie Scott's on a regular basis for a couple of nights a week to cover for me?' Ronnie asked one evening after one of our long discussions. 'You're cool, man. Almost as cool as me.'

'Are you serious?'

'Sure.'

That was how Upstairs at Ronnie's became my second ever DJing gig.

From the outset I felt far more at home there than at the Marquee. The club had a special vibe which I quickly tuned in to. I played a lot of jazz-based and funky underground music, and I started a routine of playing vintage sounds along with newer ones, something of a novelty in those days. Along the way I met the jazz musicians who were playing the club downstairs. One of them was one of my all-time heroes, Eddie Harris, who introduced the electric sax and played 'Listen Here' and 'Get on Down', a song that I want played at my funeral.

I settled into my role and other clubs started offering me gigs. Soon I was working six nights a week at various London clubs. Still, I remained true to my original determination. I was a silent DJ, I avoided chart music. I played only what I thought of as 'real music'. But the experience at the Marquee had taught me something, and I was better tuned in to the audience's taste and mood. I watched them carefully, trying to anticipate their collective frame of mind, to pick the best records for the ambience. I'd play some music I knew they'd be familiar with as a way of introducing them to new sounds. I learned how to work the crowd.

As well as providing a good living, there's a status that comes with being a DJ. One night, in a club called Lulu's where I worked regularly, I spotted three girls dancing. One in particular caught my eye, throwing back her hair and shimmying extravagantly. I smiled at her as I walked to the bar during a break, and she came up and introduced herself as Karen Friedman. She and her companions were the backing group Thunderthighs. They lived in New York and provided the backing vocals for Lou Reed's hit single 'Walk on the Wild Side'. It struck me as ironic that the line 'And the coloured girls go "Doo do doo do doo do do doo . . ."' was sung by Karen and her white friends.

They'd heard about the music I played in New York, she told me. The word was that you couldn't find sets like mine anywhere else in London. I'd lived up to her expectations – she loved the music I played and the fact I didn't talk over the records. She just wanted to get lost in the music and dance, not listen to DJ chatter. My face must have registered my astonishment. I could hardly believe that my name had reached the ears of the music industry on the other side of the Atlantic, but I grinned and after that night we met again and soon became firm friends.

My reputation was growing but my mother's criticisms were still embedded in my psyche. I wasn't comfortable being the focus of attention. I'd always been interested in fashion, I loved good design and well-made clothes, yet this passion was inseparable from my self-consciousness. So dressing smartly was my shell – to divert observers from the flaws of the man beneath.

I'd go to Laurence Corner on Tottenham Court Road, to buy army surplus gear, or a shop opposite the British Museum called Westaway & Westaway that was a favourite for jumpers. When I was working in a club I'd dress with care. I was into the vintage 1940s look, and I'd often wear a white double-breasted zoot suit, with high-waisted, wide-legged trousers and a long jacket with wide lapels and padded shoulders. It was a style popular in the US in the 1930s and 1940s, especially in African-American communities, where jazz singers like Cab Calloway wore them. To complete the look, I'd team it with a chocolate-brown voile shirt, a white hat and white buckskin shoes that I'd had specially made. Around my neck I wore a thin gold chain with multiple gold rings that I'd collected. This was my armour and it made me feel strong.

One place I'd often visit on evenings off was the Speakeasy Club in Margaret Street where A-list celebrities from the world of music were invariably among the clientele. I remember a great evening there in 1969 with a friend called Jackie Davis, a beautiful mixed-race woman whose boyfriend, Peter the Pirate, was doing a stretch in prison. Peter had asked me to look after Jackie, so I took her to the club on the night that an American funk collective called Parliament-Funkadelic* were playing. The group (really two sister bands: Parliament and Funkadelic) was fronted by George Clinton, a musical innovator who later on had a big hit with 'One Nation Under a Groove'. Funkadelic's second album was the poetically titled *Free Your Mind . . . and Your Ass Will Follow*.† Clinton came on stage wearing combination long johns and a floor-length Comanche Indian chief's headdress. The shaven-headed bass player wore a US flag and high-heeled boots, with one trouser leg rolled up and the other down. Another band member was clad in a purple Ku Klux Klan outfit.

At the time this was strong stuff – I was in the audience along with Mick Jagger, Keith Moon and countless other musicians of the day, drinking in this extraordinary performance. Suddenly I felt a searing pain in my leg. I looked down. 'Hey, man, you just burned my leg,' I said to the guy smoking next to me.

He took a long drag, exhaled, and scanned me through narrowed eyes. 'Yeah, man, you shouldn't stand so close,' he replied. It was Chuck Berry.

Dancing was central to my life – for a while I seriously thought about going professional. During the day I was taking dance

---

* They became known as P-Funk.
† They followed this with an album named *Maggot Brain*.

classes in Covent Garden with Molly Molloy, an inspirational American jazz dancer and choreographer. I continued with her until she left to go to Paris and handed over to Arlene Phillips. At night I'd go to clubs frequented by black professional dancers, many from France or the US. Women came too, but these weren't pulling joints. We went to dance, seriously. The movement was high-energy and I'd be on the floor nonstop from midnight to 5 or 6 a.m. A group of us would get together to show off jazz techniques like slow-motion dancing, dropping low to the ground, improvising fake fights, like Charades. People would gather round watching as we slowly revolved, our chests three inches from the ground, then lifted ourselves back up. Afterwards I felt as if I'd done a five-hour workout. I'd be drenched and would have to change my shirt before I left.

I sometimes worked at a small club in Jermyn Street called Maunkberry's, and when Neil Young came over to the UK on tour in the mid-1970s I was booked to DJ for his birthday party. There was a pre-arranged break in the music when his birthday cake was brought in, and I joined the guests in a birthday toast. The cake was an American-style recipe with lots of mousse and cream. Neil Young was stoned, and I remember him putting his finger in the cream and flicking it over the guests one by one. Everyone laughed, seemingly they didn't mind, but when he came up to me with a hand full of cream, I shook my head firmly as a warning, thinking, If you flick that over me you will get your face in the cake. He must have sensed my mood because he moved on to someone else. I felt that people let him do it because he was famous, and I was furious. I think I was the only person who didn't get sprayed with cream.

It was also in Maunkberry's that I met Rudolf Nureyev. As a trained ballet dancer his movements seemed stiff and staccato compared to the fluidity of the jazz dancers on the dance floor. And yet I sensed his incredible energy, and when he spoke he did so with such animation, in heavily accented English, that I wanted to listen to whatever he said. But he would always stand too close and tell me how much he liked me in a way that felt uncomfortable, and that it was important to keep a safe distance between us.

While my DJ work was flourishing, things weren't so harmonious back at the flat. It turned out that Sue and Jane had a highly charged relationship, and I was aware of altercations between them that often turned heated and cruel. My room was up a flight of stairs, theirs was on the basement level, and I tried not to get involved. I was out most nights until late, but sometimes the shrieks and yells woke me in the morning.

One night I came home late from a gig, sporting a lime-green zoot suit with a black-and-white striped lining that I'd bought from Mr Freedom. It was three-thirty in the morning. As I took my key out of the lock Jane came into the hallway. 'You're up late,' I said.

'I think Sue is trying to kill herself,' she replied in a half-whisper. Her eyes were red, one looked puffy, and her hair was a tangled mess. They'd had another fight.

'Where is she?' I said.

'Bathroom – the door's locked.'

I walked down the dark corridor and knocked. No reply.

'Sue? It's Ronnie. Are you OK?'

Silence. I tried the door but it wouldn't give. I rattled it. Nothing. 'Sue, please open the door. It's Ronnie. I need to come in.' Still nothing. Anxiety mounting, I took off my jacket, put my shoulder against the door and gave a sharp push. The bolt gave way easily. As the door flew open a fountain of something dark and warm sprayed me. I looked at my hands then down at my trousers. They were now covered in dark liquid – it didn't take long to register what it was: blood. I shut the door, thinking, involuntarily, My trousers are going to be ruined. As soon as I had this thought I was struck with shame. Sue's life was endangered and all I could worry about was my suit. What kind of callous person was I?

I opened the door again and peered in. The bathroom was long and narrow, illuminated by one weak bulb, but it was enough for me to see it resembled a slaughterhouse. Blood had sprayed over the ceiling, it ran in rivulets down the walls, the bath was covered in it and the floor was invisible beneath a sea of red. Where was Sue in this carnage? I couldn't see her. Gradually my eyes adjusted to the dingy light. I made out a mound of matted red clothing lying against the bath. It was Sue, every part of her so saturated she was barely recognisable as a human being. I knelt down and wiped the red mass of hair from her face. She was unconscious, and her limbs felt floppy. Blood was still pulsing out of cuts on her wrists – one gash was so deep I could see bone. Realising I needed to staunch the flow fast, I grabbed the first thing to hand, an old cotton pillowcase, and tore off a strip. The fabric must have been old, and with the tension it seemed to disintegrate in my hand. I needed something more robust, I realised. Still full of shame, I peeled off my heavy silk T-shirt, ignoring the thought that it was my favourite, cut it into strips, and bound her wounds tightly while shouting to Jane to call an ambulance.

The paramedics arrived in time to save her life.

After that I decided that flat-sharing was no longer for me. I moved into a studio flat in Hornton Street, Kensington. I bumped into Jane in the King's Road eighteen months later. 'How's Sue?' I asked as the terrible scene that night replayed in my head.

She looked at me with a steady gaze. 'Six months after you moved out, she did the same. Only this time there was no one to save her.' Hearing this I felt a sense of profound deflation. I realised that I had just intervened in her determination to terminate her life. The suicide attempt had been serious; it wasn't just a cry for help. And now she'd achieved her aim.

13

A Cartier Driver's Watch

Mrs Mitchelson was a glamorously coiffured Eastern European Jewish woman, with a strong accent, a business-like manner, and a marked fondness for designer labels. She had a small shop specialising in vintage Cartier in Bond Street which she stocked with canny finds from private clients, local markets and sales. Her prices were high, four times what you might pay elsewhere, but her knowledge was extensive, and I visited her shop from time to time, just to look at what she was selling and learn from her.

One day, early on in my dealing career, I noticed an exceedingly rare Cartier watch, known as a Driver's watch, on display in her shop. It was triangular in section, a bit like a Toblerone bar, which meant that the face was elevated, so you didn't have to twist your wrist to see the time if you were driving. The design is said to have been created in the mid-1930s for the actor Stewart Granger, a Cartier aficionado, and they were only ever made in limited numbers. It was the rarest Cartier watch I'd seen at that point, so I asked how much she wanted for it. I was expecting the answer to be at least £10,000, but Mrs Mitchelson shot me one of her offhand looks. 'It's an unusual piece, but you can take it for £450,' she said, unsmiling.

At first I thought I'd misheard. 'Four hundred and fifty pounds?' I said, poker-faced. Her steel-grey hair gleamed, helmet-like beneath its heavy sheen of lacquer. She nodded, lips pursed, raising herself up, as if bracing herself for a fight.

I didn't waste time bargaining. 'OK, I'll have it,' I said. Paying quickly, I thanked her and left. I was smiling to myself all the way home at the great purchase I'd made.

About a month later Mrs Mitchelson contacted me. 'Ronnie,' she said, with no preamble, rolling the R of my name extravagantly, 'I think I made a mistake with that watch I sold you. Would you care to sell it back for a profit?'

'Thank you, Mrs Mitchelson, but no,' I said. 'I want to keep it for myself. I like wearing it.'

I kept the watch and wore it for about ten years. Over that time many people offered to buy it from me, and several new clients came to me through it, but I always refused to sell. It suited my small wrist so well it could have been designed for me, and wearing such a rarity made me feel special. Eventually, a decade later, when I had a tax bill to pay, the time had come to dispense with it. I approached Keith, who had a shop in the Royal Arcade off Old Bond Street, and who usually bought my best watches. Keith and I had a rapport. He often admired the things I wore, and we trusted one another. I showed him the watch and told him the price – £20,000.

'It's a wonderful watch, but that's a lot of money, more than double what I'd usually spend. I should be able to do it. But I'd like to talk it over with my wife first,' Keith said. 'Come back on Wednesday.'

I returned, elated at the thought that my financial worries would soon be over. I would be able to clear my debts. But I was taken aback when I entered the shop and saw Keith's face. There was no affable greeting. His brow was ridged, his mouth glum, his expression almost sheepish.

'So,' I said, 'what do you think about my Driver's? Yes or no?'

He shook his head with an air of finality. 'I can't buy it, Ronnie,' he said.

'I'm surprised. I thought you liked it?'

'I love it. But just after you came in, someone else offered me these.'

He showed me two watches. One appeared to be a Driver's, but larger than mine. The other was another extremely rare Cartier. 'I talked it over with my wife, and we decided to go for these two rather than your one. I paid £65,000 for them, which is more than yours, but this Driver's is larger,' he said, 'so I think it will bring in more.' He tailed off.

As soon as I handled them, I knew the watches he'd bought weren't right. By then I was so experienced I could recognise what was genuine and what wasn't. But I couldn't say anything because to do so would have seemed like sour grapes, and I still urgently needed to sell my watch. What were the chances of two such watches turning up together – even if one was a fake? The following day I contacted Cartier's offices and proposed a deal. They responded, we agreed a fair sum, and I was satisfied with the transaction. On reflection, it was gratifying to think that such an important watch had ended up where it originated.

I didn't see Keith again until several years later when I bumped into him at an Olympia antiques fair. 'Ronnie!' he greeted me warmly. 'I haven't seen you for ages.'

'Good to see you, Keith. How are things?'

'You know, I went out of business thanks to those two watches I showed you. They turned out to be fakes and the loss broke me. I never touch watches now. I'm selling shabby-chic furniture in Rye.'

Riding home on the bus, after seeing Keith, I pondered the unfortunate coincidence that had brought about his downfall. I took no pleasure in his misfortune. If I had taken my watch to him a week earlier, he wouldn't have bought the fakes, and in all probability his business would still be flourishing. But although I felt no sense of *schadenfreude*, neither did I feel any guilt. Experience has taught me that sooner or later everyone experiences misfortunes and unexpected disruptions to their lives. None of us are safe, we survive as best we can. Keith seemed happy with his new business. I too had reinvented myself after unforeseen setbacks, on more than one occasion. Somewhere, my driver's watch was preserved in good order, measuring the passage of time as it was always intended to do. But whatever the precision of such an instrument, it didn't alter the fact that from a personal perspective, time itself is subjective and prey to the whims of fate. Everything can change in an instant.

There was a super-trendy club in Kensington High Street called Yours or Mine – also known as El Sombrero because of the hat hanging at the door. It was small and intimate, with a Perspex underlit flashing dance floor where a large gay clientele danced alongside a mix of flamboyant fashionistas, wealthy City types, pop stars and an eclectic racial mix.

I worked in the club as a DJ and was still living not far away in Hornton Street. One evening, after the crowd had gone wild to Donny Hathaway's 'The Ghetto' and then been wowed by the iconic intro on the seven-inch version to 'Slippin' into Darkness' by War, I went back to a friend's flat on the Edgware Road for a nightcap. When I left I decided to walk home to wind down. It was a mild, breezy night, and leaves and litter gusted along the pavement. The street was empty and I was only a few minutes from my flat when a beaten-up Morris Minor pulled up. Inside were a group of people, two of whom I recognised from the club that evening. The girl who was sitting behind the wheel had smiled at me a lot, so I suspected she liked me. As a DJ, I often attracted attention from the clientele, but I'd been busy playing the music and talking to friends so I hadn't spoken to her.

She wound down the window. 'Hi, Ronnie. How are you doin'? Would you like a lift?' she asked, as if she knew me.

The car seemed full – there was someone next to her in the front and another couple in the back. As far as I could see they were all men, apart from the girl driving. I said thanks but no, I was happy to walk. But she persisted: 'Don't you like us then? Is there something wrong with us?'

There was an edge to her voice, and I didn't want to upset clients of the club. It wouldn't look good if they came back and told the owner they thought I'd been unfriendly, so I said, 'Of course not – there's nothing wrong. But I only live a couple of minutes away. I don't mind the walk. It's kind of you to ask – but you don't need to drive me.'

'We're just being friendly – or are you a snob or something?'

She wasn't going to let it go. I smiled. 'OK – I only live round the corner though.'

I got into the back of the car and told the girl where I wanted her to drop me. After following my directions for a minute, she took a different turn. 'We just need to make a detour to Chelsea to drop these guys off first.'

What could I say? I was in the car now. We drove to Chelsea where she slowed and dropped off one passenger, then in a back street by the King's Road she pulled up and she and the remaining passengers got out. 'I just need to pick up something. You wait here and I'll be right back,' she said before she slammed the car door and disappeared.

I sat there for five or ten minutes, irked by the thought that if I hadn't accepted the lift, I would be home by now. Then, as if from nowhere, blue lights flashed, and a dark car screeched to a halt, angled in front of the Morris Minor to prevent any attempt at departure. A tall freckle-faced red-haired policeman flung open the door, leapt out and stood in front of the car.

'Get out – now,' he barked. 'Turn round. Spread your legs. Hands on top of the car.'

There was further tyre-screeching. Two more police vehicles pulled up behind our car.

I followed the order. 'What's all this for?' I said, as the first policeman patted me down. 'I haven't done anything – I'm just getting a lift home.'

'Oh, come on. You're with them,' he said. I turned round

to see the three others reappear. Only now they were handcuffed and being steered by three more police officers into the back of the parked cars. From the officers' conversation I gathered that they had broken into a shop and stolen some shirts while the girl kept watch. As far as the police were concerned, I was part of the break-in plot.

'He's got nothing to do with it,' the girl insisted. 'We don't even know him.' But the police weren't interested in her protests, or in mine. As they saw it, I was waiting in the getaway car and therefore I must have masterminded the entire operation. 'We're arresting you on suspicion of robbery,' said the red-haired officer. 'You'll be taken to the station for further questioning and to make a statement.'

I was ushered into one of the police vehicles and taken to an interrogation room at Chelsea police station, where they searched me again. A dog handler came in with a large Alsatian growling and straining on a lead, and stepped just close enough to let the dog jump up at my throat before yanking it away until the interrogating officer intervened.

'So tell us the truth,' he said, standing deliberately on my feet with some force. 'You set the whole thing up, didn't you?'

'No,' I said, and reiterated what I'd told them earlier. I was a DJ in a club in Kensington High Street. I lived in a flat in Hornton Street. I was walking home, the girl had stopped and offered me a lift. My only involvement with the gang was accepting a lift from them. I'd never met them before – and I knew nothing about any robbery.

No matter how many times I repeated it, they refused to believe my story. The questioning went on and on all night. I asked for my statutory phone call but was fobbed off with excuses. I'd only be allowed it when I told them the truth. I'd be allowed it in a couple of hours. I'd be allowed it in the morning. But there was no phone call in the morning, nor was a lawyer summoned. Instead, I was bundled into a police meat wagon, locked inside a small wire cubicle with a tiny window, and driven to Rochester Row police station.

'Can I make a phone call, please? What about my legal representation?' I said on arrival.

'No, no, no.' Every request was refused. In another interrogation room came more questioning, returning over and over to the same sequence of events. Then, in the late afternoon I was pushed into another meat wagon and taken to Brixton prison. I had now been charged with robbery and would be held in prison until the case came to court.

For the first week I shared a cell with two housebreakers from the East End. The cell was furnished with bunkbeds. The small floor space next to them was almost entirely taken up with a third bed, a washbasin and a single chair. There was no space to walk around, and if you sat on the lower bunk you had to do so bowed over forward, so your head didn't scrape on the bed above. Apart from allocated time for ablutions, an hour or so for exercise, and mealtimes, we spent all day in the cell.

My fellow cellmates were a rough but pleasant enough pair who scoffed at the idea of rehabilitation and passed most of their time planning their next robbery and playing cards. I was bored and fretful. I felt abused by the failures of the justice system but each day I told myself it would be the last. Someone would realise there'd been a miscarriage of justice. I hadn't done anything wrong. I would be saved.

A week later I was told I was being moved to a larger cell. Aren't I lucky? I thought.

The cell I'd been allocated was shared with a racist Scottish alcoholic. He was a large threatening man and every day he'd bare his nicotine-stained teeth and say, 'You wait till night-time comes, laddie. I'll fuckin' murder ye. I hate n*****s. I want them off the face of this earth.' Every night I went to bed wondering whether I was going to wake up, and I'd fall into a fitful sleep, dreaming that I was falling into a bottom-less abyss, or being pursued by a faceless, nameless aggressor. All day, for hours that seemed unending, I'd sit, eyes cast down to avoid my cellmate's gaze, fearful of provoking his hatred. I recently learned that sometimes the police deliberately imprisoned young black men in cells with violent racists; it was some kind of perverse strategy.

I still had no contact at all with the outside world, and as far as I was aware, no one knew where I was. From the moment I'd arrived in Brixton, I'd complained that I had not been granted a phone call. I was told it was too late for that now since I'd already been charged. As a substitute I could write letters and they handed me a pad of paper and a pen. I wrote to Jo Hawkey and to my flatmate, Serge. I told them where I was, and what had happened, and handed the letters to a guard who assured me they'd be sent. I waited and waited but nei-ther of them replied. I discovered later that the letters were never sent.

Three and a half weeks into my incarceration, a minor mir-acle took place. My saviour, Jo, arrived with her sister, Chris-tine. They hounded the prison officials, demanding to know why I was being denied basic legal rights. Jo had grown worried when she hadn't heard from me and had phoned my flat. Serge had answered and told her he hadn't seen me and didn't know what had happened, but that the police had come round to search the flat looking for stolen property, which they hadn't found. Serge was leaving, and as I wasn't around to pay the rent, the landlord was repossessing the flat. Hearing all this, Jo had made urgent enquiries and discovered where I was being held. Like a woman possessed, she was now taking the police to task for their discriminatory treatment of me.

Two white professional women petitioning on my behalf noticeably shifted the police's attitude. Suddenly they became conciliatory. My release was arranged that same day, on the proviso that I reported to the police station every night. Jo, generous as ever, said I could have a bed at her flat for as long as I needed it. I gratefully accepted the offer and slept on a camp bed, returned to my job as a DJ, and waited for my case to come to court.

14

Bob Dylan's *Blonde on Blonde* Album

Blonde on Blonde came out in June 1966 when I was sixteen years old. Dylan's seventh album was and still is regarded as a landmark. It's the first double rock album ever,★ but there was more to it than that. Compared with his earlier music, *Blonde on Blonde* marked a turning point and had a new slickness about it. Dylan began recording the album in 1965 in New York with the Hawks, his backing band. But when things didn't go well, production moved to Nashville, Tennessee, where top session musicians were brought in to collaborate. Most of the songs were recorded there, fusing Nashville talents with Dylan's poetic lyricism. The finished album included two hit singles, 'Rainy Day Women #12 & 35' and 'I Want You', as well as two

★ The Mothers of Invention's double album *Freak Out!* was released a week later.

other songs regarded as Dylan masterpieces, 'Visions of Johanna' and 'Just Like a Woman'.

For me, the album jacket was as memorable as the music within. It was a gatefold, with a slightly fuzzy out-of-focus image of Bob Dylan, dressed in a suede jacket and checked scarf, stretching across both sides. Dylan is shown with wild, curly hair, pale-faced, a concentrated expression in his eyes. The photo was taken by Dylan's friend Jerry Schatzberg on a cold day in Greenwich Village, 375 West Street at Morton Street, in the Meatpacking District of New York. Critics at the time took the blurriness of the photo to be a reference to drug use, although the photographer claimed it was because the shot was taken on a bitterly cold winter's day and his hands were shaking. I do know they made a promotional poster of the same shot. I don't remember whether I had one of them or if I just used the jacket of my album as a poster, but I thought the photo was the epitome of cool and the album was a favourite of mine, many of the lyrics seeming to echo my own sense of late-night isolation. 'Hearing *Blonde on Blonde* puts you in the position of the night watchman who clicks his flashlight at all the losers and freaks and neon madmen and wonders if it's him or them that's insane,' wrote Rob Sheffield in *Rolling Stone* magazine fifty years later. I couldn't agree more.

Five years after the release of *Blonde on Blonde*, that sense of alienation, of introspection, of being somewhere I didn't belong, struck me forcefully. I was at the Rainbow Theatre in London's Finsbury Park. My hands shook as I found myself impaled by the glare of the spotlights, mounting the steps and walking onto the stage, my body clammy with apprehension, my legs weak. The auditorium was packed, the audience were going mad, whistles and cheers ricocheted so loudly that I wondered how I'd ever make myself heard. Turning to face the screaming crowd, I waved, as if I were a star in my own right, swaggering across the stage with a bravado I didn't feel. Dressed in a black satin suit, tight flared trousers, a banana-yellow Viyella shirt trimmed in satin and heeled black plat-form boots, I knew I looked the part. Andy, a shoemaker in Goldhawk Road, had made my boots specially. They fitted me perfectly. But clothes can't transform you into something you're not.

My job was to introduce the acts. I knew the score. I'd been on the road for several weeks. I loved the touring life, talking about music with people at the cutting edge of a new exciting scene. But I hated the falseness of the way we had to introduce the bands, hamming it up for the audience.

The line-up that night was a medley of star acts brought over from the US by music impresarios Dave Godin and David Nathan, whom I'd got to know through years of buying records at Contempo Records. I was steeped in their music. We'd become friends over the years and when they had acts coming over from the States, they passed my name on to the festival organisers, who recruited me to tour with their revue. As the compere, I'd got to meet people like Bill Haley, Jerry Lee Lewis and Little Richard. So now here I was, a minor part of the show, but still uncomfortable in the role.

On this memorable night the stars were Tami Lynn, a soul singer from New Orleans, who was at the height of her fame, Rufus Thomas, an R&B musician of 'Walking the Dog' and 'Do the Funky Chicken' fame, and, at the top of the bill, Al

Green, a soul musician whose 'Tired of Being Alone' was the first of a string of big hits in the 1970s. Tami was due to receive a silver disc for 'I'm Gonna Run Away from You' from the English DJ Emperor Rosko. First up, though, was a support act called Bloodstone. They were a tough R&B, soul and funk band from Los Angeles who had signed a contract with Decca and released two singles, 'That's the Way We Make Our Music' and 'Girl (You Look So Fine)'.

The audience hadn't heard Bloodstone before, but they embraced the funky, raw sound – a mix of Jimi Hendrix hard rock with gospel and doo-wop. When the band's set came to an end the audience were fired up. They wanted an encore – and they didn't want me, regardless of my black-and-banana finery, announcing Emperor Rosko and Tami Lynn.

I told myself I just had to get the job done. 'Good evening, everybody. Now, we've got a great surprise in store,' I began, holding the microphone tightly so my hands didn't shake. But the audience weren't interested in my announcement. They couldn't have cared less about the silver disc. They wanted Bloodstone. A great crescendo of booing and foot-stamping filled the auditorium: 'More! Bloodstone! More! More! More!'

I raised my hands in a gesture of defeat. 'OK, OK,' I said. 'You win. I'll see what I can do. I'm not promising anything though . . .' The boos and stamping turned to wolf whistles and cheers, and then more ear-pounding stamping. I bowed in mock deference and walked, with as much aplomb as I could muster, off the stage. The cheers followed me. They thought this was all part of the act.

In my hurry to descend the steps and get away, I caught

my platform boot heel and pitched forward. I grabbed the handrail to save myself, but not before the heel of my left boot came loose. I tottered down the steps, trying to hide the fact that I was now wobbling unsteadily on one side, stamping down on it to press it back into position, but that made it worse – the entire heel came off. Clutching it in my hand, I hobbled down the dark off-stage corridor. 'You've got to go on now,' I told Rosko, putting my head in through the dressing-room door. 'It's your cue.' Tami was in there with him and she didn't look too pleased, although she didn't say anything.

'No way, man. You promised them Bloodstone. So go ask them,' Rosko replied.

Earlier, just as I'd left the backstage area to do my bit, he had given me a friendly pat on the back, and that had helped to calm me down. Now his tone was markedly less friendly, and to underline the message, he kicked the door closed.

The stage manager was nowhere to be seen so I hobbled down the maze of dingy corridors to the band's dressing room and knocked. In the aftermath of their triumphant set, they were lounging around, smoking, swigging beer, and passing a large bottle of vodka around.

'Guys, you were great . . .' I began. 'Unbelievable . . . And the audience is still going mad for you. Can you hear them . . . ? They're calling for an encore.' Silence overlaid the sound of the still-yelling audience before lead vocalist Charles Love growlingly responded.

'Piss off, man. We ain't doin' no more.'

None of the other band members spoke to me – they barely looked my way, too intent on drinking and smoking and laughing among themselves. But Charles wasn't joking. And I wasn't going to ask him twice.

'OK. I get it, man – thanks.' I held up my hands and retreated before I was ejected forcibly.

I went back to Rosko's room. 'No go. They won't do it.'

He wasn't pleased. 'You'll have to give the audience the bad news before I go on. Otherwise it won't work.'

I could see he had a point. Trying to walk normally and mask the fact that my left boot now had no heel, and the right was stacked up four inches high, I tottered back onstage. The audience saw me and roared. I held up my hands, waiting for them to calm down. To my utter amazement silence descended almost magically. The expectation was palpable. I broke it to them as gently as I could. Bloodstone couldn't do another set but were proud they'd been asked. 'They thank you all for being such a great audience and hope to see you all again soon. Meanwhile they hope you'll enjoy the new singles—'

The booing started before I could finish. Then the stamping. Then fists were waved, and a deluge of empty drink cans and cigarette packets rained down onto the stage, aimed at me. I was terrified. Was I about to be lynched?

'And now – without further ado – let's give it up for Emperor Rosko – he's coming on to present Tami Lynn with a silver disc!' I yelled out before I made a speedy, limping retreat to the steps, and mercifully out of the spotlight.

As I reached the sanctuary of the corridor, I caught a glimpse of Rosko. He was emerging from his dressing room. But it didn't look as if he was heading for the stage. He was going at some speed in the opposite direction – towards the stage door.

I found the stage manager. 'It's Rosko's cue now,' I said. 'I don't know where he's gone, but you'll have to deal with it. I've had enough.'

I took a taxi back to the Royal Garden Hotel, where we were all staying that night, and went straight to my room. A few hours later, I'd just about recovered when my hotel phone rang. It was Tami. She told me that Rosko had eventually come back. They'd waited for the crowd to calm down and had done the presentation. It had gone OK. So how about coming up to her room for a nightcap, to celebrate?

'Thanks, Tami, but I don't drink,' I said, untruthfully. From the tone of her voice, I knew that a drink wasn't all she wanted. I'd had enough excitement for one day though. I packed my bag and slipped off home.

My trouble with the police was always at the back of my mind until my case finally came to court, almost a year later. In a fiasco that further highlighted the corruption within the legal system, the police constable who gave evidence against me, claiming to be the arresting officer that night, was someone I'd never set eyes on before. I hadn't forgotten the red-haired, freckled officer who had taken me into custody the night of the robbery. I'd been reporting to the station every day and knew what he looked like. This man swearing on the Bible to tell the truth, the whole truth, didn't have red hair – nor was he even an officer I recognised from the station.

I informed my defence counsel of the discrepancy. I felt certain that since the police were perjuring themselves, the case would be dismissed, and I was filled with a sense of relief. It didn't last. The magistrate overheard the exchange and told my counsel to shut me up. My counsel did as he was ordered, ignoring my frantic protestations, and the hearing continued as if the false testimony of the police was relevant. My belief in the justice system was bruised before, but now it was in shreds. Remembering this blatant miscarriage of justice still angers me profoundly. Until that moment I had trusted that truth and justice would prevail and that the laws I'd been brought up to respect would triumph. But now that confidence disintegrated and the subtext was clear. Whether or not this officer or another had arrested me didn't matter. In the eyes of the authorities I was black and therefore, in some unspoken way, undeserving of fair treatment. The magistrate's main concern was that nothing should be done to expose the deficiencies of the police.

I was found guilty but was given a conditional discharge for a year. Should I be convicted of another offence within that time then that charge would also be held against me. Should I manage to stay clear of trouble then the slate would be wiped clean. Thankfully, although I've had numerous encounters with the Metropolitan Police, I have never been charged for anything since, and have never had a criminal record. But through this and many other bitter experiences, I've learned that the prejudiced treatment I received on this occasion wasn't an anomaly.

15

Ottoman Calligrapher's Scissors

Calligraphy is central to Islamic culture, and ever since the early days, Muslim scribes took pride in the elegance with which they could transcribe the Qur'an and other sacred texts in highly decorative Arabic script. In the Ottoman Empire, calligraphy flourished in the city of Constantinople (modern-day Istanbul), where it became highly refined, and the strong tradition was passed down through the centuries until the introduction of the Roman alphabet in Turkey under Kemal Ataturk's Westernised reforms in the early twentieth century. Under Suleiman the Magnificent in the sixteenth century, a special school of calligraphy was founded in the Topkapi Palace, and the decorative writing was used to transcribe court writing as well as religious texts. The tools associated with the specialist work were often exquisite works of art in their own right, and some may even have belonged to a sultan, prince or sheikh who had trained in the art.

Scissors were used to cut the paper, parchment or vellum a calligrapher wrote on, and they are distinctive in appearance. Their proportions are strange. The blades are long and narrow, the handles relatively small. They're usually wrought from iron and their surface is often beautifully decorated with gilded or damascene decoration in the form of foliage and flowers. You have to look hard to find the Arabic inscription concealed in the design on the blades of some Ottoman scissors. It reads '*Ya Fattah*' – meaning 'O Unfolder'. In the Islamic faith, *Ya Fattah* is one of the ninety-nine names of Allah and reminds believers that God is the opener of all doors.

I have handled a few pairs of these scissors in my life, and always appreciate their exquisite craftsmanship. I also love to imagine the hands that used them and the elaborate manuscripts they must have fashioned and trimmed. The inscription resonates too: it's a potent reminder that whatever your faith, courage and integrity will combat setbacks and uncertainty. For me, though, scissors of a different kind hold personal significance. For a decade or so, they were one of the key tools of my trade – my livelihood depended on them and with them I was brought into contact with an extraordinary array of prominent people.

At the age of twenty-three I had an epiphany. DJing six nights a week wasn't a long-term career option, I realised. Yes, I was still enjoying myself, but if I imagined myself at the age of forty, playing records for a living, I felt less content. Forty seemed ancient, a lifetime away, but it would arrive, and when it did I needed a way of earning a living.

Fun though it was to hold court in a club every night, my creative energy felt unfulfilled. I loved music but playing one record after another, however cleverly merged they were, was just fusing transient sounds, and sound was invisible and ephemeral. I wanted a different occupation, something tangible, that would satisfy my creative yearnings, yet still give me access to the fashionable world I enjoyed.

My friend Pat King had a brother I was close to, who was known as Ike (his real name was Dwight) and was a hairdresser at Smile, an ultra-fashionable salon in Knightsbridge. He planted the seed that hairdressing might answer my needs. I weighed it up: hairdressing was a profession that linked neatly into my interest in fashion and art. I saw it as a form of sculpture which would satisfy my creative drive. And, depending on the salon, I could remain in the heart of fashionable 1970s London. Perhaps there was another motive behind the decision, although I didn't say so or acknowledge it at the time. I was happy and free in my frenetic life, but my sense of self remained damaged. I was still shadowed with anxiety about how I looked. Consciously or not, I thought that helping to make others feel good about their appearance might help bolster my confidence in my own.

I had a contact at Vidal Sassoon, the most prestigious international salon of the day, and I approached them for a place as a trainee. 'You're a bit old,' I was told by the stylist who interviewed me. 'Most juniors are fifteen or sixteen years old. What have you been up to until now?'

I listed my various occupations. 'I was a technical draughtsman and modelmaker at Imperial College. Then I did an art foundation year at Hornsey. I ran a boutique in Greece, and these days, or rather nights, I'm working as a DJ.'

He looked at me as if I was mad. 'If you've had all that experience, why do you want to climb down from your podium, wash hair, sweep floors, run errands along with teenagers? You do realise you won't earn anything like a DJ's wage?'

It was a reasonable comment. Juniors usually lived with their families – for good reason. The pay was appalling – a derisory £7 per week. My family circumstances weren't the norm. I hadn't lived at home since I was eleven, and since I was sixteen I'd resided independently. I kept in touch with the Hoads; I saw my sister occasionally, but my mother never made contact. Though I often thought about her, I wasn't ready to see her, so living with her wasn't something I could ever contemplate. Despite needing to pay weekly rent of £14 my eye was firmly fixed on the goal ahead and I didn't care about the loss of status, or income. If I worked hard, within two years, rather than the usual three, I'd graduate to becoming a fully fledged stylist, and earn a reasonable wage.

I told the stylist about my enthusiasm for the profession and my commitment to learning new skills. Whatever I said was convincing enough for Vidal Sassoon to take me on.

I didn't explain how I'd resolve the question of surviving the training on such a meagre salary without any other means of support, and no one asked. But I'd worked out that the hours at the salon, 7 a.m. to 7 p.m., would dovetail into those at the nightclubs where I worked from 8 p.m. to 3 a.m. I would be sleep deprived, but I was young and fit. And I'd be able to subsidise my training with the money I earned.

Amy, a more experienced junior, initiated me into the basics: how to secure the towel around a client's shoulders; how to administer a backwash shampoo without getting water in their eyes; how to massage their heads and comb out their hair afterwards. Then two unsmiling senior stylists called H and Heinz (Heinz Schumi, who later opened his own salon chain) gave me guidance on interacting with the clients.

'Be friendly and welcoming but don't overstep the familiarity. Keep talk to a minimum if the client clearly wants to be left in peace. You'll be working with me to begin with,' H said. 'I'll have a coffee, no milk, one sugar. Then you can sweep the floor.'

Once I'd shampooed a client's hair, I'd stand next to H or Heinz and watch everything they did, handing over whatever piece of equipment they needed, like a theatre nurse waiting on a surgeon. I learned by watching, and gradually progressed. I was allowed to blow-dry easy and then more complicated styles. Once a week models came, and a stylist instructed us on cutting a particular style. There were also regular classes in Sloane Street or Davies Mews off Brook Street to attend. I threw myself into the new world with gusto. I was impatient to try out what I learned, and used friends as guinea pigs, trimming their hair and graduating to more ambitious cuts when they let me.

Perhaps because I was older than most juniors, none of the work seemed problematic. I had to swallow my pride when it came to menial tasks but chatting to clients came easily. I had many older friends, and I was used to making conversation, equally comfortable talking fashion, music, art, shopping or politics. Hairdressers aren't just hairdressers, I realised. They are sounding boards, confidants, therapists. They alter the way a person thinks of themselves. The best immeasurably enhance a client's mental wellbeing by adjusting the way they present themselves to the world, and in boosting a client's self-esteem the hairdresser gains a sense of satisfaction too.

But I'd totally underestimated the physical rigours of the work, and how, combined with DJing most nights, the lack of sleep would affect me. Standing for hours with hardly any time to rest took its toll. Juniors were meant to have half an hour for lunch and two shorter breaks mid-morning and mid-afternoon, but in practice this rarely happened, because if their stylist didn't need them, someone else invariably did. I saw juniors in tears from physical exhaustion, and the frenetic pace led to little camaraderie among trainees. H and Heinz had been through the same process, but they were unsympathetic to our plight, taking the attitude that this was just the initiation process. After three months I'd had enough. I didn't want to give up on my hairdressing dream but I decided to leave Sassoon, vowing that when I qualified I'd never treat a junior the way they'd treated me.

I asked Ike to get me an interview at Smile, the salon in Knightsbridge where he was a stylist. Keith Wainwright, one of the directors, gave me an interview. I told him I was desperate to become a stylist but hated the ambience at Sassoon. I also told him about my work as a DJ. He seemed to like me and said he'd take me on but that I'd still have to go through the training process on the measly junior wage. Once I'd learned the trade there was lots of potential to work on fashion shoots and location work as well as in the salon. 'That's fair enough,' I agreed. He probably only gave me a second chance because he was into music and was interested in my life as a DJ. But that didn't matter. I was in.

★

Smile was the coolest salon imaginable in those days. Its narrow door fronted on to Knightsbridge, opposite the Scotch House. Inside, a narrow staircase led up to an airy salon that stretched across the width of two shops beneath. Huge windows flooded the space with light and there were mirrors everywhere with stations for a dozen or more stylists. The salon was famous for its celebrity clientele. Cilla Black, Felicity Kendal, Leo Sayer, Lynda Bellingham, Chris Bonington, Bryan Ferry, Michael Parkinson and many other familiar faces all came and went. The salon directors also nurtured close links with the fashion departments of the legendary art school Central Saint Martins, as well as magazines and advertising agencies, so there was always a huge variety of work on offer.

Although it was always busy, the relaxed atmosphere was very different from Sassoon. I settled in and, as Keith got to know me, he asked me to make cassette tapes to play in the salon, and took me with him on commercial shoots around London. Still, the long hours were gruelling, and I found myself falling asleep on location more than once. One morning I woke up feeling so wiped out I could barely stand. I struggled along to the salon, ready for opening, but was so dizzy standing by Michael, the stylist I was working under, that I was worried I'd collapse. Michael was a kindly man and I told him I was feeling sick and wanted to go home. 'It's a really busy day, Ronnie, and we're short-staffed. I just can't manage without you.'

As the morning wore on I felt worse. 'I've really got to go,' I said. 'My head's spinning, I'm worried I'm going to faint.'

'You can't leave, Ronnie. Have a cup of tea, that'll perk you up.'

'I'm sorry,' I said after the tea made no difference. 'I just can't go on.'

He could see the state I was in but put his workload before my wellbeing, insisting I had to manage somehow and back him up. He looked at me blankly as I staggered out of the salon.

I made it home and went straight to bed. A few hours later I woke drenched in sweat. I stumbled downstairs, desperate for some water. My flatmate Tony was there. 'You're home early – are you OK?' he said, alarmed at my feverish appearance. I lost consciousness and crashed to the floor before I could explain I was unwell. An ambulance took me to hospital. Multiple tests were run, including a painful lumbar puncture. None were conclusive but I was kept in under observation. After ten days, fearing I'd lose my job if I didn't go back to work, I discharged myself. I'd concluded by then that I was suffering from nervous exhaustion. Jo agreed. 'You'll have to ease off, Ronnie.'

'I will,' I promised. After that I limited the DJ jobs I took on as much as I could, although the money was still essential to supplement my income.

Eighteen months after joining Smile I graduated to becoming a fully fledged stylist. I built a growing list of regulars, many of whom were involved in the film, music and fashion industries. I remember creating Leo Sayer's Afro hairstyle and cutting the Oxo lady Lynda Bellingham's hair into a new style that I like to think helped propel her to prominence. I was overwhelmed the first time the actress Hayley Mills came to me. I remembered being infatuated with her when I was nine or ten and saw her in *Whistle Down the Wind*, but we built up a rapport and she became a friend, inviting me to see her in her shows and go backstage afterwards.

Absorbing though all of this was, money remained a contentious issue. Keith was still paying me a junior's wage even though, as a fully qualified stylist, I felt I was due a raise. After a few weeks of waiting for my new role to be acknowledged in my pay packet to no avail, I raised the matter with him. 'Don't worry, we'll fix it, Ronnie,' he said, patting me on the back. 'Of course, you will get what you deserve. We don't want to lose you.'

The next Friday, my pay packet still hadn't changed. I raised the matter again. They'd made a mistake, it would be next week, and the next, and the next. I began to feel that Keith and the others were exploiting me.

The singer Sandie Shaw was a regular client of Leslie Russell, one of Keith's co-directors. Sandie enjoyed her celebrity status and was to be treated as a star whenever she came in. One Saturday, just before lunchtime, she arrived without an appointment. Leslie wasn't there and the receptionist told a junior to come and ask me if I'd do her hair. I was meant to be working a half-day, and it was ten minutes until I was due to leave. If I took Sandie on I knew I'd be there for an hour or more. 'Tell her you can't find me and I've gone home,' I said to the junior, as I slipped out of the salon, darting from mirror to mirror, so neither Sandie nor the receptionist saw me.

On Monday morning I was summoned to the directors' office. 'You deserve the sack for refusing one of our most important clients,' Keith said. 'Sandie wanted you to do her hair and you refused.'

'I didn't know she wanted me — she's Leslie's client,' I replied as innocently as I could.

Keith was furious but he let me get away with it. 'Never do that again, or that's it,' he warned.

'What about my pay rise?'

'Yeah. Don't worry. We'll sort it. This week.'

Two days later, when I was home in my flat, the phone rang. 'Is that Ronnie?' an oddly familiar female voice asked.

'Yes. Who's this?' I countered.

'Sandie Shaw. I've got an event on Friday night, and I'm stuck for a hairdresser. Would you come to my house after work and give me a wash and blow-dry?'

'Certainly,' I said.

I arrived at her house at the appointed hour not knowing what to expect. Was she still annoyed I'd refused to do her hair the previous Saturday? Was she planning to humiliate me in some way? I needn't have worried. She was gracious, and we got on well. She didn't mention the previous Saturday's 'mix-up', but after that I was regularly booked to do her hair at home. I never discovered how she got my private number and neither did I ask.

My pay rise still hadn't materialised, but Keith gave me Liz, a junior, to train up.

'Good luck with her,' said Ike when he saw who I'd been allocated. Liz had a reputation for being tricky and answering back, but she reminded me of the girls at Beechholme: I could see she was keen and would have talent if she could lose the hostile attitude she had acquired from people treating her so badly. I didn't expect her to do anything I wouldn't do myself.

Nor would I allow other stylists to take advantage of her. I made her take her breaks at the same time as me, and if someone came along and told her to do something I'd intervene, and say, 'She's been working all morning. I'll sweep the floor if you can't do it.'

I was aware that with her tiny salary Liz didn't have much to spend on clothes and so one Monday I handed her a bag.

'What's this?' she asked.

'It's a vintage coat. Thought you'd look good in it.'

Her face was a picture – no one had ever given her a gift like that. After that she became incredibly loyal to me. Whatever I asked it was never too much trouble.

One warm September evening in 1976, Ike and I asked Keith if we could stay on in the salon after closing to listen to a new cassette tape I'd made. 'That's fine, guys,' he said. 'Just don't forget to keep the front door locked.'

'No problem,' I promised.

At six-thirty, the last clients trickled out. I went out to get some beer while Ike tidied up. We were happily listening to the tape and were halfway through our first beers when there was a lull in the music.

'What's that?' Ike said.

I turned down the music to listen: footsteps and men's voices on the stairs were audible. My heart plummeted. I'd forgotten to lock the door. Before I could say anything the silhouette of a well-built man appeared in the shadows of the salon desk; another figure stood behind him as the jazz-funk instrumental from Donald Byrd's *Places and Spaces* came on the tape. A horrible vision of the robbery in Brixton replayed in my mind. For what seemed an eternity no one said anything. The intruders' faces were concealed in the unlit reception area; I couldn't gauge their intentions or see whether they were armed. Was this another raid, in which property that didn't belong to me would be smashed and stolen? If so my career at Smile was finished.

The figures came towards us, looking around as though they were surprised to find themselves in a hairdressing salon. Both were black, dressed in cool, casual clothes. The figure in front was stocky and clean-shaven. The one behind had a neatly clipped beard and moustache. It was he who broke the silence. 'Hey, guys, sorry to butt in like this but the door was open. We're not from round here – we're looking for Knightsbridge?'

I recognised the voice with its honeyed deep American drawl. His face, now illuminated in the evening sunlight flooding the salon, was also suddenly familiar. It was Marvin Gaye accompanied by a burly minder.

'Knightsbridge?!' I almost cried, with astonishment and relief. 'Mr Gaye – Marvin – good to meet you. You're in the middle of Knightsbridge. Where are you going?'

He seemed surprised to be recognised. 'Hey, man – thanks.'

The minder extracted a card from an inside pocket and read out an address.

'That's a few doors down. Keep on this side of the road and it'll take you less than two minutes.'

'Great,' said Marvin, eyeing our beers. 'We don't need to be there for an hour or so. Can you recommend somewhere we could go for a drink?'

'There's a pub across the road from Harrods, that's not bad,' I said. 'Or you're welcome to stay and have a beer with us.'

'Cool,' said Marvin. 'It'll be good to share some time with guys who understand music.' He parked himself in one of the hairdressing chairs; I opened a beer and handed it to him. The minder settled himself nearby and I passed a can to him too. Over the next hour and a half Marvin chatted to us as if we were old friends. For a man of his reputation, he was surprisingly lowkey and unostentatious. He was here for a tour and had arrived two days earlier. The previous night he'd played to a packed Royal Albert Hall and he'd been surprised by his reception. 'I didn't know people liked my music in Europe so much. I reckon Berry Gordy at Tamla didn't want me to know, so he could screw me on royalties. You know I had to convince him to release *What's Going On* because he thought it was too political.'

I chatted to him as if it were the most normal thing in the world, and his charming manner made me feel relaxed, although my mind swam with a sense of disbelief. This couldn't be true. How could I be sitting drinking beer and talking about the music industry with Marvin Gaye?

Time passed quickly; at eight o'clock he stood up. 'Good to meet you guys, but we must get goin'. See you around sometime. And keep on listening to soul music, brothers.' Then he left.

If an encounter like that happened now, maybe I'd take a selfie of us on my phone to remember it by. In those days that option didn't exist. Afterwards Ike and I looked at each other in incredulous silence, as if it had all been a dream.

A month or so later Marvin got in touch. He wanted to

meet up before he went on to the next stage of his tour. I suggested Maunkberry's and we had a drink one evening. I remember his album *I Want You* being played while he was there, and how good it felt to be the person sitting drinking beers with a musical legend as he raised his glass in the DJ's direction.

16

A Regency Convex Mirror

Mirrors make me uneasy. Do they tell the truth or distort reality? In many cultures the reflected image represents the soul, and psychologists say mirrors link our conscious and subconscious minds – perhaps they do all of these things, and that's what I have against them. Mirrors resurrect childhood memories so painful I prefer not to look in them.

Convex mirrors are different. They fascinate me because they make no pretence about the altered reality they reveal. I used to have one hanging in my hallway and always felt strangely drawn to the misshapen reflection of the surroundings in its domed surface. Mirrors of this kind were the height of fashion in well-to-do Georgian homes, in the Age of Enlightenment. They're the only variety of mirror mentioned by the furniture designer Thomas Sheraton in his 1803 book *Cabinet Directory*. He notes they collect 'the reflected rays into a point, by which the perspective of the room in which they are suspended, presents itself on the surface of the mirror and produces an agreeable effect'. In other words, they made a room look good. Convex mirrors had other benefits too. Servants could keep an eye on the people in a room without openly staring, and at balls, spectators could watch discreetly to see who was dancing with whom. Mirrors are important, not just to show us our reflection, but to reveal it to others too.

One of the most mysterious paintings in the world, *The Arnolfini Marriage* by Jan van Eyck, features a convex mirror that shows the backs of the couple as well as two figures near the entrance to the room – presumably one is the artist, but who is the other? Why is he there? What does he represent?

It was when I found myself trying to work out a route that avoided the mirrors at Smile that I knew I had a problem. Mirrors were everywhere, entire walls of mirrors. I faced them every time I styled someone's hair. Avoiding my reflection was an impossibility. It would pop up unexpectedly, a profile here, the back of my head there. I'd speak to clients, standing behind them looking in the mirror, trying to glue my eyes to theirs to avoid seeing myself. Suddenly I'd forget. My eyes would focus on my lips and mother's words would echo in my head – 'Your mouth is ugly, your eyes are ugly, your nose is disgusting . . .' – and I'd wrench my gaze away, trying to think about what I was doing or what the client was saying, but a horrible sense of dread would seep into the pit of my stomach and something inside me would shrink back as if I'd been struck.

What was going on in my head? My rational self knew my mother was wrong about me. She had said no one would like me and that I was a bad person, and yet I had lots of friends and a job I enjoyed. My life was full and rich. I was free of her, I reminded myself on a regular basis. Why then did those memories still disturb me? Why did the sight of my reflection still make me recoil?

Maybe the answer was that I was in denial. I had locked the traumas of childhood away in a mental closet, to avoid thinking or talking about them. But in doing so I had never confronted my relationship with my mother or properly understood it. I thought that by moving on with my physical life, filling days and nights with work and friends and music, I could outrun the past. But it was always there with me, even when I chose to ignore it, and whenever I paused, or saw my reflection in a mirror, those memories crept up, poisoning me all over again.

Clement Freud, the Liberal MP and raconteur who was a regular client at the salon, made things worse. The first time he came to me, I had hardly started to trim his thinning hair when he said, 'You don't see many black hairdressers. So tell me, how does someone like you come to be working in a place like this? Where are you from?'

'I was born not far from here,' I said, evenly. 'In Kensington.'

'Where were your parents from?' he probed.

'My father was a Welsh engineer. My mother came from Sierra Leone.'

'So she's an African immigrant. Comes over, ensnares your father. I see.'

'Not quite. They met in Sierra Leone. She came from a prominent family. They married here.'

'I doubt that very much.'

'I've seen the marriage certificate,' I replied, discomfited by the way the conversation was going.

'That means nothing. Probably fake. But I can easily find out. You have no idea the information I can access. Where's your father now?'

'He died before I was born.'

He let out a snort of laughter that sounded like a bark. 'Ha! That's what your mother told you, is it? And you believed her?'

'I've seen his death certificate,' I said, recalling the visit I had made to the Public Record Office with Ann Barraball, my childcare officer, when I was at Beechholme, and how she had helped to reassure me that my mother's account of my father's death wasn't made up.

Freud, however, wouldn't back off. 'Perhaps you have. But as I said, these things are often fabrications. I expect, should we trouble ourselves to look into it, we'd find your mother's background is nothing like you imagine it to be. They probably never married. I'll bet she was no more than a one-night stand.'

Crushed by his withering tone, I finished his hair in near-silence. My father hadn't been present in my life, but he was still my father, and despite his absence he was in some way fundamental to my sense of self. I liked to think of him as a dependable, solid and kindly man who would have loved me had he not died. It helped counter my difficulties with my mother. This conversation was making me question those assumptions. From the way he scrutinised me I could sense Freud enjoying the effect his interrogation was having. After he'd gone I felt drained, undermined, belittled. I tried not to dwell on our conversation, and worked through the rest of my clients, but his words echoed in my head and I had to force myself to concentrate. By the end of the working day I was shattered, as if I'd been up all night. Before I left, Sylvie the receptionist handed me an unusually large sum from my tip box. My surprise must have shown itself on my face. 'Most of it came from Clement Freud,' she said.

Over the months that followed Clement Freud became a regular client. Sometimes he would sit in silence, knowing he held me hostage. Sometimes the hectoring about my parentage and colour resumed. If he was silent he didn't leave a tip. If he was offensive he was invariably generous. His tips let me know that he was being deliberately abusive. They left me feeling sullied and violated, but because they were left at the reception desk and I collected them after he went, I didn't refuse them.

My client list grew. I was booked out weeks ahead, for in-salon appointments and for location shoots. Keith finally acknowledged that I was worth paying a qualified stylist's wage. But my sense of grievance didn't disappear with my pay rise. I felt I had been exploited and discovered I could earn more as a freelancer. Clients often gave me their cards; I started to keep them. Within a few months I had a long list of contacts. I found an agent and handed in my notice. I was sad to say goodbye to Keith, Sylvie, Liz and the others at Smile but we parted on good terms and I was excited to be branching out again. Liz cried when I broke the news. 'We'll keep in touch,' I told her. 'You have a great future ahead.'

Going freelance was a decision I never regretted. Work was

plentiful and much better paid, but there were often gaps between assignments, and when I had time to think, childhood memories increasingly disturbed me. Seeing myself in a mirror still made me curl up inside, and I could always hear my mother's voice telling me my face was ugly. I needed to address this, and I convinced myself that the only way to do so was to try and reconnect with my mother. Surely now I was an adult and had established a successful career she would respect me and explain her side of the story. We would resolve our differences, make peace, and move on together. And then maybe I'd be able to tolerate my own reflection.

We met in a small restaurant in Kensington, a stone's throw from where I was born. I had contacted her through my sister, Lynette, whom I still saw from time to time. I was early and chose a table by the window. I watched her approach. She was dressed as elegantly as ever, but the purposeful look in her eye didn't escape me. I stood up as she came in, conscious that just seeing her had sparked a surge of anxiety and that my heart was going wild.

'Mummy,' I said, as I pulled out her chair. 'You look well. It's good to see you.' This conventional greeting was a big mistake I realised as soon as the words left my lips. I made no attempt to kiss her, and she didn't attempt physical contact with me. Instead, she shot me a reproachful look and I felt as though her eyes had drilled into my soul. There was a long pause while she sat down, shifting heavily in the seat. 'If it's good to see me – why has it been so long since you got in touch?'

I took the seat opposite, recoiling at the rapier response.

Confrontation was the last thing I wanted. I reminded myself I had planned this lunch. I was in control. I was an adult, with a good job and an independent life. I would not allow myself to regress to the terrified boy I had once been. But I could feel the power she still wielded over me. 'I've been busy with the salon, and DJing at night. Now I'm qualified things have calmed down – I've got more time. So I thought it would be good if we could get together. To talk things through.'

Her brow furrowed in a way I knew signified silent rage. 'Talk things through? What things do you want to talk through, Ronnie? You want to tell me why you were such a bad boy when your sister was so beautiful and good? Is that what you want to say? You want to explain why you don't come to see me? Go on then. Say it. Let me hear what you've got to say.'

As her voice reached a crescendo my stomach turned to water. This wasn't how I'd envisaged things going. 'What will you have to drink, Mummy?' I said, trying to lighten the tone and regain control of the situation.

Ignoring me, pursing her lips, she surveyed the menu with narrow eyes. Then looking over her shoulder away from me, she waved her arm at the waitress.

'I'll have a lemonade,' she said.

'And I'll have a beer,' I hurriedly interjected. 'And if you could give us five minutes we'll be ready to order.'

While we waited for the food I tried to make conversation. 'How's Lynette coping with Kelvin?'

'You want to know, ask her.'

'I saw her two weeks ago. Kelvin seems a good boy. She said she's trying to get a flat in the same block with you.'

My sister had a five-year-old son. The child's father wasn't in her life and she had been living in a home for single mothers.

'If you know so much, why ask me? Lynette is a wonderful daughter. Thank God! Shame my son wasn't more like her.'

The conversation didn't get any easier. As the meal progressed she became virtually monosyllabic. If I asked a question she looked at me mutely with a dour expression. If I waited for her to speak the embittered silence seemed interminable. If I made general conversation about something I'd done she shrugged her shoulders dismissively. If I ate in silence, she fixed me with a glare that made me shrivel inside. If I looked away from her, out of the window at the street, I sensed her revulsion lasering the side of my head. Sitting there for an hour and a half was sheer torture. I was a defenceless child, mentally flogged, burned, poisoned and drowned. Once again she had rendered me helpless.

I have to get through this, I kept reminding myself. I will never be free unless I can face her as an adult and reconcile myself to the past. I wanted to run and scream but I forced myself to sit there and endure it even though afterwards the experience left me shaken and flinching inside. A month later I tried again. The result was the same. The month after that I arranged another meeting. But each time my mother's anger and animosity were unbreachable. She would never let me near her and something about her still terrified me. Eventually I had to confront reality: the meetings were making me worse rather than healing me. I couldn't face any more of them. I broke off contact, telling myself I would see her again when I felt stronger. Meanwhile my hectic work life would take over and allow me to forget.

Three years later, I came home late to my flat in Chelsea Cloisters with Jane, my girlfriend at the time. It was past midnight and the phone started ringing almost as I closed the door. I answered it.

'Ronnie?'

'Yes? Who's this?'

'It's Lynne, from Smile.'

'Lynne — whyever are you calling me at this hour?'

'I've just found a message. A woman called Christine phoned for you a couple of months ago. She said she wanted to talk to you urgently. I tried calling you a couple of times but there was no reply, and then I forgot. I've just found the note in my pocket. I'm sorry.'

'Don't worry,' I said.

Since leaving Smile to work freelance, I'd kept in touch with many of the staff and they knew where I lived. But I couldn't blame her for not being able to get in touch. I was often away on advertising shoots over several days, if I was in London I was often out clubbing or DJing late, and I didn't have an answer phone.

But something about this message worried me. It was a while since I had spoken to any of the Hoads. My sister hadn't been in touch either. Was someone ill? Mummy Hoad? Jackie? Christine? I wouldn't sleep until I knew, and despite the late hour I decided to call Christine straightaway. I dialled her number. It rang and rang. No answer.

'She's probably asleep,' Jane said.

'I'm going over to Wimbledon to see.'

'I'll come too.'

Jane flagged down a cab. In those days cabbies were often reluctant to stop for black passengers, so we had a routine whereby I would wait in the shadows, and emerge only when the taxi stopped and she had told him the route. This driver was unconcerned, and there was no issue when I gave him the address in Wimbledon where Christine lived. Half an hour later we pulled up outside the house. By then the driver had gathered the gist of the mission and said he'd wait in case she wasn't in. I jumped out and rang the bell. No answer. I knocked. Nothing.

A woman from the house next door must have heard the taxi idling and my knocking. A curtain drew back and a head emerged. 'What do you want? You do realise it's one-thirty in the morning?'

'I'm sorry to disturb you. I'm looking for your neighbour, Christine – it's urgent,' I said.

'She's been away for a fortnight,' the neighbour said. 'Don't think she's back for another few days.'

'Thank you. And apologies for the disturbance.'

She nodded and pulled the window closed.

The only solution was to go and see Christine's sister Jackie, who lived in Morden.

By the time we arrived, it was after 2 a.m., but before long an upstairs light came on, and then another in the hall and the door opened to reveal Jackie's face.

'Ronnie!' she exclaimed, still half asleep. 'Whatever are you doing here at this time of night?'

'I had a message from Christine, but she's away.'

'She wanted to see how you were. Your mother's dead!' she blurted out.

I looked at her, scarcely able to take it in. Had I misheard? 'What did you just say?'

She blinked and looked at me. Gradually, the reality of the situation dawned on her. 'Oh my God. You didn't know, did you? I'm so sorry – you'd better come in.'

I couldn't process this information. How could my mother have died without me being told? It was inconceivable surely . . .

'My mother's dead? When? How?'

'It was two months ago, after a short illness. Bone cancer I believe,' Jackie explained. 'You weren't at the funeral. Christine wondered why, but she didn't like to ask your sister – she was in such a state.'

'She didn't tell me. I didn't know.' I welled up, unable to say more, numb with the shock, but tearful.

Jackie could see my torment. 'I am so sorry. If I'd known I'd have come and found you myself.' She put a motherly arm around me and I rested my head on her shoulder but I felt as if I was drawn into a maelstrom of conflicting emotion. My mother was dead. I hadn't known. I hadn't said goodbye. It couldn't be true. But it was true. Now we would never be reconciled.

I hadn't seen Lynette for over a year, I'd been so busy. But I rang her the following day. I knew better than to confront her and ask why she hadn't told me our mother had been taken ill and had died. I didn't want her to break off contact with me – she was now the only means I had to find out what had happened. 'I only heard she'd died last night,' I said. 'It must have been terrible for you, all on your own.'

'It was,' she said sharply. 'And it still is. I miss her every day. So does Kelvin.'

'Was Mummy Hoad at the funeral?'

'No, she couldn't make it.'

Mummy Hoad was now living in the village of Santa Eulalia, in Ibiza. I knew she'd have wanted to be at the funeral. And I wanted some answers. Unless I could understand what had happened and why I'd been ignored I would never find peace. A few days later, I rang Lynette again. 'Why don't we go and see Mummy Hoad this summer?' I said. 'It will do us both good. I'll pay for the trip. It will be nice for Kelvin to have a proper holiday.'

'OK,' she agreed.

The events surrounding my mother's death remained at the forefront of my thoughts. I had yearned for her to explain things from her point of view, to demonstrate some warmth towards me. Remembering the criticisms she had made about my father when I was a child made me suspect I had once represented her pain at his loss. But I wanted to believe that despite her cruelty she'd only intended the best for me, that her mental illness had been to blame, and that she'd been proud of what I'd achieved. I'd wanted us to grow together harmoniously. None of that could happen now, our relationship was unsalvageable. I would never have closure.

For a while I was unable to grieve. A week later, alone in the flat, I went to bed around midnight. Suddenly, without warning the tears came. I cried for my dead mother. Great wracking sobs convulsed my body. For the next seven hours

I wept and wept, then, eventually, as dawn came I grew calmer and fell asleep. When I woke up I felt as if I had run a marathon, or survived an emotional tsunami. I could barely move, my mind was exhausted. But I still couldn't face unpicking my dysfunctional relationship with my mother, or explaining the real reason for my anguish to anyone else.

Lynette, Kelvin and I went to see Mummy Hoad in Santa Eulalia that summer. Over the three weeks we were there I was careful not to push my sister. There were so many things I wanted to ask her, but I didn't want to make her defensive. I would wait until the time was right. One day I gently raised the subject. Little by little, Lynette revealed that our mother had been in hospital for two months before she'd died. She had visited every day, but one day our mother had written her a letter that mentioned me.

'What did it say?' I asked tentatively.

'It said, "Ronnie doesn't like me. I know that, but he doesn't understand that everything I did was for his own good."'

I thought about this, then I carefully said, 'And you didn't think to tell me she was ill and wanted to speak to me?'

'No one ever knew where you were. Ronnie, you never stayed in touch. You were always doing different things.'

Her voice had a brittle edge. She was growing impatient, and I was afraid of her losing it altogether. I can't do this, I thought. She doesn't comprehend: the most important thing in the world to me was to be able to have a final conversation with my mother, to say goodbye. Now I never will.

I changed the subject.

★

For the next six or seven years, each summer, Lynette, Kelvin and I visited Santa Eulalia. Kelvin and I became close. I saw myself in him and felt that having time to really talk to him and guide him was beneficial to him and in some way consoling for me. Over the years I waited for Lynette to express some sense of regret for not having told me that Mummy was dying. I still couldn't understand her reason for not letting me know. One evening the four of us were sitting on the terrace. The sun was sinking over the olive trees, and in the distance the sea glinted with orange and gold light as we reminisced about summer evenings in Eastbourne. 'I remember you so well, Ronnie. How independent you were,' said Mummy Hoad. 'At the age of seven or eight you'd come down with Poppet on the train, and then you'd go off on Christine's bike, which was far too big for you. But sometimes you could be naughty. So naughty I'd threaten to send you home. I could never understand why you were like that when Poppet was always so good and you had such an incredible mother.'

The reference to my mother wounded me. I turned to Lynette, hoping she would intervene to explain what I never could: Mummy hadn't been the maternal paragon she'd seemed; she hadn't treated me kindly. But as I turned, I saw my sister, her eyes with a glazed look, lost in a reverie. A thought began to take shape in my mind. Had Lynette not told me our mother was dying because she feared my mother and I might somehow be reconciled? Did she prefer to bask in our mother's love alone? Maybe she didn't want to meet at our mother's deathbed because she didn't want to share her affection with me. I couldn't understand her actions. I just felt as if the pain I suffered maybe didn't count in the equation somehow. But I could say anything then and haven't spoken with her about it since, so I will probably never know the truth.

Perhaps my mother would never have told me she loved me and she would have remained embittered to the end. But at the time I felt as though I'd undergone a seismic shift and my mental landscape changed. I could no longer bear to spend time with my sister, and despite my love for Kelvin, our holidays to Ibiza were over.

After that I saw Kelvin regularly, and built a strong bond with him, but I only saw him on his own. Spending time with my sister risked bringing up those thoughts and my own feelings of worthlessness.

Mummy Hoad died in the middle of August 1998. I heard the news from Jackie, who told me that the funeral would be the following day, in Ibiza. Since it was high season and flights were scarce, she didn't expect Lynette or me to attend, but she just wanted us to know we'd be welcome if we did.

'I'll be there,' I said without hesitation.

I went to the travel agent I often used and said I needed to get to Ibiza the following day.

'You'll be lucky,' the agent said.

'It's my foster mother's funeral. I have to be there.'

'I'll see what I can do.'

Miraculously, she found me a standby seat. I landed in Ibiza mid-morning with less than an hour before the service started. Not knowing the Spanish word for 'cemetery', I mimed being dead to make the taxi driver understand where I wanted to go, and changed into a suit on the journey. The service was held outdoors and had started by the time I arrived. I quietly joined the back of the group of mourners. I could see the coffin, and I felt the emotion of my childhood wash over me as I recited the Lord's Prayer. My two mothers were now both dead. Without Mummy Hoad my childhood would have been infinitely bleaker – perhaps I would not have survived it. She had shown me love, warmth and care when my own mother had had none to give. The home she'd created was my blueprint for a happy family life. Tears began to fall as the service progressed. I sobbed and sobbed, but was thankful to be there, to be able to say a final goodbye to someone so pivotal in my life. Afterwards, Martin said he'd never heard anyone cry so much, and Derek and Doreen comforted me. I didn't tell them the truth: that my tears weren't only for the wonderful Mummy Hoad, but for the other mother to whom I had never said farewell.

17

An Indistinctly Signed and
Inscribed Oil Painting

My passion for art started partly through my interest in illustrated books. I mostly bought children's books, but I was also
keen on a series featuring the Gibson Girl, the ideal woman of
the late nineteenth and early twentieth centuries. The Gibson
Girl had an elegant physique, fine features and an independence of spirit, all of which I found hugely appealing. The
books were published in large format, and I'd accumulated
quite a collection of them when I was aimlessly wandering
through the basement in Alfie's Antique Market near Regent's
Park and a painting caught my eye.

There was something about it that I found compelling. It
was painted in a loose, post-Impressionist style and had a soft-
ness about the handling of paint that reminded me of a Monet
haystack. Except this painting featured a ramshackle agricultural building set in a deftly painted landscape against a streaky

orange-sunset sky. At the bottom on one side, a signature had been scratched in the wet paint, probably with the end of a paintbrush. On the other side, in vivid red, there was a scrawled inscription.

'I don't know who it's by,' said Cyril, the old-school picture dealer. 'I can't read the signature or the inscription – they're both illegible.' I went closer and peered. I couldn't decipher the signature either. Squinting at the inscription, I could just about make out: 'To Waldorf from Dana.' Dana must be a female artist, I thought, but that didn't shed much light either.

Yet when I looked at the painting from a distance again, I felt a strange sense of recognition, as though the artist was one I knew. Intending to do some research and find out more, I bought the painting and took it home to my flat. A year or two later, I was sharing a small rented gallery in Knightsbridge. I wanted to make it feel like an elegant interior rather than a conventional shop, so I hung the painting as a focal point on one wall.

My main stock in trade in the gallery was jewellery, watches and small works of art. I also had a few miniatures for sale. But I knew I didn't want to sell this painting. It was just there to enhance the gallery display, and it did that so brilliantly that when the sun streamed in it looked almost like a window in the wall.

Several people offered to buy the anonymous landscape, but I refused them all. Then one day, and I can't remember why, the pieces just came together. It wasn't really a eureka moment, more like frost on a window pane had melted and I saw clearly something that perhaps I'd known all along, subconsciously. Dana wasn't a female artist. The scribbled signature on the painting was identical to the one reproduced on the illustrated Gibson Girl books I'd collected: by Charles Dana Gibson, the series creator. The painting was dedicated to his friend, the American-born press baron and politician Waldorf Astor. He'd probably painted the landscape while he stayed on the Astor estate, Cliveden, which Waldorf had been given by his father-in-law on his marriage to the famous society hostess Nancy Langhorne Shaw – better known as Nancy Astor.

Afterwards I often thought about the moment the realisation had finally dawned. The whole time I had owned the painting and had collected Gibson's printed books and yet I hadn't realised I owned one of his original works. I still have the painting now, hanging in my office, a reminder that sometimes instinct is more powerful than the conscious mind. In searching for distant treasure, you can overlook what's right in front of you. Precious things may be so close to hand you don't see them. But occasionally the same applies to dangerous things too.

My career as an antiques dealer had started almost accidentally. When Keith had finally given me my long-awaited pay rise at Smile, I had treated myself to a vintage watch from the 1920s, paying £20 for it in a London market. It was exquisite: square-shaped, with no name on the dial, but made from solid 18ct gold. In those days vintage watches hadn't become the popular collecting area they are today, and my watch drew attention, because as a hairdresser your hands – and wrists – are a focus of attention. 'What a great watch!' clients would often say. 'Where did you get it?'

When I said I'd bought it at an antiques market several clients offered to buy it from me. I always said no, until one day someone was so insistent that I said, 'Out of interest, what would you pay for it?'

'I'll give you £200,' he said without hesitation. My expression must have revealed my astonishment. 'A new one in a Bond Street shop is over £1,000,' he explained.

It didn't take more than a second or two to do the maths. If I sold him a watch I'd make more than I made in a fortnight at Smile, even with my pay increase. What did I have to lose? 'OK,' I said, 'I'll see if I can find you something similar.'

Within a week or two I'd bought another watch and sold it to him, and from then on, if someone admired my watch I'd offer to find one for them. I was still DJing a couple of nights a week and at the club I'd met a young man called Martin Kay who was a scrap jewellery dealer, buying and selling gold and silver just for the value of its base metal. Martin started coming to me to have his hair cut, and when he saw my watch he told me he was scrapping all the old watches that came his way. 'I'll pay £5 over scrap for any good ones you bring me,' I said. He thought that was wonderful, more than he made from the Hatton Garden dealers. After that, whenever he came in to get his hair cut he'd bring me a bag of vintage watches and I'd slip the money over to him.

The watches sometimes needed restoring or fitting with a new strap, which I would sort and then sell them on for hundreds of pounds more. No one taught me about watches. I learned from buying, selling, handling and reading, and was helped by my enthusiasm and an eye for detail that linked back to my days as a modelmaker and technical draughtsman. If I could, I'd have a look inside the watches I bought, so I could familiarise myself with the inner workings, and I taught myself basic repairs. The weight and the thickness of the metal all revealed something about the watch, I discovered. After observing a jeweller replace a mainspring I tried it myself and was able to do it, although it took me five times longer. By handling watches every day I learned to distinguish quality and worked out that Patek Philippe, Cartier and Rolex were superior watchmakers. Apart from the money I was making I enjoyed building up knowledge and bringing something unloved and undervalued back to life.

But progress wasn't all smooth. Within a month or two the directors at Smile realised what was going on and told me they didn't want watch-dealing going on in the salon. I'd have to stop or leave. I suppose it was a fair enough objection. But by then I was well and truly into my newly developing business. I'd started to think about leaving and going freelance and I wasn't about to give up such a promising new venture. But even so, I didn't want to have a fight with Keith, so Martin and I would meet surreptitiously off the premises and exchange watches and money.

When I left the salon and started to take on hair assignments on a freelance basis, the watch business continued to flourish in tandem. Having time between assignments gave me more time to source good stock. The dealers I bought from in those days all said I was mad. 'No one will buy them,' they'd say, not realising that by then I had an address book full of clients in the media, film and fashion who hungered for accessories that were different from the norm. I pressed on, branching out into other items that caught my eye. On location, there was often time between shoots to explore the local area. If I came back with something interesting I'd often show it to the production staff, who would sometimes offer to buy what I'd bought.

Meanwhile, I'd met Ric Saunders, who loved a drink and smoked heavily. He was a part-time model, with chiselled features that gave him more than a passing resemblance to Clint Eastwood. Ric and I had overlapping interests. As well as film work he also dabbled in antiques, specialising in vintage lighters. We decided to set up a business together and rented a stall in Antiquarius, the upmarket antiques forum on the King's Road right by Chelsea Town Hall. Ric's wife, Vansi, manned the stall while I supplied watches and arranged them in an eye-catching display, and Ric did the same with his lighters and other accessories. Soon I'd built up such a reputation for buying watches that the fashionistas and some dealers gave me the nickname Ronnie the Watch. It was partly a joke – most of the dealers still couldn't see any future in the things that fascinated me.

To keep a stall well stocked meant much of my time was now spent on the road, scouring sale rooms, fairs, markets and dealers for things I could sell. Once or twice a week I'd go down to the south coast, touring Brighton, Hove and Hastings. Then every couple of months or so I would take trips up north, sometimes up as far as Scotland.

As I travelled around looking for watches, I noticed other things: beautiful vintage luggage by Louis Vuitton, crocodile briefcases, wallets and cigar cases mounted in gold and silver made by big brand names like Hermès, Dunhill and Asprey. Considering their intricate craftsmanship, sumptuous materials and their technology these items were hugely undervalued, I thought. And so, despite more raised eyebrows within the trade, with naive enthusiasm, and a confidence that came from recognising excellence when I saw it, I started buying those too. I soon discovered that buying was easier than selling: no one in England wanted vintage luggage – but in Paris the market was burgeoning. A dealer called Annette had a shop in the Champs-Elysées. If I brought her thirty or forty pieces she would buy them all. This spurred me to turn to something new: I started to buy handbags.

Soon I was branching out further, buying not just watches, luggage and handbags, but objects of vertu* by Fabergé, Cartier, Dunhill and other top makers, as well as interesting jewellery. If you knew where to look and had a good eye, you could buy incredible things in those days for relatively small sums. I remember buying a Cartier handbag with a solid gold handle like a thick snake for £20. The gold alone was worth £1,000. Then I found an incredible cigar box made of Russian karelian birch, inlaid with tendrils of gold entwined like seaweed, the crossing of each tendril studded with a cabochon sapphire. The box was signed by Louis-François Cartier himself – I paid £50 for it.

Alongside my growing passion for antiques my love for music hadn't waned. I took on DJ jobs, and when the opportunity arose I accepted assignments to do the hair on advertising shoots and I'd also play music at high-profile fashion shows. I was frantically busy, making more money than I ever had before. The money made me feel good but it wasn't my driving motivation. My frenetic life was an escape from painful

* An object of vertu is a term used to describe small, highly refined works of art made from precious materials, but distinct from jewellery because they are not made for a person to wear.

recollections. By filling every moment, I wouldn't have to think about them.

The world of antiques is a cliquey, opportunistic one, and not all partnerships end well. Some of the pieces I bought weren't right for the stand I shared with Ric, so I'd sell those through Marika Johnstone whose stall, also in Antiquarius, specialised in luxury accessories. Marika was well spoken, always immaculately dressed, and possibly the most brilliant salesperson I've ever encountered. But, I came to realise, there was another side to her. The deal we had was based on trust: I'd supply her with items and set a figure that I wanted for them. She would add her margin to that sum. When the items were sold, she would pay me the price I'd originally asked, and keep the profit for herself. It didn't worry me that even when I was supplying 70 to 80 per cent of her stock she couldn't bring herself to acknowledge me properly. But I was concerned when I realised she'd sold some of the items I'd supplied but hadn't paid me for them. I needed the cash in order to invest in more stock – that was how the business worked. I explained this to her and said that I thought she owed me a lot of money. It wasn't an easy exchange and she made me feel I was taking advantage of her. I held my ground for weeks and eventually we settled up, but it had created tension between us that I knew I wouldn't be able to forget.

When I heard various dealers talking about a gold Cartier clock that a jeweller in Wimbledon was selling, I decided to investigate. It was a gold travelling carriage clock dating from the mid-1920s with an enamelled case. There was a small square cut in the gold clock doors so that you could see the time, but when you pressed a button on the top, the doors pinged open and the full dial with its enamelled figures and diamond hands was revealed in all its splendour. The clock was made from solid gold and the dealer was asking £2,000 for it. He wouldn't negotiate on the price. All the other Bond Street clock dealers said this was too much. But with my income from hairdressing and DJing as well as from my growing antiques business, I had money, and I wanted to spend it on the best objects. I regarded it as investing in my reputation, and I felt willing to take a risk, not really caring how much profit I made. I paid the Wimbledon dealer his price, and because things were strained with Marika, I gave the clock to Tanya at Cobra & Bellamy, dealers in objects of vertu, and I was delighted (and a little relieved) when she sold it for £3,750. Today it would fetch nearly ten times as much.

Friendships are often complicated and it's a sad fact that close friends are not always happy about each other's success. I realised this when Ike, my best friend who'd got me the interview for the job at Smile, and who was with me when Marvin Gaye walked in, started to distance himself. Through a friend of a friend I heard that he was spreading rumours about me – saying I was dealing in stolen goods. I was livid and hadn't decided how to deal with it when I bumped into him at Legends, a popular nightclub.

'Hi, Ronnie. Long time. How you doing?' he greeted me.

'Not too good, Ike,' I replied.

'What's wrong, man?'

'You are,' I said, and I challenged him over the things I'd heard he'd said about me, telling him I no longer regarded him as a friend.

He looked hurt and mumbled some vague excuse, then

disappeared looking sheepish. About a week later he sought me out at Maunkberry's. He was sincerely sorry for the things he'd said. It was just a stupid response to the fact we no longer hung out like we had done. 'Can we go back to how it was?' he asked.

I thanked him, saying I was grateful for the apology and I'd like to heal our rift too, but I was still hurting. 'I'm off to Ibiza tomorrow,' I told him. 'I'll try and forget what you did, and call you when I'm back.'

Looking relieved he said, 'OK, that's cool. See you around in a few weeks then.'

On my return from Ibiza, three weeks later, I went into a shop on the King's Road. The assistant there was a girl I vaguely knew. 'You're a friend of Ike's, aren't you?' she said.

'Yes,' I replied.

'You've heard the news?'

'No – I've been away. What news?'

'Ike's dead.'

My face must have registered my shock. 'What?'

'He died in his flat, alone. He took a drug overdose about three weeks ago,' she said.

I shook my head. I couldn't believe what I'd heard. 'What did you just say?' She repeated it. 'Are you sure it's the same Ike?' There was no doubt, she was absolutely certain: my best friend Ike – Dwight King, the hairdresser – had killed himself. He was just twenty-eight years old. We had been so close: we'd worked together at Smile, and when we weren't working we'd spent so much time clubbing together. It was like losing a brother. I've never got over it.

★

221

Gemma and Alison were beautiful identical twin sisters and models whom I'd met through hairdressing. They'd been on a shoot with Dustin Hoffman, and when he'd mentioned that he was interested in antiques somehow my name had come up. Dustin had heard about Bermondsey Market and wanted someone to show him round. Would I do it? Of course, I'd be delighted, I said.

The four of us met early one morning and I stepped into tour-guide mode. By then I had worked with so many celebrities that I was adept at behaving normally in the presence of stars. Even so, I felt that Dustin Hoffman was in a different league. He was at the zenith of his fame. I'd seen all his films and was a huge fan. But I held myself together and was gratified when he stopped and looked at everything I pointed out, and even bought one or two pieces. He was more extroverted than I'd expected, unworried when people recognised him, relaxed, happy to talk. But it was a freezing winter's day, and as we lingered over candlesticks and medieval carvings and Tunbridge ware, the girls were shivering with cold. Dustin was wearing a Burberry trench coat with a removable winter lining. Without a word he took off the coat and gave the lining to Gemma and the coat to Alison. Afterwards we all had breakfast in a cafe and eventually went our separate ways. I'd forgotten all about that day until five years ago, when I was standing on the pavement at the bottom of Bond Street, waiting to cross. I was agitated, running late for a meeting, wondering when the lights would change, when something made me look to my right. The man standing next to me was Dustin Hoffman. We looked each other in the eyes and he smiled as if to say he remembered me and was inviting me to speak. But I just thought, I'm late and I can't get involved, and walked on. Afterwards I thought how stupid I was. I'd love to have talked to him again.

The watches were going so well that one day Ric said, 'Ronnie, you sell one watch and I have to sell twenty lighters to make the same money. I want to learn about watches – will you teach me?'

After all the years of being told I was mad to take an interest, this represented a turning point – validation that my judgement was spot on. I told him I'd be happy to share my knowledge, and so once a week I'd visit him at his flat with a roll of watches and teach him what I could. He was starting to buy the odd watch for the stand when Vansi happened to mention that someone from Sotheby's had come in and spent some time on the stand looking at all the watches we had on display. 'He must have spent half an hour looking at everything, and he asked if he could talk to someone who owns the pieces about them. I don't know what he wants. Do you want to call him?'

I arranged a meeting at Sotheby's with David Battie. He told me that the auction house had recognised the growing market in wristwatches and wanted to start holding specialist sales. An expert from one of the Art departments, Nigel Sullivan, was going to head the new department, but he didn't know enough about watches. Would I help him catalogue the sale and teach him what I knew?

'Of course, I'd be honoured,' I replied.

With the benefit of hindsight, I should have agreed a fee, but naively, I presumed I would be remunerated on a standard consultancy basis. I also reasoned that the kudos that came with my association with the illustrious sale room would help my status as a dealer. Needless to say, without any financial agreement, Sotheby's didn't pay me anything, and I found myself donating my expertise on a voluntary basis. When the sale was on view Sullivan called with a query and I went along to have a look. I picked up a copy of the catalogue. There was no acknowledgement that I had helped in any way. 'We're charging £10,' Sullivan said.

I looked at him long and hard. 'You want me to pay for the catalogue I've helped you write?'

He flushed. 'No. Of course not. Have it with my compliments.'

I took on a gallery in Montpelier Walk in Knightsbridge with a new business partner, James Stewart, who lived in the basement flat under the premises with his wife, Vanessa. James had played in a band so we shared a love of music and went to concerts together – Santana and Jaco Pastorius (the bass player with Weather Report) being two memorable highlights. The fact that he also dealt in jewellery and objects of vertu and liked the same things gave us myriad overlapping areas of interest. The main difference between us was that James was white. Even though he'd sometimes sail much closer to the wind than I ever wanted to, he never had to navigate the pitfalls that beset me because of the colour of my skin.

One day I had arranged a meeting with a potential client at Grays Antique Market. I put some jewellery in my briefcase along with my Filofax and some money. As usual, I was running late, and the rendezvous was a good fifteen minutes away, so I decided to jog along the pavement to make up time. Bad decision. As I turned a corner, two police constables, a man and a woman, were walking a few yards ahead. Knowing from experience that their suspicion would be easily raised, I slowed my pace. But my shoes had metal toecaps, and as I drew closer and was about to pass them, they heard me approach and turned.

'Where are you off to in such a hurry?' said the male police constable, coming to a halt in front of me to block my way.

'I'm late for a meeting with a client,' I replied.

'What's in the bag?'

'My address book, some money and some jewellery.'

He raised a sceptical eyebrow. 'Jewellery? Let's see.'

I opened the briefcase. There were perhaps a dozen items each in individual plastic bags.

'Where did these come from?'

'I run a gallery round the corner. I deal in jewellery,' I said, irked to be put on the defensive. 'If you don't believe me, all you have to do is walk round the corner with me. My partner is there. He'll vouch for me.'

'I'm not taking orders from you,' the constable replied, glancing at his female colleague. 'Drop the bag. Put your hands on the wall. Spread your legs.'

I snapped shut the briefcase. 'Why should I do that? I'm cooperating with you. I've shown you what's in the bag. If you want me to empty my pockets I will.' I handed them my keys and a few coins. 'Why should I be demeaned by being searched in the street, for no reason?'

'If you won't do as I say, I'm going to have to restrain you,' the constable said. He grabbed my right arm just above the wrist and tried to force it behind my back.

I flexed my arm, resisting his attempts to force my arm back, even though he was using two hands. 'I haven't done anything. I am cooperating with you. All you have to do is to walk round the corner to verify my story. You have no reason to harass me like this. I refuse to be humiliated when I've done nothing wrong. Allow me some dignity. Call a car if you need to do this, and question me privately in a room at the station.'

'Get on the radio,' he said to his colleague. 'Say we need a car to arrest a suspect.'

With him clinging to my arm, we stood awkwardly in the street. By the time a car came and I was ushered into it, a small crowd had gathered to see what was going on. I forced myself to remain outwardly calm but I was incensed with the indignity and injustice of the situation. My annoyance was overlaid with shame and a sense of powerlessness. I had missed my meeting. What if one of my clients happened to walk by and saw me? I hadn't been doing anything unlawful or suspicious. The only reason I'd been apprehended was the colour of my skin.

At the station I spoke to the desk sergeant. 'I'd like a phone call, a sandwich, a coffee and an apology,' I said. He let me phone Jo, who said she would be there in half an hour with Huw to vouch for me. I was put in an interview room. Eventually, someone brought me refreshments and told me I was free to leave. Jo and Huw had arrived and were waiting for me. As I walked past the sergeant, he mumbled his regret at the inconvenience I'd been caused. 'They were just doing their job,' he said by way of explanation. It wasn't much of an apology.

18

A Van Cleef & Arpels Concealed-Watch Handbag

When Estelle Arpels, the daughter of a dealer in precious stones, married Alfred Van Cleef, the son of an artisan jeweller, in 1895, their union gave rise to a new luxury brand. A few years after the wedding, Alfred joined forces with Estelle's brother Charles, and Van Cleef & Arpels opened their doors in 1906. The shop in the Place Vendôme, Paris, has remained in the same premises ever since. Van Cleef & Arpels soon established a reputation for innovative design and fabulous quality and their illustrious clients included countless celebrities and fashion icons, among them Grace Kelly, Marlene Dietrich and Elizabeth Taylor. Royalty were also drawn to their jewels. The Duchess of Windsor was given a spectacular ruby and diamond necklace for her fortieth birthday by the Duke, and these days the Duchess of Cambridge is also a fan.

I've traded in Van Cleef & Arpels jewellery, watches and

clocks of one kind or another for as long as I can remember, so it made sense that when it came to collecting handbags, they would draw my eye, and I like to think I played a small part in establishing them as the flourishing collectors' market they are today.

A watch handbag is a particular rarity, and I've only owned or even seen two of them. Made from black antelope, my one had a gold clasp mounted with cabochon emeralds. When you pressed the emeralds, they released the catch, which opened the miniature gold louvre blind, and a hidden watch was revealed. A watch concealed within a handbag held obvious appeal to me – combining two areas of interest in one beautiful object. Added to that, I love to imagine the elegant lady who once owned it. Perhaps she used its hidden device as an excuse for a speedy getaway from unwanted advances. Maybe her lover gave it to her as a token because she was always late for their rendezvous. Whatever its hidden truth, the bag was redolent of glamour and subterfuge and here too it has relevance to my story. Bags of a similar calibre gave me entrée to new cultural circles in Paris, New York and London. Thanks to a handbag, I became friends with one of France's most iconic screen celebrities. And in hiding their function, in a sense, such bags represent characters I've met within the antiques world. Some are exactly what they appear to be, others mask their true character. Even with experience, what lies beneath the outer shell is often unexpected.

In 1981 I had a 6ct diamond ring that I wanted to sell. I was at Portobello Market when I spotted a woman I recognised from the Lanes in Brighton. I was well aware by then that some of the Brighton dealers were dodgy, but I had no reason to feel wary of this woman, and seeing her out of context made me drop my guard.

'Let me show you this,' I said, and I took out the ring. As soon as I did so I realised I'd made a mistake, and even when she'd gone my uneasiness didn't fade. All day I felt jumpy and apprehensive and at closing time, for safety's sake, I went home in a taxi. I was living in a studio flat in Chelsea Cloisters at the time, and when I got in I realised I needed some provisions. There was a shop not far away, but something told me not to leave the expensive jewellery unguarded in the flat. I put the ring and one or two other things in my pocket, leaving the rest in my bag.

There was a long narrow corridor shaped like a boomerang with doors to the street at either end. The door to my flat, number 10, was at the kink in the boomerang; a storeroom was opposite. I left by the street door closest to the shop, a different door from the one I'd just entered. Returning fifteen minutes later, I rounded the bend and found that the door of the storeroom opposite my flat had been hacked to pieces. Splinters of wood lay on the carpet like confetti, leaving a gaping hole large enough to crawl through.

I knew instinctively that this was meant for me. Someone had watched me go down the corridor and stop; perhaps they pulled back so I couldn't see them and mistakenly thought the door to the storeroom was the one I'd entered. They'd waited until they saw me leave and had broken into what they thought was my flat. The violence of the attempted robbery shook me. What would have happened if I'd come back a few minutes earlier? I didn't want to think about it. The time had come to move.

Someone I knew had a property for sale in North London. A friend organised a mortgage; I just needed to raise a £10,000 deposit. I had been thinking of promoting vintage handbags through an exhibition for a while. With a new sense of purpose, I approached a friend who dealt in twentieth-century works of art, and invited him round to my girlfriend Jane's house in Knightsbridge. Before he arrived with his partner, I set the stage: I selected some of my best bags, arranging them beautifully, making sure they were all carefully lit.

They were suitably impressed. 'They look fabulous, like works of art,' they said.

'They are works of art,' I said. 'And they could be a huge new market for you. Why don't you buy the whole collection – there's three or four dozen in total – and hold an exhibition? I've got connections in the fashion press I can give you. It's a whole new field – one that's virtually untapped.'

They loved the idea and agreed they would pay £5,000 for my bags. 'But the deal is you don't get to come to the exhibition. We don't want anyone knowing where they came from.' I was too desperate to make the sale to argue but I was deeply hurt. It wasn't just my bags they were buying but my concept. There had never been an exhibition of handbags in London before, and I suppose they wanted the kudos of discovering and developing this new area. Even so, I'd thought we were friends.

Perhaps my face showed my feelings because a few weeks later they relented. 'You can come to the exhibition, but only if you promise not to tell anyone the bags were yours.'

'OK,' I said. It still didn't feel right. Needless to say, there was no mention of my name in the catalogue either. But the bags did what I wanted them to do, providing half the deposit I needed for my flat. I was able to move in soon after.

The further I got into the world of dealing, the more I realised my approach wasn't the norm. My motivation wasn't making money. I never went to a museum and wondered how much something was worth – it seemed almost sacrilegious to do so. When I looked at lovely things, I just thought, I want to get to the soul of the person who made this and understand something about them. I need to make a living, and eventually I'll pass them on and make a profit. If I could be the custodian of something that cost me very little, then that was part of the fun, but it wasn't the key. What did the object teach me about the human condition? What did it say about the ability of humankind to rise above avarice, cruelty and selfishness – to make beautiful things, to create, to care?

My knowledge grew, piecemeal, by buying whatever interested me. Things that I could afford and that others didn't want: wristwatches, Bakelite jewellery, crucifixes, tribal currency, tribal bangles. If someone said, 'No one wants those,' I'd think, I do. And amassing a collection propelled me to a greater understanding of the object and its place in society, because when you see a corpus of items, they start to make sense. You see how they developed, what they meant to a community, a society, an age.

Travel became an integral part of my trading life. Whether I was with friends or alone, I always felt especially comfortable in France, particularly in Paris. My interest in fashion echoed the national preoccupation. My style wasn't dissimilar to French tastes, and I blended in, whereas in England no dealers dressed like me. Paris inspired me. Its sinuous Métro signs, its elegant art deco bars, its street fashion, its hauteur, its markets, its minimalism, its extravagance – all of it seeped into my soul, enticing me to learn about an ever-widening range of objects.

I explored a different part of the city each time I went. I walked to most places, but if I wanted to venture further afield, I would sometimes take the Métro and get off at an unfamiliar place just to see what was there. On one of these forays, I emerged from the Métro and found myself in an unremarkable residential area. I walked on, hoping for shops or some point of interest, but nothing captured my attention. I was starting to think about heading back when the sound of music became audible above the buzz of passing cars and trucks. Perhaps there's a record shop nearby, I thought. Parisians love jazz – maybe I'll find a treasure trove of the vintage records I collect. I followed the music. Still no shops materialised, but I found myself standing in front of a break in the endless facade of apartments.

Set back from the street frontage stood a dilapidated theatre. The music was coming from within and something about the melody drew me towards it. I walked up the steps, through the open doors of the foyer, and into the auditorium where I could make out the backs of two people's heads. Other than them the theatre was deserted. The men were watching a woman on the stage. She had hair cropped short and bleached yellow-blonde. Presumably she was rehearsing for a performance that evening. Her voice, rich and mellifluous, was one I recognised: I'd lucked out, I realised with a shiver of excitement. She was a musical heroine of mine, one of the best post-war singers of all time. I silently took a seat and stayed there, hardly daring to move for the next hour while she practised song after song, including her stunning 'I'd Rather Go Blind'. I'd stumbled into a breathtaking rehearsal performance by the legendary Etta James.

As my interests expanded and my knowledge grew, I was drawn to works from the fifties, sixties and early seventies: things I couldn't sell to other dealers but that I felt would find an appreciative audience if they were properly presented. I took a share in a large stall at Alfie's and stocked it with Danish-, Scandinavian- and Italian-designed pieces, as well as the odd handbag and anything else that caught my eye.

One hot mid-summer afternoon I came back to the stand laden with finds from my weekly South of England run. I wasn't feeling my best, having driven for hours in a car with no air conditioning. My T-shirt felt damp, my trousers were creased. At the counter stood an elegant French woman with a pile of my stock around her. She was complaining loudly about the price of a bag. Initially I was all set to give her short shrift, but then I realised who it was: Catherine Deneuve, wearing no make-up but still looking beautiful. Since I've always had a soft spot for beauty of every variety, not to mention French cinema (plus it isn't every day you get to meet a screen goddess), I reined myself in – as best I could.

The bag she was looking at was made from crocodile skin; it resembled a miniature duffel bag and had been originally made to hold gentlemen's collars, although it would make a perfect ladies' handbag. The price, £80, was 'trop cher' she told my business partner.

'If that bag was in Maud Frizon it would be £1,000, and you think £80 too expensive?' I interjected.

'Who is this?' said Catherine, swivelling round, evidently bemused by my sudden appearance.

'Oh – he's just someone who brings stuff in,' said my partner dismissively.

'No,' I said, infuriated. 'I buy it all. And I've just come back with a carful now.'

She softened and raised an eyebrow. 'What have you bought? Any *bijouterie*?'

'Yes, as it happens. A wonderful RAF airman's diamond winged brooch. It's so romantic – an airman would have bought it for his sweetheart.'

'May I see?'

I took out the brooch, which was shaped like a circle with wings on either side, and placed it in her hand. '*C'est ravissante,*' she said, holding it to her shirt lapel. 'How much do you want for it?'

'It's platinum, set with diamonds, so I think £180 is a fair price for it,' I replied.

'*Trop cher,*' she said, pursing her lips.

'You think everything is *trop cher*,' I said, unable to contain my exasperation. 'In Asprey it would be £2,000.'

'Can't you do a better price?'

'Not really.'

'If you do a better price I will buy it.'

I smiled. 'I will do it for £160 – if you give me a kiss,' I said, testing my luck.

She threw her head back and laughed. 'OK.' She went to kiss me on the lips, but I turned my cheek before she made contact.

'We've got a deal,' I said.

'What do you have at home?' she asked.

'Amazing things.'

'Can I come and see?'

After that, whenever she came to London, Catherine Deneuve visited me at home, and when I was in Paris I often went to her home near Saint-Sulpice. She was a wonderful client and friend for many years, and introduced me to M. Hébé, a renowned collector whose apartment overlooked Notre-Dame. I remember the first time I went there: M. Hébé sat at a desk designed by Emile-Jacques Ruhlmann, with a life-size bronze feline by Bugatti striding past. He was surrounded with exquisite objects by Lalique and Maurice Marinot. A huge painting by Matisse hung on the wall – I felt I had entered a world of dream objects, beauty and creativity, to which I would always aspire.

When dealing was going well I would sometimes extend my trips to Paris and explore further afield in France with friends. One of the most memorable times was in the mid-1980s when I stayed at La Colombe D'Or, a hotel in the medieval hilltop town of Saint-Paul de Vence. During the Second World War the hotel was a popular refuge for artists and writers. Some paid their bill with paintings, and as a result there's an astonishing collection of works by luminaries like Picasso, Matisse, Léger, Braque and Chagall hanging on the walls. I was in the bar after dinner with a couple of friends when a man sitting at the bar signalled me over and asked me to have a drink with him. I told my friends I would meet them later – I'd recognised the man as one of my literary heroes, the writer James Baldwin. Jim, as he told me to call him, explained he had left the US for Paris as a young man and had lived in Saint-Paul de Vence since 1970. He asked me what I was doing in Vence and I explained I was an art dealer enjoying a few days' holiday. 'How do you find the French attitude towards you?'

I told him that I felt I was more readily accepted here than in England, partly because, from my experience, if the French saw you making an effort to integrate – in the way you dressed and attempted to speak their language – they were usually hospitable. He agreed, there was a tolerance here which he hadn't found in the US and that was why he had decided to settle here and become a transatlantic commuter. I told him I was a great admirer of his work and had read three of his books: *Go Tell It on the Mountain*, *Giovanni's Room* and *The Fire Next Time*. My favourite was the first. 'That's my favourite too,' he agreed.

We spent an hour talking, discussing black civil rights issues and his experiences as a black American. I felt honoured to be passing time with such a leviathan, although I had a feeling he was lonely.

Sometimes I went to Paris with Linda Rogers, a dealer friend who had been brought up in a family of jewellers. Linda said she'd tutor me in a subject about which I'd already gleaned some basic knowledge but wanted more. I understood construction, I recognised good craftsmanship from my model-making days, but Linda was a gemmologist and knew much more about gemstones than I did. She also had a wealth of connections in the cliquey world of vintage jewellery, and while we were browsing an antiques fair in Paris one day in the early eighties, she introduced me to an American friend, who wanted to meet me. 'Ronnie – meet Izzy Fischgang.'

'I've been watching you for a few months now,' said Izzy with a warm handshake and a shrewd gaze. 'I admire your style and the things you buy. I have a shop in New York, dealing in vintage jewellery. I have a proposition for you.'

Over a coffee he explained. 'I'd like you to buy for me. I'll give you £25,000 to spend on jewellery, and you can take 10 per cent. I'll pay all your expenses, and I don't mind where you stay when you come to New York. It's up to you.'

It didn't take me long to decide. 'That's a generous offer. Thank you, Izzy, I accept.'

I went back to London walking on air. James, my business partner, said he knew of Izzy Fischgang. His shop was on 47th Street, in the heart of the Diamond District, where about 90 per cent of New York's jewellery trading takes place. 'I went to visit him once, a year or two ago,' James said. 'The shop doesn't look much when you walk in, but he has an incredible stock. The back is crammed with huge safes full of jewels.'

A fortnight later I checked into New York's Plaza Hotel. 'When you get in, you must look up Alessandro Magliano,' James had said. 'You'll love him. He'll show you round and he'll really look after you – and I mean *really*,' and he'd given me a knowing look that I hadn't quite understood.

Telling myself I had nothing to lose, I phoned Alessandro, and told him I was a jewellery dealer and that James and I ran a business together. 'You are a friend of James's, you are a friend to me, Ronnie,' he said, in a strong Italian-American accent, and he invited me round for a drink the following afternoon.

His apartment was just a block from the Plaza, overlooking Central Park. I took the elevator up to the seventh floor and found myself in a vast space furnished in a glitzy style, with cut-glass chandeliers, French giltwood furniture, and brightly coloured porcelain on every surface. Alessandro greeted me. He was good-looking in a chiselled way, with a body like an ancient Greek statue: perfect and every bit as hard. He was also possibly the tallest man I'd ever met, standing at least 6 foot 8 inches. I'm not tall in stature and when he bent over to give me a hefty handshake I felt I was being dwarfed by a giant. We sat down and exchanged pleasantries about my visit. It was the first time I'd been to New York, I told him. He gave me a wolfish grin. 'Anything you want you just ask, I'll get my pets to look after you. But first, what will you have to drink?'

I wasn't sure what the reference to his 'pets' meant, and I didn't like to ask. 'A cup of tea, please,' I said.

Alessandro raised a wedge-shaped black eyebrow. 'You can have anything you want. Just ask.'

'Thanks, tea is just fine,' I replied, shifting a little on my gilded chair.

He clapped his hands and a minute later a woman appeared who looked as if she'd stepped out of a lingerie advertisement.

'Ronnie – meet Gina. She'll make you happy any way you want.'

'Hi, Gina.'

Gina gave me a toothy smile and waved a perfectly manicured hand at me. Lace and champagne silk fluttered. I smiled. 'Helloo, Ronnie,' she said with a smoky-voiced drawl. 'It's lovely to meet with you.'

'Likewise,' I said and looked at the table.

'He wants tea, babe. Will you get it for him? And I'll have the usual,' Alessandro said, an edge to his voice.

A few minutes later, Gina brought a tray set with tea and biscuits for me and a large glass of bourbon on the rocks for him. She handed Alessandro his drink, poured my tea, then glanced back at Alessandro who jerked his head at the door. 'See you later, Ronnie,' she said, before sashaying out.

I stirred my tea, conscious of Alessandro watching me. 'So you're buying for Izzy Fischgang, James tells me?'

'That's right.'

'Well – as I said, I know a lot of people in this town. You need anything, diamonds, sapphires, rubies, you just shout.'

'That's really very kind of you,' I said. 'But I've brought stock with me from Europe.' This wasn't entirely true. I planned to trawl New York's jewellers the following day, but some gut instinct told me I would be better off without his assistance.

We made polite conversation about how he knew James, and half an hour later I stood up to leave.

'Say, why don't you join us for dinner tomorrow? It's a family party. Nothing fancy. I'll pick you up at seven. No excuses.'

'Thanks – that sounds great.'

'How about company tonight? Say the word and I'll send a pet round to take care of you.'

The thought of ruby-nailed Gina or one of her colleagues was the last thing I wanted. 'Thank you – that's kind, but I'm tired after the flight,' I said. I wished I didn't have to join him for dinner, but it was awkward to refuse both offers, and I felt I'd ended up with the least precarious option.

★

The next day I'd decided to explore 47th Street and its jewellery shops before going to see Izzy. The area was dominated by Jewish merchants; Orthodox Jews dressed in black overcoats and fedoras hurried past, or stood huddled in groups on the street, briefcases tightly clutched in their hands, and I heard Yiddish and Hebrew spoken almost as often as English. I chose a promising-looking shop and entered. The shopkeeper, a tall bespectacled gentleman with a long black beard, took one look at me, then pressed a bell that sounded in the back room and scuttled out from behind his counter. He took up position standing in front of it, legs braced, eyeing me, as if he expected me to cosh him at any second. In their eyes, a young black man wasn't a regular visitor in this part of town – unless he meant trouble.

'What d'ya want?' he said, as another stocky figure materialised in the doorway to the back storeroom, and sidled up next to him to form a human wall between me and the counter, in which the jewellery was displayed.

'I'd just like to take a look at what you've got,' I said. 'I'm interested in pieces by Cartier, Chaumet, Asprey.'

'Sure you are.' Neither man moved.

'I'm buying for Izzy Fischgang.'

The men's shoulders dropped; their defensive stance relaxed. 'You're buying for Izzy? Why didn't you say so?' They stepped away so that I had a clear view of the jewellery display under the glass counter. The stocky man shook my hand and introduced himself. 'Come in the back and we'll fix you a drink and something to eat. So, you're not from round here?'

'No, London.'

'London! Would you like some champagne, smoked salmon, caviar?'

It was the same story every time I entered a shop. As an unfamiliar mixed-race man, I'd be greeted with hostility and suspicion until I mentioned Izzy's name. Then everything changed, and I'd be offered VIP treatment and whatever I wanted. I hadn't experienced prejudice like this when I'd travelled on the continent and I still recall how unprepared I was for it.

I took the stock I'd bought to Izzy, then went back to the hotel in time to get ready for the evening outing with Alessandro. James had just flown in and joined the party. We drove over the Brooklyn Bridge, crossing the East River, then took a turn towards a parade of shops and cafes. We stopped outside an Italian restaurant, which had a terrace that overlooked the water and the twinkling lights of Manhattan beyond. The restaurant was packed, but Alessandro was obviously a regular, and as we were ushered to a large round table by the window, people nodded in recognition or raised a hand in greeting.

Four or five people were already seated at the table. Introductions were made. The atmosphere seemed relaxed as the wine flowed and the food was brought out. Alessandro, the benevolent host, sat opposite me. Gina and James were seated between us. Alessandro was regaling his guests with an anecdote about various people I didn't know. He repeated a conversation he'd had with someone called Marvin, when Gina laughed and intervened. 'No, honey, Marvin didn't say that. Don't you remember – it was Chuck.'

Alessandro shot her a quizzical look but didn't respond.

With quiet deliberation he dabbed his mouth with his napkin and stood up. Standing to one side of her he drew back his right hand and slapped her, hard, across the left side of her face. The blow came without warning, and with great force. Her head whipped diagonally back. In that second she looked like a smashed doll and I thought he'd broken her neck. The conversation dried up immediately. Gina didn't cry out or touch her face. She just sat there looking at him, round-eyed, as an angry red welt appeared on her left cheek and a silent tear rolled over it. As the blow had connected, I'd noticed many of the men seated elsewhere in the restaurant swiftly reach inside their jacket pockets. The atmosphere was intense. I sensed it wasn't the first time something like this had happened, and I felt as if I was taking part in a gangster movie. Then someone said, 'Cool it, everyone, let's have more wine,' and the conversation bubbled up again as if nothing out of the ordinary had happened.

But the brutality of the incident shook me. Physical violence had repelled me ever since my unhappy childhood. I had experienced too much of it then, and I didn't want to be around people who thought it was the norm now. James saw Gina whenever he was in town, and she visited him later that evening. In the morning I asked after her. James assured me that she was fine. Sadly, I concluded Alessandro's assault wasn't anything out of the ordinary for her.

I returned to New York regularly after that first visit and always stayed at the Plaza or the Waldorf Hotel. But I never again contacted Alessandro. James didn't share my antipathy. If I visited with him, he always insisted on contacting Alessandro, and invariably a couple of his 'pets' came round to see

James, who would send one on to me. I'd buy the girls drinks on Alessandro's account and chat to them, but nothing more ever happened. In the morning, over breakfast, the girls would tease me, because all I'd done was talk. I let them laugh. As I saw it, becoming beholden to Alessandro was a far more terrifying fate than their jibes. I'd had a lucky escape. They were less fortunate.

New York didn't have the monopoly on unsavoury characters. Plenty skulked the corridors of London's art and antiques world too, but through my dealings with Izzy and James's transactions with Alessandro, America infiltrated my life on both sides of the Atlantic. The main difference was that in London I felt at home, so I was more gullible: if I crossed paths with someone I liked, I treated them as my friend, until they proved otherwise. Usually, I escaped unscathed. Sometimes I didn't.

When James and I decided the gallery in Montpelier Walk wasn't earning its keep, we gave up the lease, took a large stand in Grays Antique Market in its place, and joined forces with a third partner, Peter Kleiner. Peter was James's friend, a charming ex-public-school boy who dealt in jewellery and art deco works of art. At the time I was amassing a collection of wristwatches. For safekeeping I stored them in a safe deposit box at Selfridges, along with other items I didn't want to sell immediately. From time to time Peter also had items of jewellery that he held back for special clients, and so he offered to share the expense of the box with me. Every month or so I would place a few watches in the safe deposit box, storing them in a special jeweller's roll, and adding them to the inventory I kept.

Peter's jewellery was stored in a separate roll, so there was no confusion.

For me this was a frantically busy time, travelling to Paris, Brussels, Amsterdam and New York to buy and sell, as well as scouting the big antiques markets and fairs throughout the country for stock. On top of that I was still taking on DJing jobs and the occasional hairdressing assignment. As a result, I didn't get round to checking my stock each time I visited the box. I just put whatever I had in an empty pouch, or a box of some sort, and kept an inventory, so I knew exactly what was there.

Six months or so went by. I was planning a trip to Paris and decided I would take a rare Louis Vuitton crocodile gentleman's case, fitted with silver and enamelled bottles, to sell to Annette. I'd bought the case several months earlier and had left it in the box for safekeeping. I went to Selfridges, found our box, and unlocked it. Peter's roll lay next to mine. Underneath was the cardboard box in which I'd stored the Louis Vuitton case. I moved the jewellery to one side, and took out the cardboard box. It felt lighter than I remembered. That's odd, I thought, as I lifted the lid.

The box was empty. The case I'd left there three months earlier had vanished. I stared blankly at the evidence in front of me, thinking I must be dreaming. Half in a daze, I untied my jewellery roll and started looking through the pouches. The first pouch I opened contained a metal watch strap. The next a valueless piece of jewellery that I didn't recognise. My heart plummeted as one by one I opened each pouch, only to discover either a piece of worthless junk or nothing at all inside. The Rolex, Cartier and Patek Philippe watches that should have been there had vanished along with the Louis Vuitton case. In a roll that should have contained thirty-five to forty watches, just two or three remained. I stood there frozen, trying to process what had happened. My thoughts were racing incoherently: who had done this? It couldn't have been Peter. Could it? If not Peter then who? He was the only person with access to the box apart from me. But he was my business partner, a friend, a public-school boy. He'd been at Gordonstoun with Prince Charles! He was a respectable dealer.

Wasn't he?

I took out his roll and opened it – inside was a further unwelcome revelation. Every glinting emerald bracelet, every sapphire ring or ruby necklace was cheap paste. With hands now trembling so wildly I had difficulty coordinating them, I took both the rolls and put them in my briefcase and slammed the lid closed. Leaving the empty safe deposit box open on the table, I pressed the buzzer and signalled to the security guard outside to let me out. As I left I handed the key to him. 'I won't be needing the box any more,' I said, mumbling my words with the emotion of this discovery.

I headed straight to Grays, walking blindly through the crowds of Oxford Street and South Molton Street, my mind still scrambling to assemble some sort of reasonable explanation for the disappearance of so many valuable watches.

'Where's Peter?' I asked James when I arrived.

He was polishing a Dunhill lighter. He looked up. 'Pass. Why? What's up? You look weird. Has something happened?'

'I've just been to my box at Selfridges. My watches have disappeared,' I said. 'Peter wouldn't have taken them would he?'

A pained look flickered in James's eye. He carried on

polishing the Dunhill, avoiding meeting my gaze. There was a long silence. 'James. Please tell me the truth. You know something, don't you?'

'Sorry, Ronnie. But it's common knowledge that Peter has a serious coke habit. I thought it was risky you two sharing a box, but I didn't want to interfere.'

'Oh my God!' I said, scarcely able to take in what I was hearing. 'You knew, didn't you? All along, you knew, and you didn't warn me?'

He swallowed. There was an uncomfortable silence. 'Some of them are pawned at Suttons,' he said eventually. 'You'll be able to get them back.'

I shook my head in disbelief. 'That makes it OK, does it?' He didn't reply.

I tried to contact Peter but he never took my calls. A week later James handed me some pawnbroker tickets for ten of the missing watches. Suttons demanded £6,000 to relinquish them to me. I paid up and made no profit from their eventual sale, to say nothing of the lost items. Every time I saw Peter Kleiner afterwards he sprinted in the opposite direction. I later heard he'd died from a drug overdose. I was sad to hear this as we'd once been friends, but my sorrow was still confusingly laced with hurt at the dishonest way he'd behaved.

Emporio Armani had by now recruited me (in a freelance capacity) to buy vintage watches, fountain pens and cufflinks to supply their shops worldwide. I was scouting for them at Portobello one day when a dealer I knew showed me a watch. It was what's known as a tonneau shape, with curved sides, designed to elegantly contour the wrist. The shape alone made the watch rare, but what propelled it into a different sphere was the fact that it was a single-button chronometer, so all the functions – stop, start and wind – operated from one button. The watch dated from the mid-1920s. It wasn't signed on the dial, but as soon as I examined the movement and saw 'EWC' I felt the hairs on the back of my neck prickle: I recognised it as an incredibly rare Cartier model.

The dealer had paid £50 for it but he was now asking £1,000 and wouldn't budge. He had shown it to a few people in the trade but no one would give him the profit he wanted. That didn't put me off: I desperately wanted to buy it – at retail it was worth around £30,000, I reckoned. The only problem was, I was short of cash.

I went to see a friend, with whom I sometimes shared expensive pieces. I explained I needed £1,000 fast. 'OK, Ronnie,' she said, 'but I want 10 per cent of the profit, and you must promise you won't hold on to it – you will sell straightaway, so I get my money back.' I agreed to the terms, feeling reasonably confident. There was a watch sale coming up at Bonhams, all the big international dealers would be there, so I would easily sell it on.

But when I showed the watch to the trade and told them I'd accept £2,000, they all quibbled about the fact the dial wasn't signed. Undeterred, I tried to contact Harry Fane and Mark Shand, high-end dealers in St James's, to whom I often sold top-quality pieces. However, as bad luck would have it, they were abroad. I took a Polaroid of the watch and put it through their door with a note and waited to hear back. Nothing. Conscious of the outstanding debt I needed to repay, and not wanting to renege on my agreement to sell quickly, I took the watch to New York on my next trip and showed it to Izzy Fischgang. It would be worth £30,000 on the retail market, I told him; I only wanted £2,000. 'I don't know anything about watches, but I trust you, Ronnie, so I'll pay you your price,' he said and handed me a roll of cash.

He sold the watch a few years later for $75,000. I still see Harry occasionally and he has always regretted not getting back to me sooner. That was the last deal I ever did with Izzy; sadly he's dead now, but he lives on as a legend in the jewellery trade.

I met Mick the Murderer (so called by a few people in the trade because of his aggressive manner) and his son Elliot at Camden Lock in the nineties. The pair had emerged from nowhere as dealers in luggage. They had some good-quality stock on their stall, and I was interested in a vellum attaché case they were selling. I asked them the price and tried to negotiate. 'Fuck off,' was the unceremonious reply.

'That's a bit aggressive!'

'We don't want the likes of you slagging off our stuff.'

'I wasn't slagging it off – just trying to negotiate.'

'Well, don't. Now we've told you once already – fuck right off.'

The animosity continued. Every time I saw them, which was fairly regularly, since they also had a stall in Antiquarius, I would be subjected to a barrage of abuse, often racist. When I asked around I discovered they were rude to everyone, so I didn't take it too personally – although it didn't make it any more acceptable.

I was wandering round Antiquarius one morning when I

bumped into Mick. 'Fuck off out of here,' he said by way of greeting.

I'd been to the antiques fair at Kempton early that morning and I was feeling tired, but Mick's uncalled-for aggression woke me up. 'What did you say?'

'You heard.'

'I used to have stalls here. You can't talk to me like that.'

'I can – now get lost. We don't want your sort in here.'

I'd let this go unchallenged for too long. I decided it was time to call a halt. 'Mick, if you want me to fuck off, let's go outside. Because I can't do this every time I encounter you. I'm in this business, whether you like it or not. And I'm free to go where I like. So if you're not happy about it, let's go outside and sort it.'

'OK. Come on then,' he said. He leered at me with an unpleasant gleam in his eye. He was about 5 foot 11, at least four inches taller than me, probably three stone heavier, solidly built, but I wasn't going to let that get in the way of resolving matters. Rage had made me fearless.

We went out of the door leading on to Flood Street at the side of the building. A few people who had overheard the altercation followed. I stood facing Mick, my hands in the back pockets of my jeans. A sense of calm had come over me. I was deadly focused. I didn't care if I lived or died, I was sick of his bullying and I'd prove my point whatever the outcome.

'Now you just tell me what you said in there, and see if you can make me do it, if that's what you want,' I said. Then I braced myself and waited for him to try and hit me.

Nothing happened. He didn't reply, and as I stared at him his face turned ashen and his nasty smile faded. Instead of lashing out as I'd expected, he just stood there, mute. His arms and legs had started visibly shaking. After a minute or two he shook his head, spat on the pavement, and shuffled away.

Someone patted me on the shoulder. 'Well done, Ronnie.' The crowd dispersed. I thought that was the end of it, and got on with my day.

Two weeks later I was back at Kempton. I arrived at 5.45 a.m., ready for the doors opening at 6 a.m. Not long after I got into the first hall I saw Mick and Elliot walking towards me, a look of intent on their faces. 'Fucking n*****,' Mick said when he got close. Oh God, here we go, I thought.

Mick swung a punch at me. I dodged and instinctively returned a blow that connected with his jaw. As I did that I was aware that Elliot was bouncing around like a trained boxer. He was shorter than his father but still taller than me, and stocky. But my attention was mainly focused on watching Mick, so when Elliot threw a punch, it took me by surprise. He hit me square on the jaw, splitting my lip. I was about to retaliate with a swing at him when an arm came round from behind, yanking me back out of reach. A third member of their party – a man I hadn't recognised – was also joining the attack. Holding my neck in a vice-like grip he forced me down to the ground. Now I was lying on my back, across his body, pinioned, so the other two could work me over. Expletives poured out of the three of them in a torrent. 'We're going to fucking do you, n*****!' Mick shouted. 'You fucking black c***. Think you got the better of me? Think again, you bastard.' Meanwhile he and his son did their best to stamp on my face, kick me in the stomach and boot me between my legs. I'm going to die here unless I fight for my life, I thought.

I fought back as I never have before or since. I thrashed my legs, kicking out at their shins, grabbing their feet whenever they came anywhere near my face, elbowing the guy under me as brutally as I was able. He let go and I scrambled to my feet. The three of them couldn't take any more and ran off. I gave chase. They saw me and yelled some further expletives at me, waving their fists, and headed for the exit. And at that point I suppose shock or self-preservation must have taken over and I let them go.

I'd lost my hat and bag in the fracas and went back to the scene of the attack to retrieve them. People were still milling around and looked at me with open curiosity. Someone had my belongings and passed them to me. My head was buzzing with the attack I'd survived, but when I surveyed the crowd, a surge of despair swamped me. My mouth was bleeding, my neck hurt. I had some bruises and grazes, but the fact I wasn't badly injured was no thanks to anyone here. I could have been seriously injured, maimed or killed while they just stood by, watching an innocent man being lynched, doing nothing.

'Three against one – why didn't you help me?' I said, emotion welling audibly in my voice.

'We thought you'd nicked something,' someone said. I shook my head, incredulous. I wanted to ask them, if they'd seen three black men jump on a white man, would they have stood by? But why bother – I already knew the answer.

Word spread. As I walked around a few of my friends came up and commiserated. 'Who are these people? We'll go and get them,' someone offered. The sentiments helped restore my battered sense of justice, but I didn't condone retaliatory violence.

'No,' I said. 'That's not the way to deal with it.'

Later that day I went to Chelsea police station and asked for the detective inspector. A female officer appeared and when I said I wanted to report an assault she took me to an interview room. Her manner seemed sympathetic. I explained what had happened and told her I knew the names of two of my attackers and that their business address was in Antiquarius. As well as the physical assault I had also been subjected to racial abuse. I had witnesses who would corroborate my story.

The DI's eyes narrowed. 'Were your attackers white?'

'Yes. All three of them.'

She nodded and looked at me evenly, as if I were a piece of evidence. 'I can see you are injured, and I don't doubt your story, but I have to tell you that the Crown Prosecution Service will never take up the case, because the chances of conviction are minimal.'

'But there were witnesses to the attack. I can identify them.'

'I don't doubt it. But I'm sorry to say that if they are white and have a business in Chelsea, no jury would accept your version of events and convict them against you.'

Her polite sympathy combined with her unequivocal acceptance of the situation amplified my sense of outrage. What sort of society can condone an innocent man being beaten and refuse to bring the perpetrators to justice because of the colour of their skin? Numb with disillusionment, I sat there, not knowing what to say. The DI did her best to console me. But her verdict that I would never win a case against the thugs was utterly immutable. I'd have to put the attack down to experience and live with the injustice. To attempt any form of legal redress through the courts would be pointless.

I walked away from the police station weighed down by the realisation that even here in London, racial equality was a chimera. Justice was moulded by prejudice, slanted against the likes of me. Until that changed I had no option but unwillingly to follow her advice.

19

A Keith Murray Vase

If I had to list my top twenty favourite objects, I think a Keith Murray vase would probably make the grade. But it's not just the pots he created, rather his wide-ranging talents that I admire, because Murray had an incredibly varied career. Born in New Zealand, he trained as an architect in England, after serving as a fighter pilot in the First World War. After qualifying, he struggled to find work and so turned his attention to glass, ceramic and silver design. His vases were first made when Wedgwood employed him as a freelancer in the 1930s. At the time the company was experiencing serious financial difficulty. Some say they avoided ruin only because Murray's designs attracted new style-conscious young buyers with a taste for modernism.

Murray's vases always draw the eye. Whether ovoid, bomb shaped, flying saucer shaped or tall and tapering in form, they have a powerful, innovative simplicity. Decoration is pared down to basics. Ribbed panels emphasise structural contour, and single-colour glazes in subdued hues of cream, moonstone and green amplify the sense of restraint. The rarest vases of all, and to my mind among the most stylish examples of English modernism, are those in black and brown basalt signed in red. I'm always on the lookout for such examples.

I've admired Murray's vases ever since I started to take an interest in modernism, but the connection between them and my visit to Zimbabwe and South Africa is perhaps less obvious . . .

Apartheid has both appalled and fascinated me ever since I was a teenager. Brought up in England, my experience of racial integration, whether in institutions, foster families, school or the workplace, was broadly positive. Yes, I had frequently encountered racism from the police, and had grown to expect it. Further incidents had taken place but, weighed against them, the support and guidance of friends such as Jo and Huw and the Hoads allowed me to write them off as aberrations rather than pervasive norms. Travel through Europe and America hadn't greatly altered my view that most white people would be friendly towards me if I was friendly to them. So the notion of a country whose legal system was underpinned by racial segregation, where white supremacists forced black people to live separately, in subjugation, in their native country, and denied them the right to use the same facilities and amenities as whites, seemed to me to belong to a dystopian novel rather than reality. Could such a place exist in the world I knew? What was it like? I wanted to find out the truth.

In 1984 the opportunity arose. Jo's brother, Roger, invited me to stay with him at his home in Harare, the capital of Zimbabwe. He was going through a difficult time. His marriage had broken down, but he and his wife were still living together, while future living arrangements were made. It would be good to have a friend around to be a mediator, he told me on the phone.

'If you're sure I won't be in the way?'

'No, truly – you might dilute the tension, if you can bear it.'

Roger was a language officer for the British Council. Prior to his posting in Zimbabwe, he had worked in Nigeria for several years. By staying with him I would gain the insider's view of the country – albeit a view filtered through the life of a privileged white man. Staying with Roger would also allow me to travel into South Africa to see for myself what the country was really like. It would be an expensive trip – tickets to Zimbabwe weren't cheap in those days – but I was confident I would be able to cover the costs by seeking out some top-quality pieces of African art, a growing interest of mine. I knew my experience as a black man would be different from Roger's, but I didn't anticipate quite how extensive the differences would be.

It was an interesting time to visit Harare, a tipping point in the relationship between the old colonial and new independent regimes. Robert Mugabe, head of the ZANU-PF party, had been prime minister since independence was granted in 1980. But Ian Smith, the white former prime minister, who had led the country during the transition period, was still leader of the opposition and a fierce critic of the changes being implemented. How would this new era manifest itself to a black British visitor? I was curious, if nervous, to find out.

Roger lived in a comfortable leafy suburb made up of spacious single-storey houses with large shady verandas and gardens blooming with tropical plants. His work provided him with a Land Rover and a Zimbabwean driver called Oliver, and we soon settled into a comfortable routine. Every morning after breakfast we would set off for a different institution where Roger needed to supervise the teaching. We would drop him off and Oliver was then at my disposal until whatever time Roger needed to be collected later in the day.

Some of the colleges Roger supervised were in remote villages deep in the bush. Waiting for the doors to open at seven-thirty or eight in the morning, the assembled students would gather in the yard or grounds in small groups and sing, in exquisite harmonies, pieces as beautiful and pure as anything you'd hear in the Royal Albert Hall or at St Paul's Cathedral. The students could have been singing Western classical choral pieces, but they sang without direction, in such an effortlessly natural way, simply to pass the time before lessons. It made me realise the parallels between the aural traditions of African and Western music and understand that people from separate environments may have many unexpected cultural crossovers. It was the most beautiful expression of human spirit.

I had never been in a tropical country before, let alone experienced anything like the Zimbabwean bush, with its sweeping horizon and vast unpopulated spaces in which animals roamed freely. It was a steep learning curve, and there was so much to absorb and take in. As a black tourist, people viewed me as a novelty. Wherever we went, people were as curious about me as I was about them. Despite the fact I had taken great care to wear nothing that might attract attention, I didn't look like a black Zimbabwean, and nor – obviously – was I white. I stood out. Where did I come from? What was I doing?

Oliver was the best guide I could have asked for. He knew

everyone, and he was open and happy to talk about his life in Zimbabwe. Sometimes he took me to townships and introduced me to his friends and family, sometimes we drove out into the bush to safari parks. Once when we were in a park, he stopped the car so that I could watch a herd of zebra grazing. In the distance a pair of giraffes slowly meandered through a thicket of thorn trees. I was mesmerised and wanted to get closer. I got out of the car and started walking towards them. Oliver probably thought I wanted to relieve myself and didn't say anything. But when I kept on walking away from the Land Rover he must have realised my intentions and panicked. What if a lion or a hyena or a buffalo should see me? He threw open the door and rushed after me, shouting crossly that I should get back in the car. 'It's not safe, Mr Ronnie,' he said. 'The animals here – lion, leopard, hyena, buffalo, crocodile, hippo – they can be very dangerous.'

I couldn't ignore the cultural chasms. One day Oliver took me to the Eastern Highlands, a spectacular mountain area on the border of Zimbabwe and Mozambique. The climate here was cooler and damper than Harare, and I was fascinated by the colonial architecture of the Leopard Rock Hotel, with its towers and terraces that looked as if they could have been transported directly from the Highlands of Scotland. When we stopped for lunch Oliver didn't join me and the waiter who served me was clearly astonished to see a black man seated at a table. He treated me with such deference, as if I were a god rather than another human, so that eventually I said, 'You don't need to call me "sir" all the time.' But that only made things worse: he looked as though he would burst into tears.

★

Bulawayo is the second largest city in Zimbabwe. I'd heard Roger's friends talk about it often and someone said it had interesting Victorian architecture and a museum I could visit. I asked Roger if it was safe for me to go. There had been reports of military activity in the area due to civil unrest between the Shona people, supporters of Mugabe's ZANU-PF party, and the minority Ndebele, who supported the opposition ZAPU party. 'You'll be fine,' Roger said airily. 'But it's a five-hour trip to get there, so take my car, and drive yourself.'

It was early afternoon by the time I arrived to find the streets teeming with a sea of uniformed and heavily armed African military. I would later understand that this army presence was responsible for *Gukurahundi* – a Shona term meaning 'early rain that washes away the chaff' – the massacres and atrocities perpetrated by army loyalists against the local people from 1983 to 1987. There was no one, black or white, in civilian dress anywhere to be seen.

I parked the car and walked slowly along a main street. I felt myself being scrutinised by what seemed like a thousand soldiers and my head tingled with apprehension. The atmosphere felt almost palpably threatening. All the shops and public buildings looked shuttered. A few minutes of walking around was enough. This plainly wasn't a safe place to explore with a camera around my neck, and there was nothing to visit anyway. It would only be a matter of time before someone pounced and asked my business. And then what? I swivelled round, carefully avoiding looking directly at anyone, and walked purposefully back to the car.

Driving through the outskirts of Bulawayo I saw huge clouds piled up in the distance – mounds of grey and white contrasted against a vivid blue sky. A pewter triangle of falling rain misted the horizon. Thunder rumbled far away, and the occasional flash of forked lightning flared. A tropical storm was coming, and it looked like a big one. Not wanting to be caught by a Zimbabwean tempest any more than by the Zimbabwean military, I pressed down hard on the accelerator and raced north as fast as the bumpy roads would allow, determined to keep ahead of the storm. I was conscious that if it caught me and I had to stop, I might draw the attention of an army patrol and place myself in a vulnerable situation. I don't know what damage I did to the car's suspension, but I got back to the sanctuary of Harare just as the first fat drops streaked the dusty windscreen like tears.

A few days later I'd arranged to spend a couple of nights visiting the Victoria Falls, one of the seven natural wonders of the world. 'Local Kololo tribesmen call it Mosi-oa-Tunya – "the Smoke that Thunders". You will see why,' Oliver said, smiling.

I booked myself into the Victoria Falls Hotel, an atmospheric colonial building that dates from the early years of the twentieth century, built originally to provide accommodation for workers on the Cape to Cairo Railway commissioned by Cecil Rhodes. The railway was never completed, but ever since the first trains brought visitors from Cape Town in 1913, Victoria Falls became a key tourist destination and the hotel flourished.

I checked in to my room and then, drawn by the thunderous sound of the nearby falls, I decided to explore. In those days there were few readily available guides, and no organised tours around the falls: in fact, I saw very few other visitors.

Colonies of potentially aggressive baboons squatted in the undergrowth near the path. Some carried babies slung under their stomachs, some had them clinging on their backs. Remembering the warnings I'd been given ('Don't try to touch or feed them, sir,' the hotel doorman had said), I didn't stop; instead, picking up my pace, with my eyes fixed ahead, I followed the track to the falls.

Guidebooks tell you that the falls measure more than 5,600 feet wide, and that they are the world's largest sheet of falling water, forming the border between Zambia and Zimbabwe. But nothing really prepares you for their immensity, or what you feel the first time you take in the spectacle of a huge river, a mile wide, plummeting into an abyss to a boiling torrent 350 feet down. Nor can you imagine the great column of spray shooting upwards into the air – more than 2,500 feet high at certain times of the year.

I was soaked by the spray within seconds, but I didn't care. I was utterly mesmerised and wanted to capture every view, every angle I could. I stopped on bridges and in the bends of the track, clothes drenched, taking photographs with a misted lens, trying to imprint this incredible phenomenon in my memory, so that it would always remain there. I must have succeeded because I have never forgotten my sense of awe, nor my amazement at seeing for the first time a multitude of completely circular rainbows. They weren't rainbows, I would tell everyone for years to come, they were rain circles.

I decided to fill the second day with a hike along the Zambian side of the river. I was due to leave the following morning and as a final highlight of my trip I'd planned an aeroplane flight that evening. It was going to be a hot day, so I took what I thought were appropriate precautions. I wore a singlet, shorts, hiking boots and a cap and took with me a single bottle of water, a bottle of mosquito spray and my camera.

From the hotel I took the road that leads to the main bridge crossing over the river. From there I climbed down a creeper-and-foliage-covered rockface, my face pressed against the rocks, with the thundering water to my right. Near the bottom of the gorge, the incline wasn't so steep, and I was able to walk carefully forward, with the water to my left, crossing rocks before I reached a section of river, then known as the Devil's Punchbowl. The sun was already high in the sky, and the river coiled ahead, like a fat serpent. I was sweating profusely. I knew there were dangers in this solitary excursion, and I would have been safer with a guide, had one been available, but I told myself I was fit and strong, and I'd be able to defend myself should I need to do so.

I was picking my way along the bank of the Zambezi when, twenty metres ahead, I spotted a crocodile lazing on the bank. I froze. He was at least five metres long and a metre wide, immobile, one glassy yellow eye open. His head was facing the path, towards me, his tail just brushing the water's edge. Some-where a parakeet screamed. Large insects danced in the air around my head. I waved them away, wondering what I should do. Did the crocodile know I was there? Could he smell me? More importantly, was he hungry? Pulses of trepidation coursed through my veins as the realisation dawned that I was an interloper here. But I wasn't going to give up on the chance to trek along the Zambezi. As I stood watching, the crocodile flicked his serrated tail and slid back into the water. Heart racing, I turned to my right and scrambled through some undergrowth for a few metres until I found another path, parallel to the river but a safer distance from the water's edge.

From the safety of the forest path, I spotted five or six more huge crocodiles sunning themselves on the bank. Then a colony of fifteen or so small vervet monkeys appeared, swinging and playing in the trees above my head. They had a kittenish look about them and leapt closer and closer, as if they wanted to make contact, but each time I reached towards them they leapt away. I was lucky they did so: I found out later they are carriers of rabies, and had they bitten me I would have needed urgent medical attention.

A short way on a boy of about fourteen was sitting on top of a high, smooth rock on the edge of the river, fishing. He looked at me as I passed, his expression openly curious. I suppose a black tourist walking alone in the jungle was as remarkable to him as the sight of a five-metre croc to me.

I was beginning to think about turning back in good time for my flight when through the trees I glimpsed a bend in the river and a crescent of ochre sand edging the water. A white man walked slowly along the strand, stooped over as if searching for something he'd lost. Curious as to what he was doing I went over and introduced myself. He told me he was an archaeologist and that primitive Palaeolithic and Neolithic people had inhabited this region more than 10,000 years ago. They had manufactured tools from flint or stone to skin and scrape the hides of animals they caught. The sandy beach was a good place to unearth them. He showed me some of his finds, and we discussed archaeology for about half an hour.

I suddenly remembered my flight. Anxious not to miss it

I said a hurried goodbye. 'Here, take these as a souvenir,' the archaeologist said, handing me two of the flint tools he had found.

Realising I would miss the flight unless I made up time, I ran back along the track. The sun was still high, it was an oppressively hot afternoon, and very quickly my water supply ran out. I jogged on regardless, increasingly parched as the sun beat down and the skin on my shoulders blistered.

I made it to the airstrip with minutes to spare and took my seat on the plane. Almost immediately the propellors started to build up speed and we taxied out onto the airstrip. We circled the falls, then meandered up and down river in a wider circuit. I looked down on a large herd of zebra and gazelle grazing on the grassy plain. A huge bull elephant stranded on Livingstone Island flapped his ears, showering himself with dust; a family of hippopotami wallowed nearby. I saw the vivid red blooms of the flamboyant trees and the tiled roof of the hotel and then the great schism in the earth into which the Zambezi plummets to create the mighty falls. Dehydration was making my head spin, my stomach felt nauseous, the skin on my shoulders was raw, but looking down on this panorama, discomfort was overlaid by exultation. I could understand why settlers who saw Africa for the first time fell so deeply in love with it. For a moment the thought came that my mother's heritage linked me to this continent, but my feelings towards her were tainted and the pride I felt in the connection was fleeting.

One of the first questions I'd asked Roger when I arrived was if he thought it was safe for me to travel alone to South Africa.

'No problem if you go by bus – people come and go all the time. But don't drive. There are always police checkpoints. They want you to pay bribes and it can be risky if you don't. Don't forget South Africa isn't like Zim – you can't stay in a white hotel. You'll have to find a multiracial one. I'll help you if you want.' Roger also explained the importance of my British passport. 'Keep it safe at all times. And keep copies as an insurance,' he said. I listened and followed his advice. I hid copies of my passport anywhere I could think of: in my shoes, pockets and the lining of my bag. And then at last I was ready for the journey of discovery that for years I'd dreamt of making.

It's a twenty-hour journey by bus to Johannesburg, and from there another bus and another eight hours gets you to Durban. The first bus left Harare in the early afternoon, taking the A4 highway, a bumpy thoroughfare that despite its name consisted of two strips of concrete, with just dirt in the middle. On either side of the route there were cultivated areas of farmland, fields of tobacco, maize, sorghum, sugarcane, cotton and beans, and groves of oranges and banana. In between, tracts of bushland stretched to the horizon. Some of the bush was open scrub and grassland, some was punctuated with thickets in which baobab trees – squat yet weirdly jagged in form – reared up from the blur of surrounding undergrowth.

My fellow passengers were mainly black South Africans and Zimbabweans, travelling to visit friends and family, interspersed with a handful of whites. Across the aisle sat a blond-haired blue-eyed backpacker. He told me his name was Matt, and like me he came from England. He had relatives in Cape Town and was on his way to stay with them. It was the first time either of us had visited South Africa and we talked about apartheid. 'I'm horrified by the system, so I'm going to document my experiences and write about them when I get back,' Matt said. 'People in the UK need to do more to protest or the inhumanities will continue.'

I told him I shared his interest and his outrage, and that the purpose of my trip was also to discover the truth about apartheid – although I would leave the writing and changing the world to him. I just wanted to talk to the local people, find out what they thought, and tell them about the culture I came from. Matt would be coming back to Harare on the same bus I'd booked onto, and we agreed we'd share notes on our return journey.

It was dark by the time we reached Beitbridge, where a bridge spanning the Limpopo marks the border with South Africa. 'Everyone out of the bus to clear immigration,' the driver said.

A cheerful Zimbabwean official examined my passport, scribbled something, stamped it a couple of times and waved me through. On the South African side, it was a different story. The scrutiny was intense – suspicions about a black man with a British passport were overt. Why did I want to visit South Africa? Where was I staying? What was I taking with me? The contents of my case were sifted through. Their manner gave me cause for concern, but I wasn't unduly troubled. Officials are not representative of an entire country, I told myself, thinking of my experiences with the Metropolitan Police. Just because they are unfriendly doesn't mean everyone will be the same.

Eventually I was cleared and re-joined the bus. I was the last to do so, all the other passengers had been processed before me.

By now it was after midnight. I reclined my seat and fell into a deep fitful sleep, dimly aware of the bus stopping now and again and people getting on and off. At dawn, when I next came to properly, the bus had reached Pretoria. I got off, stretched, bought something to eat, then took my seat again. It was lunchtime when we finally disembarked at Johannesburg.

I had two hours to kill before the bus to Durban. I said goodbye to Matt and went in search of a snack, hoping that I might meet some friendly locals and hang out with them. But it wasn't to be; in fact, the atmosphere on the streets was overtly hostile. If I walked on the pavement I was elbowed into the road by white people, and within the space of half an hour I was approached by three black muggers, one of whom held a knife to my ribs. I managed to ward them off, but I felt under siege and lost all desire to explore. If it was like this in broad daylight in the city centre when the streets were busy, what would it be like at night? I navigated myself back to the safety of the bus station, profoundly unnerved by the aggression I'd encountered.

The bus route from Johannesburg to Durban crossed three provinces: Transvaal, Orange Free State and Natal. Roger had warned me that Orange Free State was notorious for its draconian implementation of apartheid rules. 'Keep a low profile, and avoid any confrontation,' he'd advised. I'd thought he was probably exaggerating, but after Johannesburg I wasn't so sure. A roadside sign showed when we'd crossed the Transvaal border and were now in Orange Free State. Not long afterwards we encountered the first police checkpoint. The bus was waved to a halt. All the passengers were told to disembark.

This was a normal occurrence, nothing to worry about, someone said. Our papers would be checked and then we'd be cleared to proceed.

Two armed Afrikaner policemen stood by as a senior officer examined each passenger's papers and nodded to indicate they could get back on the bus. I stood in line, passport at the ready. As soon as he saw that I was British he gestured over his shoulder to the other two and all three officials homed in on me, pointing their rifles at my head. What was I doing, where was I going? the senior man asked. I replied politely. Did I have any biltong? he demanded.

'No – I don't even know what biltong is,' I said. This wasn't the right answer.

'Get your bag.' He steered me at gunpoint towards the bus, watching while the driver opened the luggage compartment and I scrabbled inside for my case, pulled it out, and placed it on the ground in front of him.

'Open it,' he commanded, diverting the muzzle of his rifle away from my head to point it at the bag.

I nodded and obediently did as he requested, unzipping the case on the side of the road while all the other passengers looked on.

'Stand back,' he ordered, and when I complied, he stood over my case and using the barrel of his rifle like a pitchfork, he tossed every item of clothing and every other possession I had with me into the road. Not daring to object, I looked on wordlessly. Eventually, when the case was completely empty and all my belongings were scattered in the dirt, he nodded, grim-faced, and walked off.

'You can put everything back now,' the driver said.

I scurried around, thoroughly humiliated, and put the bag back in the locker. The other passengers avoided looking at me as I got back on the bus.

Twice more we were stopped at roadblocks. Each time I was subjected to extra scrutiny because of my colour and my British passport. Without this harassment the route would have been a wonderfully memorable experience. The bus wound its way through the Drakensberg Mountains, some of the most stunning scenery I've ever seen – a landscape of verdant plains, river valleys and the mighty mountain peaks above. But my appreciation of the beauty I saw was overshadowed by the experiences in Johannesburg and on the road. What would I encounter in Durban? Would I be subjected to more bureaucratic intimidation? How safe would I be walking about in the streets? We approached the city as the sun slipped low, gilding Cape chestnut trees laden with fluffy pink blooms, and making the crimson flowers of the Kaffir boom trees fluoresce against the gathering shadows like blood.

In Durban, true to his word, Roger had booked me into a multiracial hotel. I was the only non-white visitor as far as I could see. Most of the staff were South Asian. If they were curious to see a black guest, they didn't let on, treating me in a reassuringly hospitable manner.

I wanted to put the experiences of the previous day behind me and went for a walk after breakfast. Durban didn't have the same dangerous vibe that I'd sensed in Johannesburg, but I still found myself jostled off the pavement if a white person passed, and none of the black people I encountered seemed to invite conversation. It quickly dawned on me that there was an unspoken protocol: if you were black you would cross the road or move away when a white person approached. But even after I'd grasped this, I still felt vulnerable. What other rules might I transgress unwittingly? This country felt like a jungle as dangerous as that around the Zambezi, and far less appealing. I didn't know where I could walk, which areas were safe, what the curfews were. But I had a week to fill, an opportunity I couldn't waste sitting in the hotel.

I decided I would use up one day by going on an organised safari. I found a travel agent near the hotel. A blonde woman in her mid-twenties asked me in a strong South African accent what I wanted. Her eyes widened when I told her: black tourists were an anomaly in those days, but it would be no problem to organise a day's safari for the following morning, she said. 'Where are you from?' she asked. 'I love your accent.'

'I'm from London,' I explained.

She ran through some safari options. I started to feel more relaxed. At last, a friendly South African, someone who isn't full of hate and suspicion, I thought. Her friendly enquiries continued as she organised my itinerary. Where was I staying in Durban? Did I want her to arrange transport to the safari pick-up point? I told her the name of my hotel and said yes, if she could organise transport I'd be grateful. 'You can get there by bus, but you'll have to change a couple of times.'

'No problem,' I said.

The conversation went on. What was London like? What was I doing here? For a few minutes longer we chatted easily. What a lovely young woman, I thought. How can you live in a place like this?

But then unexpectedly she looked up, frowning. 'Oh my

goodness, I've just realised I've made a dreadful mistake,' she said.

'What's that?'

'I haven't thought about it till now. But I've booked you on buses that black people aren't permitted to travel on. I'm so sorry.'

'I don't mind sitting at the back,' I said.

'No – blacks aren't permitted, even at the back. And I'm afraid I don't have any information on the black buses that will get you there.'

'Never mind. Just write down the name of the place I need to get to, and I'll work it out,' I said.

She shook her head, furrowing her brow. 'You can't do that.' She paused a minute. 'I know. Why don't you take the buses I've booked for you? When you get on, show them your British passport. The rule really only applies to black South Africans – it's not for British visitors like yourself. Some of our rules are so embarrassing.'

After the altercations on the buses to Durban I had no desire to attract more attention. More importantly, this just seemed wrong. 'I can't. I don't want special treatment. I'd rather travel on black buses, like everyone else,' I said.

'Of course you can.'

'I can't.'

She shot me a look of exasperation. 'I'm telling you – you can. After all, you're not a bloody *Zulu*, are you!'

Her words hung there, floating like balloons in the air. How should I respond? I was bemused and for a moment it felt as if she'd punched me in the head. She had seemed so normal, the type of person I could be friends with. Yet, underlying the veneer of friendliness, her loathing towards her black compatriots was laid bare. I have never forgotten those words or the expression on her face as her prejudice was revealed.

I don't remember what I said, or how I got to the departure point the next morning. Only that when I arrived and made my way onto the safari bus, the driver looked almost comically bewildered to see me, a black person, presenting him with the papers to show I had paid for the trip. The bus was half full, everyone was white apart from me. As I walked down the aisle, the hum of chatter dried up and I was conscious of everyone watching me, as if I were a mistake. Burning with indignation, I made my way to the rear of the bus and sat down. Still no one spoke, until eventually a man seated in front of me turned and said hello.

'Hi,' I replied, as normally as I could, and introduced myself. At the sound of my English accent the atmosphere changed. Normal conversation resumed. The man told me he was from Eastbourne. I smiled and said I knew the town well, having spent many childhood holidays there. 'Where did you stay?' he asked. By some extraordinary coincidence, he knew Daddy Hoad. That connection soothed me a little, but I still felt the other passengers viewed me as a trespasser.

In the park, we transferred to jeeps to enjoy the privileged spectacle of animals in their natural habitat. During that time, I was able to forget about apartheid. Nature was a salve, it made me feel free, it was breathtaking, but a small voice in my head reminded me I was an observer, this was the animals' domain not mine. The brief connection I had felt in Victoria

Falls through my heritage with this great continent had vanished. Here my feeling was one of alienation.

At lunchtime we stopped for an hour at a small development with a cafe and toilets. I wanted to use the facilities and walked towards the entrance, when a sign above the door caught my eye: WHITES ONLY, it read. Terrified of breaking a rule and finding myself apprehended, I asked where I, a black visitor, could go. 'There are no facilities here for black people,' I was told.

I went to buy some food. Above the door to the cafe an identical sign was suspended: WHITES ONLY. As a black man, visiting a black country, I was not only proscribed from certain means of travel, and a target of the authorities whose job was to protect and ensure law and stability. I was also denied two basic necessities of every human being, whatever the colour of their skin.

That afternoon the guide led us on a hike through part of the reserve. We walked in single file, following a path that led along the edge of a thicket of thorn trees. Suddenly the man in front of me froze so unexpectedly that I nearly crashed into him.

'What's wrong?'

'Snake! Go back,' he whispered.

Over his shoulder I glimpsed a wriggling sliver of green. A snake about two metres long was suspended from an overhanging branch by its tail.

'What's that?' I said.

'Green mamba. They're highly venomous.'

The snake had dropped just as the man had walked beneath the branch, its head descending so that his face had almost collided with it. We watched it writhe and twist, tongue flickering out, small eyes gleaming. Even though we were standing back there was something unpredictable and frightening about it – yet another danger I was ill equipped to anticipate or to avoid.

Back in my hotel room I turned on the radio and heard that Marvin Gaye had died. Shot by his father after an altercation, the bulletin said. I knew his father was strange and hadn't got on well with Marvin, but I remembered the engaging person I'd spent an evening with when I was still hairdressing at Smile and couldn't believe what I'd heard. This is a fabrication, a manifestation of South African anti-black propaganda, I told myself. Only when I returned to England and read the story in a British newspaper did I believe it was actually true.

Over the days that followed I explored Durban further, but it wasn't comfortable. If I went to a mixed-race restaurant I was hyper aware that I was a curiosity: everyone fell silent and scrutinised me while I walked to my table and ate my meal.

The beaches were segregated – the best sections designated for whites, a less appealing stretch for South Asians, and the rocky end for black people.* At one end of the beach (the white end) was a large aquarium, which I visited. It had a vast, partly glass-sided central tank, shaped like a drum which allowed you to view various monsters of the deep from above

---

* At the time, the Immorality Act meant that it was illegal for different races to cohabit, so visiting mixed-race families were anomalies.

and below the water. Watching the majestic floating shadows of huge manta rays and the weird forms of the hammerhead sharks within touching distance, I felt the sense of awe that observing such a wild creature at close quarters brings. But this was an artificial environment, I reminded myself. These creatures were captives, in a setting as artificial as the one created and inhabited by the citizens of this country. Visitors were enthralled by the spectacle they saw, children shrieked in delight, but the different racial groups didn't mix. Even here, there was no avoiding the scouring reality of the divisive political system, or its invisible barriers.

I wasn't sorry when the end of my trip to Durban approached. The day before my departure, I went for a walk to the seafront. I saw a kiosk where black people were queuing for snacks. Some young black guys in their late teens and early twenties were hanging around by a bench nearby. I smiled at them, hoping they would talk to me. I still hadn't had a proper conversation with a black South African, but they glared at me with such rancour I felt compelled to look away. Was I constructing their belligerence into something more than it was? Was this symptomatic of my insecurities, my discomfort at being somewhere unfamiliar? I didn't think so — I had visited many other places and never encountered anything comparable. In London the colour of my skin wasn't something I frequently thought about. Here, in a black country, I couldn't forget it.

I bought a drink and wandered along the road that fronts the beach, watching the waves and the gulls wheeling in the sky, wondering where to go to fill the last few hours of daylight. At first I told myself I was imagining that someone was following me. Then, worried by the figure I kept glimpsing behind me, I left the seafront and diverted to a side street. Behind me I was conscious that the dark silhouette took the same turn. I upped my pace. The shadow was still with me, too far away to see clearly. Adrenalin kicked in. My pulse began to race, I kept walking at a brisk pace. Was I about to be mugged? My shadow was now maybe thirty yards away heading towards me, and there was no one else around. I had no doubt that I was his target. I sat down on a low wall and braced myself for what was to come.

This is my last day, I was thinking. So far I've survived unscathed: please God, don't let this change.

As he came closer the man's pace slowed. Three yards from me, he stopped, nodded, half raised a hand in greeting. He was of South Asian appearance, about my age or maybe a little older. Nothing about him looked remotely aggressive.

'I hope I haven't alarmed you,' he said. 'I've been trying to catch up with you. I wanted to talk after I heard you buy your drink on the beach. I've never heard a black person speak like you with a British accent. Where are you from?'

'London,' I said, my face hot. This place was getting to me. I didn't know whether to laugh or cry.

'They have black people in London?'

'They do, yes, and they don't have apartheid,' I said.

He looked at me with an incredulous expression. 'What? I thought everywhere was like this?'

'Well, it's propaganda. London isn't perfect, but we sit side by side on buses, walk side by side on pavements, eat in the same places, use the same lavatories.' I paused and looked at him. 'Anyway, you're not black – so where are *you* from?' I asked. I was still upset and there was a sharpness in my voice that I didn't intend.

He explained that he was a member of the mixed-race community, and that his forebears had originated from India. He'd never met a black Englishman before and it was good to talk.

I told him I felt the same. I was disappointed I hadn't been able to hang out with more local young people. When I came here that was what I'd intended. 'I wanted to talk to young black people. To hear their views on the situation. I wanted to talk to those guys on the beach. But everyone is so unfriendly,' I grumbled.

'The reason they are being hostile is because you don't look like them, or dress like them, or sound like them. Whatever your intentions might be, to black South Africans you stand out and you are not white. Suppressed people are angry people. This is a dangerous place for you.'

'I'm leaving tomorrow,' I said. I didn't want to say I wouldn't be back any time soon, but I thought it.

On my last morning I was seated in the hotel dining room having breakfast when the manager, a tall Indian man with a distinguished air, came up. 'I hear you are leaving us today and I would like to shake your hand before you go.'

I stood up. 'Certainly – may I ask why?' I replied.

He looked at me for a moment, a resigned sadness in his expression. 'This is a multiracial hotel. It's been open for over thirty years, and you are the first black person who has ever stayed here. I want to congratulate you and to say that I hope others will follow.'

I thanked him, conscious that his sentiments were sincere.

But I thought, Why would any sane black tourist want to come to a country that treats them like this? I've never returned – I hope it's different now.

On the bus back to Harare I met up with Matt, the blond idealist who was going to change the world and document and eradicate apartheid. 'How was it for you in Cape Town?' I asked.

'Fine,' he said. 'I had a great time. But I didn't find much to record. Black people have such a good deal and a great way of life. The whites look after them. All this business about the injustice of apartheid – it's all propaganda, isn't it?'

I looked at him bewildered. What had happened to the radical anti-apartheid champion? Had he been brainwashed in just ten days? We might have visited different planets for all our experiences had in common. He didn't ask about my trip, nor did I begin to explain. After a while I said I wanted to sit in a different seat so I could stretch out, and I moved away from him.

I had come to Africa hoping to find African art to buy. But here too my expectations were disappointed. In Johannesburg I had been too terrified to go looking. Durban wasn't much better, and in Harare I saw nothing old or of the quality I sought. One day, shortly before I was due to leave, I walked into a small second-hand shop not far from Roger's house. There, among the tarnished silver plate, chipped tea sets, crinoline shepherdess figurines and the fading prints of Turner's *Fighting Temeraire* and Constable's *Hay Wain*, something drew my eye like a beacon. Six Wedgwood Keith Murray vases: two large and four medium size. Elegant, simple, their refined clean lines stood out among the dross like a designer jacket on a rail of unshapely house coats. The price on the tickets was a fraction of what they would be worth in England. This wasn't what I had in mind when I came to Africa, I thought. I wanted to take home something quintessentially African. The vases were quintessentially English. But still . . .

I bought all six, took them back to Roger's house and thought about how to get them back to London, without breakage or paying for extra shipping. By stuffing and wrapping each vase with my clothes and arranging them in the middle of my case they made it safely back to London.

I put the vases on the stand at Grays. The profit I made paid for my trip with a little to spare. Which all goes to prove the truism of antique dealing, and life: you never know what you will find, it's rarely what you expect, but it's always worth looking. A few days after the last vase sold, a headline in the newspaper caught my eye: TEENAGER EATEN BY 15-FOOT CROC ON BANKS OF ZAMBEZI, CLOSE TO VICTORIA FALLS.

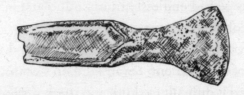

20

A Bronze Age Unlooped Palstave

Thursday, 17 August 1995. I think of my life as before and after that night. The evening hadn't started well: I'd agreed to go to Maureen's when I didn't want to. I was out of sorts because I'd tried and failed to call it off, swept away by the emotional pressure she'd applied, regretting it as soon as I'd yielded.

Maureen, Marilyn and I had become friends at group therapy meetings ten years earlier. I'd needed help to sort out my head, when not long after my return from Africa, I had a mini breakdown. It happened as a result of my relationship with my girlfriend at the time, Martine.

Martine had a dysfunctional relationship with her mother, and although I was deeply in love with her, the impact on our romance was more than I could handle. The toxic interactions between mother and daughter mirrored those I'd experienced with my own mother. My childhood nightmares returned, and I knew I'd have to end it, for my own sanity, but when we broke up there was no relief. Unresolved memories that had lain buried resurfaced. My skin broke out in sores. I couldn't sleep, yet I was tired all the time. I couldn't eat, I felt restless, panicked, unable to focus on anything other than the break-up, which replayed endlessly in my mind and left me barely capable of coherent conversation.

Friends could see the state I was in. They didn't know the full extent of my torment, because I didn't want to tell them, and I still find it difficult to think and speak about this episode today. But when they said the only way to deal with it was to seek professional help, I listened and consulted various therapists on a one-to-one basis, but they didn't work for me: I wasn't comfortable talking aloud for an hour. Group therapy felt more comfortable. If I didn't want to talk I could listen and join in when I wanted to. I discovered that hearing others' problems and how they confronted them was as therapeutic as speaking of my own experiences.

It was against the rules to meet other members of the group outside the organised sessions, but Marilyn and I bonded. She had removed herself from an abusive relationship with a Texan woman who was a reader at the British Library. They had two adopted children, one of whom had special needs and had added extra strain to their already inharmonious relationship. As a result, Marilyn suffered from acute anxiety and during bad episodes her pretty face would twist up like a knot. Having lived with Jane and Sue, I'd seen the effect of abusive relationships, so Marilyn liked talking to me and I enjoyed confiding in her.

Marilyn was already a close friend of another group member, Maureen, who was a former ballet dancer and

choreographer. Dance had been central to Maureen's existence, until she'd fallen down a short flight of stairs and damaged her back so severely that she needed a stick to walk.
Afterwards she'd struggled to come to terms with the way her
life had altered, and her difficulties were manifest in self-
absorbed disaffection. While I was at Beechholme I'd worked
as a volunteer at a local hospital for people who had suffered
physical injury and associated problems. I'd seen the psycho-
logical havoc accidents and illness can bring, so I found it easy
to empathise with her predicament too.

I didn't warm to Maureen in the way I had to Marilyn, but
I tolerated her, and the three of us started meeting up once
every few weeks, calling ourselves the Three Musketeers. By
1995, I was no longer attending therapy, but the meetings with
Maureen and Marilyn continued, and every few weeks we got
together to talk through our progress. We'd arranged our
August meeting a month earlier, before I realised I had to leave
early the next morning for a buying trip, plus I had a hundred
and one things to deal with before that. Marilyn didn't mind
me changing our meet-up to a different day. Maureen was
another matter entirely. She detested any change in arrangements and I dreaded making the call. 'You can't let me down,
I'll regress. I'm so looking forward to seeing you.'

'OK, OK,' I relented.

We agreed on a compromise: I'd arrive at 7 p.m. and leave
on the dot at 9.30 p.m. I took the bus from my house to Notting
Hill Gate, and from there walked the short distance down Hol-
land Park Avenue to Maureen's flat. I was anxious about all the
things I had to do, but I managed to put them to one side while
we had supper and chatted. Then nine-thirty came. I started

to say my goodbyes. But Maureen pleaded, 'Please don't go now, Ronnie. We're all doing so well. It's so good to be together isn't it?'

My head pounded. 'We agreed nine-thirty.'

'But you know how fragile I am. Don't leave. Just stay till ten.'

I sighed. 'OK.'

I was furious with myself. Yet again I'd given in to her, and really there was no point in my staying. I just sat there, fuming inwardly, watching the hands on the clock, waiting for the half-hour to pass. Why hadn't I just left? On the dot of 10 p.m. I said goodbye, and stormed to the bus stop at Notting Hill Gate, my mind seething with all the things I had to do when I got back.

I reached the bus stop only to find it was taped off. A make-shift sign just read: DIVERSION. Nothing to show where the diversion went, or where the next functioning bus stop was. Infuriated that everything seemed to be conspiring against me, I decided to walk the route until I came to the next stop. I turned down Pembridge Road. I knew the next stop was near the junction with Chepstow Crescent. It wasn't far. I got there to find that too had been taped off. I would have to keep walking towards Westbourne Grove, and I now needed to cross to the other side of the junction.

There was a triangular island in the middle of the road planted with flowers and there were low bollards at each end with a narrow kerb around it. I stood under a big plane tree opposite. The sky was just dark but there were streetlights and no traffic. I crossed to the island, stood on the narrow kerb and edged my way round the low wall, then positioned myself in the centre of the opposite side of the island. I looked carefully each way. In front of me were parked cars, but there was a gap for me to get to the pavement on the other side. The street was still quiet, no traffic at all, and for some reason the silence now made me feel nervous. I paused, looked left and right, then did the same again. I heard the breeze rustle the tree behind me. Nothing was coming. My fear was unfounded. I stepped out into the road just as the black shadow of a vehicle flashed into my peripheral vision. My heel didn't even touch the surface of the road.

The next thing I recall is lying in the road with my head in a woman's lap. She was stroking my head. 'Don't worry, the ambulance is coming,' she said as she soothed me. I tried to move my legs, but I couldn't. Nor could I move my head or my right arm. Only my left arm was working. I moved it a little and touched something; it was wet, warm and gritty. This was my blood, I realised. 'What a mess!' I tried to say, but the sound that came out was incoherent. It wasn't my voice. Then pain overwhelmed me and I lost consciousness.

I woke up again. The woman was still there. In my strange, semi-conscious state, she seemed angelic. 'Don't worry, help is on the way,' said the angel. I wanted to thank her for her kindness. Blackness enfolded me again.

I became aware of people milling about, the paramedics arriving. 'Oh my God, your face is a mess,' I heard a voice say. 'Your mouth is split from nose to chin.'

'Shh,' someone else said. 'Don't say that. Poor bloke.'

When I woke, I was on a stretcher in a corridor. St Mary's Hospital. I had an open head wound and a huge graze on my back. One leg was bent back towards my buttocks, the other lay at an oddly skewed angle in front. My right arm was useless. The pain was excruciating. If I tried to move my head, I passed out, but overlaying all the agony was a desperate craving for water – I was parched, I had to drink. I called out, rasping sounds that didn't sound like my voice. A nurse came. 'Be quiet, you're disturbing everyone.'

'I'm dying. I need water,' I croaked.

'We can't give you water till you've been X-rayed. You may have internal injuries.'

'I've got to drink.'

'Shh. Be quiet.'

This hell of excruciating pain and thirst seemed to last for hours.* I hallucinated. I was an injured soldier in the Bosnian War, lying on the battlefield wounded. When I regained consciousness, I was still lying on a trolley in a corridor. Where? I couldn't remember. I was still in agony. My head was still caked in blood, I was still desperate for water. Why wouldn't someone give me a drink? I bellowed for help. I was parched, I would die without water. A nurse came and told me to be quiet. I grabbed her tunic with my left hand. 'Please, if I can't have water give me something to do. Give me some dressing so I can clean myself up. I might feel better if I can do something rather than just lie here.'

She came back with some gauze and I think she helped clean me up. 'If I can't have water, could you soak a gauze dressing? Just so I can put it in my mouth and get some moisture?' I begged.

* I later worked out that I was on the trolley for four hours.

'OK,' she said. 'But I'm not really allowed.' She pressed a damp gauze into my left hand. I put it in my mouth, started to suck, and then gagged and spat it out. It was full of grit and tasted putrid. She had given me a soiled gauze. I passed out.

Sometime later when I came to again they were wheeling me down to the X-ray department. I was still thirsty. When the radiographer saw me she said, 'Not another one. I've been in this room for the last twenty hours, and I told you five patients ago not to send any more. I can barely think.'

She tried to squeeze past me and leave the room, but I grabbed the hem of her uniform. 'Please. Please X-ray me. I beg you. I'm dying of thirst.'

I suppose she must have taken pity on me and obliged, and then I was sedated. I awoke to find myself straightened out. I had been strapped to aluminium supports with bindings across my forehead, chin and shoulders, so I was unable to move my head. 'Your neck is broken,' someone said. 'A chip of vertebra has become detached. A millimetre of movement could cause damage to your spinal cord.'

The idea of not being able to move was more than I could bear. I was fit. I danced several times a week for hours on end. I walked for miles at fairs, often carrying heavy items for long distances. Now I was pinioned and powerless, fed through a tube. I was swamped by panic. Death seemed preferable to this existence. 'I can't stay like this,' I muttered because my split mouth had been clipped back together. I was raging and writhing, trying to wrench off the straps.

'Stop that. You'll paralyse yourself,' a nurse said.

'I don't care,' I replied. 'I'd rather be dead.'

They gave me morphine. I slept.

Two days later I woke still strapped to the metal plates. I would be here for two months, they told me, though I found out later it would be three – they hid the truth because they didn't think I'd cope. The prospect of bedridden immobility was devastating. But as I lay there, pondering the grim reality of my situation, some dormant desire to get better smouldered and ignited. I will not give up, I told myself. I will cope. How? I needed a strategy to hold on to. A plan materialised. For the next minute I'd see how well I could do, how calm I could be. And then I'd see how well I could do for the next two minutes. And then the next four, and the next eight. Gradually I would build up to an hour, two hours, a day. I would get through it somehow. I would get well. I would walk and dance and be free once more.

I was lucky: the bone chip fell back into place and just needed time to heal. The plates were removed. I was put in a neck brace; my three broken limbs were plastered.

It wasn't until weeks later that I discovered what had happened that night. At the moment I had tried to cross the road, a black cab had shot across the junction at speed from behind me. The rustling leaves of the tree had probably masked the sound of his approach. The impact had broken my legs and had tossed me high in the air, which is how I'd also suffered the broken neck, broken arm and facial injuries.

I was in bed in a general ward when the orthopaedic specialist came to see me. He was trying out a new method of treatment. There were no pins in my legs, but the plasters on them were hinged at the knee. Every day I would spend five hours on a machine that moved them so that I wouldn't lose mobility.

The treatment started the next day. I was propped up on pillows and one of my legs was strapped to a machine which slowly bent and straightened it. After two and a half hours it was the other leg's turn. Even on the strong painkillers, the treatment was torture. Friends who came to visit couldn't bear to watch. But it was doing me good, it was getting me out of here, I told them. Until I could walk, I couldn't go home.

I was on a large open ward with a reception desk in the middle, men at one end and women at the other. It didn't take long for me to work out that the hospital facilities were stretched to breaking point, and that tired, overworked nurses are not caring nurses.

On my first night in the ward, a woman was put in the bed next to mine. From early evening she called out in agony, crying, screaming, begging not to die. All night she gurgled and spluttered and moaned alone, and as dawn came, I heard her die, and felt that part of me died with her. Why should a woman in the twentieth century have to endure the indignity of dying in the middle of a men's ward? Why hadn't they moved her to a quiet room, so her last hours on earth were in privacy?

Indifference towards patients and their needs broke spirits. A delightful octogenarian called Perry took the bed next to mine. He was a writer and had come in for a hip operation. The procedure went well and visitors came to see him, including a former Bond girl. Perry and I chatted about books and friends. Then, one morning, he fell out of bed. With my good hand, I pressed the alarm for a nurse to come; several other patients did the same. An hour passed before anyone responded, meanwhile Perry, sprawled helpless on the floor, became increasingly distressed. The next day he called for a bedpan; again, there was no response for an hour or so, by which time it was too late and he had to endure the humiliation of curtains being closed and nurses washing and changing him like a child. All this demolished his spark and dehumanised him. He went downhill and died a few months later. I still believe it wasn't the operation but neglect that killed him.

To survive incarceration in a place like this I decided to fill my day with a rigorous regime. After a few days of strategic planning I devised a way of giving myself a bed bath. I managed to slide a towel under myself, remove my gown, and, holding a bowl of water on my lap, give myself a wash. It took me an hour or so, but it made me feel better. One day, I was in the middle of this difficult procedure when a young nurse pulled open the curtain of my cubicle and walked in.

'Excuse me, I'm washing!'

'Don't mind me – I just need to check your chart.'

'I do mind. If I was in the bathroom you'd wait.'

'Oh, we go into everyone's cubicles,' she retorted briskly. She was fiddling at the chart, not looking at me. I was outraged.

'Well, you're not coming in mine if I'm washing. Now go away, and pin my curtain closed. When I've finished you can come back. You are not taking away my dignity walking in like that.' She looked up astonished and stood there for a moment frowning, as if I was making unreasonable demands. But she didn't argue and did as I asked. Every morning after that, my curtain was pinned closed, and my sanity and dignity were maintained. A friend brought my hair clippers and razor so I could trim my hair and shave. Small things – but they break you or make you.

I don't know how my friends discovered what had happened to me, but they did, and their support was hugely consoling. I worked out afterwards I averaged about nine visitors a day, although I always told people not to tell anyone what had happened, terrified of some unscrupulous acquaintance breaking into my house.

Two weeks after my accident the ward was over capacity and I was put on a mattress on the floor. The weather was stifling and being in a neck brace and having both legs and an arm in plaster in the oppressive heat felt unbearable. I'd been given a fan to keep me cool, but they were in short supply, and when another patient developed a high temperature, a nurse took it away. Lying on the floor with nothing to relieve the heat, I thought I was going insane. Wretchedly, I dragged myself to the window – whether for air or to hurl myself out I'm not sure. At that moment two friends arrived. I looked at them unfocused, hardly recognising them, rambling about dying from heat. They held me down until the nurses arrived.

Steven, a close friend, heard the news and came back early from holiday to see me. He arrived with a portable TV and a mobile phone. He would collect my mail and deal with any bills that needed paying, he promised. He brought the police report, which informed me that the cab driver claimed it was my fault for stepping out from a concealed spot without warning. The letter enclosed the record made at the time. It read:

'Black man lying in road, blood coming from ears, nose, mouth. Cab driver says it's the *black* man's fault, therefore no need to investigate further.'

There was no way to read this other than as an example of racial discrimination. Why was my colour relevant? Would a report have read, 'White man lying in road'? Had I been white, would they have satisfied themselves the accident was my fault by asking my assailant? The police didn't interview me. They didn't take a witness statement from the woman who took care of me, or from anyone else. The cab driver wasn't breathalysed, his brakes and tyres weren't checked. Nor did he ever take the trouble to see how I was. Huw and Jo said this was outrageous and that I had a claim for compensation. Soon after the accident Huw had measured and photographed the skid marks on the road, which were more than twenty feet long, but by now weeks had passed. The police begrudgingly reopened the case, but nothing much happened and eventually it was dropped without any court hearing. I never received a penny.

Until then, I had convinced myself that I would be compensated for my injuries and the driver would be prosecuted. The realisation the case was to be dismissed filled me with dismay. Had the taxi run over someone's pet dog more would have been done. The message underlying the inaction was clear: despite the gravity of my injuries, I was black. Different rules applied. The unjustness hurt more than my injuries. I still feel aggrieved and infuriated when I think about it.

Another dealer friend visited and I asked how things were at Portobello. 'Fine,' he said. 'I've just bought a Bronze Age axe head.'

'Really? Is it an unlooped palstave?'

'What's that?'

'Show me what you bought.'

He rummaged in his bag, took out something wrapped in a grubby piece of newspaper, and placed it unwrapped on the table in front of me.

I picked it up with my left hand for a closer look. A palstave, or Bronze Age axe head, may look like a very basic prehistoric tool, but scroll back through time and you see it in a different light. It takes its name from an Icelandic digging tool, though it was actually used for chopping. Cast in a two-sectioned mould, the head would have been fitted to the V-shaped cleft of a wooden handle, then bound around with strips of hide that would have been applied wet so that they tightened as they dried. The central ridge in the middle was cleverly devised to stop the head sinking back and becoming embedded in the handle. Some even more refined versions had a loop that allowed the head to be tied to the handle to secure it. This one didn't have that feature, hence the term 'unlooped'. There were signs of wear and age that told me it wasn't a reproduction. Probably a lucky metal detectorist's find, I guessed.

'Oh yes, it's an unlooped palstave,' I said. The dealer in me hadn't died, I realised, as I heard myself asking how much he wanted for it.

'I paid £80, so you can have it for £90.'

I knew this was a good deal. 'OK. But I haven't got the cash on me. Come back next week and I'll pay you.' I handed the palstave back to him but he shook his head.

'You can keep it till then. You're not going anywhere in a hurry are you?'

I asked a friend to go and see Geoffrey Munn at Wartski. The week before my accident I had sold him an Aesthetic Movement gold chimera brooch and he owed me the money for it. With the cash from Geoffrey I paid for the axe head and then had some spare to start a float. I bought some pearls from one dealer visitor and sold them to another. Meanwhile the axe head stayed under my pillow – a talismanic, strength-giving reminder of the world to which I was still connected, and to which I intended, as speedily as possible, to return. Its magical force spurred me to heal in a way the grim medical fraternity could not have comprehended.

Then Maureen came.

I saw her before she saw me: a stooped figure at the reception desk, all dressed in black, elegant in a malevolent, Bette Davis way.

'How are you?' she enquired, taking a seat at my bedside.

I had conditioned myself to believe that every day was a good one, and I didn't want to dwell on the fact that without her insistence that we met that night, I wouldn't have been lying in this bed at all. To make things easier all round I said, 'It's great, I'm fine. When you leave I will be put on a machine and tortured for five hours. But I'm fine.'

This wasn't what she'd expected, her astonishment was obvious. 'You can't be fine. I was in this very same bed when I broke my back. And I was utterly miserable. I can't take your chirpiness. You don't know what you are doing to me . . .' And with that she stood and left.

I turned her words over and revisited that night, but I wouldn't allow myself to sink into despair by remembering what my life was like back then. I had to live in the present. A month or so later Maureen returned. I didn't dare say I was OK and prompt a repeat performance, so when she asked how I was I said, 'My legs are killing me. I've just been on that machine. It's agony, you can't imagine—'

Before I could go on she interrupted: 'I don't want to hear about your miseries. I want to be uplifted. You know I was in this ward, in this bed, and how I suffered! Talking about how bad you feel makes me feel bad.' She walked out. That was the last time I ever set eyes on her.

Marilyn was also a regular visitor, and although her presence also reminded me of that terrible night, she didn't upset me and we remained fast friends for years afterwards. When she got cancer and was being cared for in a hospice, I spent many nights with her, talking her through the suffering. I was somewhere in Kent, on a train to Hastings, when the hospice called to tell me she was in the last few hours of her life. I took the next train back to London.

I hadn't spoken to Maureen since her second hospital visit to me, but I rang her straightaway and told her Marilyn was dying. She should go to the hospice immediately if she ever wished to see her again. Maureen said she had a massage appointment which she couldn't cancel. She would go the next day.

'Marilyn won't last the night.'

'I'll take the chance.'

I made it to the hospice in time to hold Marilyn's hand for the last few hours of her precious life. She died an hour or so after I left. That night I deleted Maureen's details from my phone.

★

I filled my hospital days with small steps. Each one would transport me towards the end goal: becoming independent enough to go home. There were several flights of stairs in my home. I would have to be able to climb them unaided before I could leave hospital. Determination to put my key in the lock of my own door spurred me on. And the nurses helped me succeed – their indifference pushing me forward.

Using my good left arm, I practised lifting myself up on the bar suspended over my bed. I needed a nurse to help me at first. One day, early on, my hand slipped and jerked my neck, sending searing pain through my body like an electric shock. I grabbed out at the nurse for support, but instead of responding and catching me, she stepped back deliberately. I tumbled sideways, nearly falling out of the bed. She stood by, watching.

The weight of the plasters was making my spine curve and I was sent for X-rays several times a week. The member of staff who wheeled me down the corridor into the X-ray theatre told me, 'I hate my job. I wish I didn't have to do this.' The conversation – if you can call it that – was further stimulus to get better.

Day by day it became easier to sit up and wash myself. After ten weeks I hoisted myself into a wheelchair and was able to move around the ward. I would now also be able to use the bathroom instead of suffering the indignity of a bedpan and bottle: another milestone reached. I navigated myself to the door of the unisex toilet block and looked in. I felt physically sick. The floor was awash with urine. There were seven or eight commodes – all of them caked in dried faeces or piled with recent deposits. I wanted to throw up but instead I called for a nurse. I remember two coming, and arguing ('I'm not cleaning this up.' 'Why should I do it? It's not my job . . .'). I insisted, and begrudgingly a junior sister was directed to clean a commode for me. She scraped and chipped away the dried-on residue. 'There you are – it's done,' she said, backing away.

I shook my head. 'That's still not clean. Would you sit on it? I have no wish to criticise you, but please understand that treating patients in this way is dehumanising. And if we lose our dignity, we lose the will to live.' She relented and cleaned it properly.

When the plasters on my legs and my arm and my neck brace were removed, I was flabbergasted. My legs had previously been well muscled and strong from dancing. Now I hardly recognised them as my own: spindly chicken legs, incapable of supporting anything, had somehow replaced the well-formed limbs I remembered. 'You'll build up muscle again,' said the physiotherapist who taught me to walk again in a rehab room equipped with parallel bars. For painful hours I staggered like an old man, working my way from one end to the other, then back again. When that got easier, I graduated to crutches. I had maintained my upper body strength by pulling myself up on the bar above my bed, and the physiotherapist was right: my progress was rapid. I forced myself to walk up and down the hospital stairs on my new crutches. Home and a return to my normal life was in sight.

In the last fortnight before I left hospital, six friends invited me out for lunch in my wheelchair. One collected some clothes from my flat, and I felt like a different person when I put them on. They had booked a special cab and took me to Thomas Goode. It was my first taste of the world outside the hospital precincts, and reminded me of how it would feel to be free.

One thing still troubled me. For months no doctor had spoken to me about the nature of my original injuries or how I could expect to progress. The only conversation I'd had was in my first week in hospital when I'd woken up in plaster, heavily sedated, and I couldn't remember what I had been told. Every day the registrar walked through the ward. Every day I tried to attract his attention, but he never stopped. A week before I was due to leave, I started to petition the most sympathetic of the nurses, Christine Cross, every day. Eventually, she relented and spent fifteen minutes explaining exactly what had happened to me and how I had been treated. The prognosis was good. It would take time. But there was no reason I wouldn't be able to lead a normal life again.

The day of discharge came. Jo and Huw took me home. They had been there in my absence, tidied the place up, and bought me some food to start me off. I closed the door behind them with a mixture of anxiety and relief. I had left Beechholme aged sixteen because I'd wanted to be free of institutions. In hospital I had become institutionalised again. Now I was alone. Thank God. Could I cope? Yes, I could. I wouldn't allow myself to be reliant on friends, crutches or a walking stick for any longer than I had to. The flights of stairs in my home would be my physiotherapy. I would go out alone. And one day I'd dance and run again. For now, limping about my home, eating standing up because I couldn't carry a plate, I reacquainted myself with my pictures, books, records, and all the other things I loved. It was like a reunion of old friends after a long separation. And then I remembered I had an introduction to make. I placed the palstave on a shelf next to a tribal mask and an Inuit carving. Its power had worked; it had brought me home.

Next morning a friend came and took me out. We walked to the shops. 'Shall I come again tomorrow?' she asked as I waved her off.

'Thanks, but no, I need to do this on my own.'

I forced myself to go out alone for a walk uphill the following day. When I came to a crossing I found myself looking left and right obsessively. I was shaking in terror at the thought of stepping off the pavement, but I forced myself to do it. On day three I took a bus ride to Notting Hill Gate. It was a sparkling cloudless day in early December, and I returned to the scene of my accident. I was still on crutches, but I made myself cross the road in the same spot where I'd been knocked over. There were no leaves on the tree as there had been on that night, and its heavy black branches fretted the sky like bars. Back and forth I hobbled, across to the island, and to the other side of the road. Four or five times I repeated this. When I could do it without fear, on the far side of the road, I stopped and looked back at the tree. The branches seemed lighter from this vantage point; through them the sky shone brilliant and blue.

21

An Inuit Thimble Guard

Fast-forward fifteen years. A call from the BBC's *Antiques Roadshow* office in Bristol. Collecting was evolving. They were looking for new faces with relevant expertise. They'd heard I was a specialist in a wide range of new collecting areas. Would I be interested in coming to Bristol to discuss joining the team? The offer took me by surprise – I could hardly believe it. The show had long been a favourite of mine. Even though I don't own a TV, if I am ever at a friend's house on a Sunday evening I always ask if I can watch it. But being on the programme in front of the camera was something I had never contemplated. It scared me. I've always hated having my photo taken. My discomfort with my appearance, the legacy of my childhood, has never entirely disappeared. Besides, people brought up in children's homes who left school at seventeen don't conform to the usual expert profile.

'I can't come to Bristol,' I said.

'Our producer Simon Shaw will be in London next week. Could you meet him at Waterloo?'

'Not really.'

But my mind was racing. What if I gave it a try? My knowledge in a wide variety of subjects would be tested, but it would be an endorsement of years of looking and unconventional learning. Opportunities like this don't come every day. Was I really going to throw it away?

No.

'What about at Somerset House?'

'OK. Great.'

I wasn't sure who Simon Shaw was when I met him, but I liked the coat he was wearing, and we clicked as soon as I mentioned my work as a DJ and my connections to Contempo Records and *Blues & Soul* magazine. Simon had recently found a box of those magazines in his attic and couldn't bring himself to throw them away. We talked more about my various areas of interest within the world of collecting. 'Would you like to join the team?'

'Yes. If you think I have something to offer, I'd like to give it a try.'

Simon outlined how things worked. The show is entirely filmed on location. Each location makes at least two episodes and then there are specials for Christmas and other landmark events. Each year there is a 'feedback day' in London, at which most of the experts and production team old and new congregate. That year's feedback day was scheduled to take place at Broadcasting House in White City in a month's time – why didn't I come along? It would be a good opportunity to meet the rest of the team.

I showed up on the appointed day, feeling so weak with apprehension I nearly went home. A buffet lunch was spread out in a meeting room. There were about a hundred people, among them a couple of familiar faces that I knew from the trade. Most people, despite being strangers, were welcoming – although one person rattled me when he came up and said, 'You stay out of my way and I'll stay out of yours.'

My unease was further amplified when someone told me that after lunch, I would have to introduce myself and explain my area of interest. How would I encapsulate all I'd studied over the years? I was sick with nerves as I started. 'Hi, I'm Ronnie. I'm interested in quite a cross-section of things . . .' Afterwards I felt proud of myself for getting through it.

The first hurdle crossed, I was invited to come and observe the show being filmed at Birmingham University. Once again, nerves unsettled me as soon as I took my seat on the train. I calmed myself with regular doses of Rescue Remedy.

The main filming was due to take place the following day, but I'd been asked to go along the afternoon before for a screen test. 'Bring something you can talk about,' Michele Burgess, one of the producers, had said. 'It will be as though you are doing a recording for the show. But the public won't be there.'

I thought carefully about what to take and decided to go for something unusual, small, easily portable – the sort of thing I loved. An Inuit thimble guard. I rehearsed what I wanted to say over and over in my head.

'This might look like a carving of a seal, but would it surprise you to know it's an Inuit thimble guard? To the people who owned and used it, the tools associated with sewing were incredibly important. Their clothes were their protection from the harsh environment in which they lived. They couldn't have survived without them, and the materials they used – skins and seal guts – are not easy to stitch, which is why to them, thimbles were incredibly important implements.

'As the name suggests, thimble guards were designed to keep the thimble safe. Some of them are plain and functional; some are fashioned as talismanic symbols. This one is made from walrus ivory and takes the form of a spotted seal, a creature that the Inuit believed was a protective spirit. The woman who owned this would have seen it as much more than a functional object. She believed the seal protected the thimble just as the clothes she made protected her family. To keep it safe the guard would have been attached to a needle-case strap or stored in a "housewife", a small bag that held other implements for making clothing such as awls, needles, creasers and scrapers.'

Once the camera started to roll, I'm not sure how much of this I actually said. I wasn't as nervous as I thought I'd be, partly because I became lost in the subject which has always fascinated me. Had I rambled? No, Michele said I'd done well, and that was good enough for me.

Next day was filming day. Each specialism was spread around the location: there were tables for pictures, furniture, silver, jewellery, ceramics, glass, clocks, militaria, books and miscellaneous, where I sat along with half a dozen other experts. Our job was to deal with all the objects that came in that didn't fit into any of the other conventional categories. Long queues built up at the reception desk as soon as the gates opened. There, people's possessions were sifted through and they were directed to the appropriate experts' tables. Soon hundreds of hopeful owners snaked in a line around our cluster of tables, holding bags that bulged with scientific instruments, tribal art, Indian artefacts, dolls, teddy bears, vintage clothes, kitchenalia, textiles, film and pop memorabilia, photographs, and a plethora of other things.

Antiques Roadshow has run for so long that people greeted some of the veteran experts like they were old friends. Despite being a new face, I too was welcomed and put at ease. Talking to people about their treasured possessions was something new for me, but I found I enjoyed doing it. I was getting into my stride around lunchtime when fellow-expert Paul Atterbury came up holding something – I recognised it as a feathered cloak from the Great Lakes. 'You said you're interested in indigenous American art? They want you to film this,' he said.

'I can't,' I said, inwardly cringing. 'I'm just here as an observer.'

'That doesn't matter. Observers often film things. I did on my first day.'

'I don't feel ready.'

'You'll be fine. It's your subject,' he said reassuringly. Several other miscellaneous experts offered similar encouragement. But I still felt tension mounting. I hadn't expected to perform. No one had warned me I might be asked to film for real, and I hadn't psyched myself up for it. Michele said I had coped the previous day, but that was different. I'd prepared and chosen an object, and there was just the crew, not thousands of people. 'I need to have some lunch,' I said, and scuttled off to the canteen.

As I sat down with a plate of food, one of the other experienced experts joined me. 'Are you OK, Ronnie?' she said.

'I'm fine. I've been asked to film something. But I don't feel comfortable about it.'

She smiled and patted my arm in a motherly fashion. 'Then don't do it. There's no reason to put yourself through it if you don't want to.'

I glanced at her. I was about to agree when my determination crystallised. I thought, I've dodged crocodiles by the Victoria Falls, fought off various assailants, walked barefoot across the Jura, survived Colin Woodford – and I know about objects like this. Of course I was capable of talking about it on camera.

'No. I should do it,' I said. 'Thanks for the advice though. Knowing the door was open and I could walk away helped me want to stay.'

When the moment came a huge crowd gathered around us. We were about to film on the multi-camera set-up, Michele explained. This is a more complex operation than the single-camera set-up used to record most items, but it gives greater flexibility, allowing different angles to be mixed. I shouldn't let that bother me, though. She would direct me. Michele's face was close to mine as she fixed a mic on my lapel. I was really stressed out by then, but after working with her the previous day I regarded her as an ally. To make myself relax I said, jokily, 'Give us a kiss then.'

It wasn't a professional thing to say, and she frowned in astonishment, as if she couldn't believe what she'd heard. 'Absolutely not!' she said sternly. As she spoke we both realised the mic was switched on, and that everyone had heard. I felt ridiculous, wondering if I'd be sacked before I'd started for inappropriate behaviour, but there was no backing out now. It was time to find out if I could do it.

'This cape may have been made in Lake Erie by Native Americans. Perhaps they used it themselves for ceremonies, or maybe they traded it. If so, it could have once belonged to a Boston society lady who wore it to the opera. But equally, it could have been made in South Africa. The only way to be certain where it comes from is to identify the feathers from which it's made. To do that you need to take it to the Natural History Museum . . .'

As I spoke I felt a sense of dislocation. As if I were a member of the crowd, watching myself. It dawned on me that my curiosity and desire to understand and be able to recognise diverse objects and what they represent had an existential dimension. It had steered me through life. It had fashioned me into the man I am. Human creativity and the objects we produce tell of inner truths and beliefs. Many are made from love, and they rise above cruelty and injustice. They are important because they promote understanding of others. Knowledge had helped me to remove myself from unhappiness and to overcome racial prejudice. In communicating some of this on TV, I could help people to see their mysterious possessions with fresh eyes, to appreciate cultures and lives removed from their own. Or as the poet William Blake said, 'to see a World in a Grain of Sand'. This would be as cathartic for me as, hopefully, it would be enlightening to others.

'Cut,' Michele said. 'That went well.'

Some months later my piece with the feathered cape made the programme. At the following year's feedback day, to my surprise and delight, I was presented with a newcomer's award. A decade on, I still don't particularly enjoy the cameras, but I accept that it is part of the deal and is outweighed by the benefits that work on TV brings. Filming things is important so that people will see, understand, want to talk to me, and believe what I say. I will never enjoy talking about the monetary value of an object, because for me money has never been what a work of art represents. Knowledge is the key and brings with it a sense of value beyond price. Experience has shown me that objects often find us rather than the reverse, and that through them the past becomes personal. Over the years I've handled and been the temporary custodian of an amazing variety of artefacts. Through them, as well as through friendships, adventures and misadventures, I've learned that with an open heart and mind, the world often provides what is needed when it's needed, and thus one's spiritual development continues.

I really do think I've been truly privileged to have had all my life experiences – even the harrowing events of my childhood, if only because they taught me I could survive.

The *Roadshow* is now central to my working life. It brings me into contact with all sorts of extraordinary people, through it I've made firm friendships, and because of it I've been able to discuss incredible items: the largest was a huge totem pole dating from the 1960s, brought along to Media City in Manchester by the Kwakiutl people from British Columbia whom I interviewed.

The nature of the programme means that much of what we see on the miscellaneous table is unremarkable and of relatively low monetary worth, but we are always conscious that we are handling people's treasures, and no one is treated insensitively or turned away. Still, we always hope that the next bag that's opened in front of us will contain something jaw-dropping. To be the bearer of good news to an unsuspecting owner is one of the show's greatest pleasures.

At Crathes Castle in 2019, it was late in the afternoon of a blisteringly hot day when a woman sat down at my table and unwrapped a small domed silver gilt box. I looked at it carefully. The sides were engraved with elaborate figurative scenes and their style and the inscription told me it came from the Netherlands. If it was genuine it dated from the seventeenth century, but its perfect condition made me suspicious. Could any object survive three and a half centuries without a scratch, I wondered? I examined it more closely – everything looked right.

I began to unravel the subject matter. Every scene and every motif adorning the box related to the theme of love. The clasp was fashioned as a Cupid; the handle on top was formed from outstretched hands clasping one another. One side featured the Marriage at Cana, another a wedding dance. The more I looked the more certain I became: this was a seventeenth-century marriage casket, made to celebrate the union of a high-status couple.

As my pulse began to race with the realisation that this was really something out of the ordinary, my heart simultaneously plummeted. There's an unwritten rule among the team. An item of calibre deserves appropriate expertise. Objects of vertu such as this were once my stock in trade, but on the show I am a miscellaneous expert, and this was definitely one for the specialist silver table, so I steeled myself. 'I'm just going to show this to a colleague,' I told the owner, and marched over to Gordon Foster before I had time to rethink.

Gordon looked up distractedly when I showed him the box. He agreed that it was remarkable and definitely worth filming, but he wasn't up for it. After a long day of filming he was exhausted, and he was still dealing with a long queue that looked as though it would last till nightfall. 'Why don't you do it, Ronnie?' he said. 'I can tell you love it.'

I didn't need asking twice.

Later, on camera, I explained to the unsuspecting owner why the casket was such a standout object for me. She didn't have any idea of its age or its purpose and was thrilled to learn of its romantic associations. I kept the final piece of good news till last – she was left virtually speechless with the discovery that the box she owned was worth several thousand pounds.

The *Roadshow* takes me to fascinating places. If we film in a historic house there's often a chance to visit and to be shown round by the owner or curator of the collection. On the day after filming, I take the opportunity to visit whatever museums or other places of interest are close to hand. There are too many to list here, but one stands out in my memory. The day after filming at Media City in Manchester I visited the Imperial War Museum North. There I found photographs of the African troops who had fought in the Burma campaign. One caption read:

Jungle Commando Troops Leave Africa for Burma,
*c.*9 March 1945
More drafts of West African troops have arrived in India
for service on the Burma front. Their arrival follows
almost within a year of the arrival of the first contingent
who have since distinguished themselves in the Burma
fighting, and earned themselves the title of 'Jungle
Commando'.

This was the first time I had learned of the key role African soldiers played in the Burma campaign. It stopped me in my tracks. Why had they been virtually erased from history? What other pages of black history have we lost? I remembered how the history I'd been taught as a child excluded the story of black people, and how the absence of black role models made me feel a sense of disconnection. I hope that in today's curriculum things are changing.

And now we return to the starting point for this book: Castle Howard, 2017. A member of the specialist team for seven years, I was well used to the routine and the surprises a day of filming can bring. But nothing could have prepared me for that day, when Janet, one of the reception specialists, handed two Sooty and Sweep puppets to me. A circle in my life closed.

The puppets represented my childhood. They were not my spiritual guardians in the way the Inuit thought of the seal thimble guard, but like all the objects I have detailed in these pages, they represented something more than their physical selves: they weren't just puppets in a box, they were the repository of memory, an embodiment of childhood innocence.

A swell of emotion swept through me as I picked up Sooty and held him. I saw the little boy I was on the day that Harry Corbett visited the children's home, a time when I felt loved and secure in my world. I remembered myself without self-pity, but with sorrow for the innocence I would soon lose and for the suffering that lay ahead. At the same time, little Sooty empowered me. After all, I'd survived the journey. I knew what constituted a meaningful life, I recognised what love was.

*

But I didn't anticipate what would happen when the Castle Howard episode aired later that year. An email was forwarded from the *Roadshow* office. It had been sent by Georgina Phillips, the daughter of the foster family with whom Anna, my childhood best friend, and I had spent weekends while we lived at Westdene. She was still in contact with Anna. Would I like her to put us in touch? I could hardly believe this was happening. 'Yes, please,' I replied.

So, after sixty-odd years, Anna and I were able to write to each other. She told me she had stayed on at the home until she was able to live an independent life. She had met her husband, a teacher, while she was travelling, and they'd settled in New Zealand. She had three children, all grown up now, and an established career as a quilter. She planned to come to London the following summer, for a quilting seminar. Could she see me?

August 2019. Where do you meet someone who once filled your life, whom you haven't seen for six decades? What about the Victoria and Albert Museum? Or would the British Museum be better? We settle on the V&A. It's raining, not an auspicious start. I'm excited but I'm also sick with apprehension. What will it be like meeting someone from so long ago? I'll recognise her because she's sent me a photo. She'll know me because she's seen me on *Antiques Roadshow*, without realising who I was. But what do we say to each other, after all this time?

She's waiting on the steps when I arrive. A small figure with a broad smile and sparkling eyes that are just as warm and full of life as I remember them. After we've hugged one another, slightly awkwardly, we go inside. The entrance hall throngs with people, and the noise makes any meaningful conversation impossible. I ask a gallery assistant friend for help. She ushers us into the members' area where it's quiet. We order tea.

'I've often thought about you, Ronnie,' Anna says without preamble. 'I didn't know what had happened to you. I didn't even know your surname, or how to find it out. But the photo of the two of us in the Phillipses' garden under the parasol has always hung on the wall in my kitchen at home. My children often ask who that is with me. Do you remember we sent the picture to the Queen?'

'I have never forgotten you either,' I say as tears well in my eyes. 'I've thought of you so often.' But I confess I'd forgotten we sent the photo to the Queen. 'What made us do that?'

'I don't remember either,' she says, laughing. 'Perhaps we thought she'd invite us round.'

In between bridging the gap of more than sixty years we laugh and hug and cry. This is surreal, I think, as I pause and sip my tea. Anna's husband and her sister sit with her, quietly supportive presences in her life. I am happy for her and I'm happy for myself. I feel as though I have rediscovered a lost member of my family, and in a way I have. Anna was a sister to me. We refill our cups and reminisce some more.

Some months later, when she is back in New Zealand, a parcel comes. It's an album, compiled by her husband, filled with pictures of the two of us and letters we wrote to each other during the time we were together. There's a copy of the reply we received from the Queen. It's typed on Buckingham Palace headed paper, dated 4 March 1955.

Dear Anna and Ron,

I write at the Queen's command to thank you very much
for your letter, and for the lovely photograph which you
have sent for Her Majesty. The Queen is looking forward
to her visit to Southport.

Yours sincerely,
Rose Baring, Lady-in-Waiting

'I hope you enjoy the enclosed,' Anna has written. 'I'm coming
to London again next summer. I'll look forward to seeing you
then.'

Yes, it will be really good to meet again, I think. Perhaps
we should go to Buckingham Palace this time. And maybe I
will go and see her one day in New Zealand. I've always been
fascinated by the Maori culture.

Next day I have an early start. It's a fine morning and the
rising sun heralds a day full of promise. I prepare to leave. Putting on my hat and coat I glance in the mirror to reassure
myself that my appearance is acceptable. Not quite convinced,
I tell myself it's an antiques fair I'm off to. It's one of my
favourites, and finding something really good is what matters.
I close the door and step out into the fresh morning: I'm in an
optimistic mood, excited by the prospect of what I'm about
to find.

Acknowledgements

Writing a book is a new venture for me. My thanks go to Gordon Wise for your belief, to the late Christopher Little, whom I never met but who introduced us and set me on this path, and to Jules Bearman, his assistant, for the key role she played in this book taking shape.

I am also grateful for the encouragement, understanding and professionalism of the team at Century – especially Zennor Compton and Callum Crute. Thank you also, Rachel Kennedy and the publicity team, and Romas Foord, my talented friend who took the cover photo.

I am fortunate to work with some of the leading experts on *Antiques Roadshow*. My colleagues have been hugely supportive of this project. A special thank you goes to Robert Murphy, Gill Tierney, Fiona Bruce, Michael Welch, Andy McConnell, Mark Allum, Simon Shaw, Adam Schoon, Hilary Kay, John Foster and Paul Atterbury for their encouragement and friendship through the years.

For my friends the Hoads, the family who saved me, thanks seem barely adequate, but thank you anyway to Christine, Jackie, Gerald, Lynette, Michael, Martin and Ann and Derek and Doreen. Thanks also to John and Maureen Abbey at Contempo Records/*Blues & Soul*, for believing in me when I was